BRITAIN'S PLANNING HERITAGE

Contributors

Introduction: William Ogden, FRTPI, BSc, MICE.

Cumbria: Gordon Fanstone, FRTPI, BSc, Director of Planning, Cumbria CC.

East Anglia: Tony Bird, MRTPI, BA, Principal Planner, Urban Planning Division, Building Research Establishment. He was Director of the East Anglian Regional Strategy Team until mid-1974.

East Midlands: John Anthony, FRTPI, FILA, Principal Lecturer, Department of Town Planning, Trent Polytechnic.

London: John Craig, FRTPI, ARICS.

Northern Ireland: Geoffrey Booth, FRTPI, County Planning Officer, Essex County Council.

Northumbria: Neville Whittaker, MA, BArch, ARIBA, FRSA, Director, Civic Trust for the North East.

North Wales: Colin Jacobs, FRTPI, FRICS, FIMunE, County Planning Officer, Clywd.

North West: Graham Ashworth, FRTPI, BArch, MCD, ARIBA, Professor of Urban Environmental Studies, University of Salford.

Scotland: Urlan Wannop, MRTPI, MA, MCD, Deputy County Planning Officer for Warwickshire.

South East: David Lloyd, MRTPI, BA, Free-lance Writer and Planning Consultant.

South Wales: Tom Hughes, FRTPI, MA, MCD, Senior Lecturer and Richard Mordey MRTIPI, BA, MCD, Lecturer, Town Planning Department, University of Wales Institute of Science and Technology.

South West: Peter Laws, FRTPI, FRICS.

Thames and Chilterns: David Overton, FRTPI, ARICS, County Planning Officer, Hertfordshire, Gordon Sibthorpe, MRTPI, Assistant County Planning Officer.

West Midlands: Gordon Cherry, FRTPI, BA, FRICS, Senior Lecturer and Deputy Director, Centre for Urban and Regional Studios, University of Birmingham.

Yorkshire and Humberside: Mark Andrew, Director of Yorkshire and Humberside Council for the Environment.

Britain's Planning Heritage

Edited and compiled by

RAY TAYLOR, MARGARET COX and IAN DICKINS

CROOM HELM LONDON

ISBN: 0-85664-192-8

Acknowledgements

The editors would like to express their warm appreciation and
thanks to the following:
Guest authors – for writing and revising their articles, often
at very short notice. **Bill Ogden** – for his advice and
encouragement throughout the project. **Bob Stokes** – for his
assistance in selecting the sites and collecting the information.
Marjorie Wheeler – for so speedily typing the manuscript.
Dianne Reed – for taking innumerable telephone calls and
typing many letters. **Maureen Neary** – for undertaking extensive
photo research and continued effort on our behalf. **The City of
Birmingham Polytechnic** – for the use of facilities within the
School of Planning. **The Royal Town Planning Institute** – for
its financial support throughout the project. **Members of the
West Midlands Branch of the RTPI** – who have contributed to
secretarial expenses. **The British Tourist Authority** – for
permission to reproduce BTA photographs and **Mr Harold Booty**
of the BTA for his encouragement and support throughout the
project. All planning officers and their staffs who so helpfully
supplied information and photographs. All other people and
organisations who supplied information and photographs.
George Philip (Printers) Ltd – for their cooperation in preparing
the base maps.

Printed in Great Britain
by Redwood Burn, Trowbridge and Esher

Contents

How to use the guide

This Guide has been designed to help tourists – both foreign and native – who are interested in social, economic, political and physical history to find interesting examples of the way town and country have been consciously developed over the last four thousand years. We hope it will be as useful to the professional planner on holiday as to the interested layman who is perhaps a member of an amenity society or the National Trust.

The Guide is easily laid out for quick reference. The United Kingdom is divided into regions based on the various tourist boards (except for the Peak District which is put wholly within the North West Region for convenience) and each regional section begins with a map showing the sites mentioned and a general introduction to the history of man-made development in the region.

Within each region, the sites are divided into 'tours'. All sites on each tour are dealt with together in the text. For easy identification, each site is given a reference number, consisting of the initials of the region (e.g. NW for North West, Y for Yorkshire etc.), followed by the number of the tour within the region and the number of the site within the tour. Thus – NW 4/2 refers to site 2 of tour 4 in the North West. These reference numbers are shown on the regional maps, above the guide entries themselves, and also in the index at the back of the book. Thus quick cross-reference may be made between the map, text, photographs and index.

Reference is also made to the Ordnance Survey sheet and National Grid Reference appropriate to each site (except for Northern Ireland). The 'OS Sheet' number indicates which of the new 1:50,000 series sheets covers the area in question. The Grid Reference, 'GR', identifies the south west corner of the one kilometre square containing the whole or principal part of the site.

We have also included an index classified by type of site – for example – 'Conservation in Towns', 'Defence Sites', 'Housing Developments' and 'Industrial Towns'. This should make it easy for the person who is interested in a particular facet of the urban or rural environment to trace the relevant entries very quickly.

We hope that you will enjoy reading and using this Guide and that it will stimulate interest generally in the man-made environment, both modern and historic. We warmly thank all our contributors, but the final choice of sites and their descriptions – and any factual errors – must be attributed to us.

Introduction

In his *English Social History*, G.M. Trevelyan dates the beginning
of the 'English People' from Chaucer's time: the fourteenth
century. The English had by then become a racial and cultural
unit; the ruling class was no longer French, nor the serfs
Anglo-Saxon. The economic and social forces at work in the
building of towns and the countryside were all truly native at last.

This social and political watershed is not sharply defined but
occurred during a period of transition, marked primarily by the
growth of a wealthy mercantile class which could compete with
the aristocracy in building grand houses and providing money for
the King's and the Public Purse. This wealth was created by early
industrial revolutions in, for example, cloth making and the use
of water power. The fourteenth and fifteenth century 'wool'
churches of East Anglia and the Cotswolds, such as Lavenham,
Cirencester and Chipping Campden, still reflect this radical change in
English social life, which marked the end of the Middle Ages and the
birth of modern England, and is clearly reflected in this guide.

But the guide is concerned not only with England but with the
whole of the United Kingdom. The introductory notes to
Scotland, Wales and Northern Ireland place the national
contributions in geographical and historical context. They tell
fascinating stories of regional diversity, overlaid by differences in
culture and language. There is a similar, but not usually so
strongly marked, diversity between the regions of England. Much
of it can be attributed to variations in geology, soils, climate and
migrant peoples from many parts of Europe — Celts, Angles,
Saxons, Danes, Normans, Dutch and French — each with
differing skills and ways of life, who have settled in this country
over the past three thousand years.

It is such facets of the social and environmental evolution of
Great Britain and Northern Ireland that this book sets out to
illustrate. Planned developments do not just happen — they are
brought about by specific social, economic and political forces.
Before the fifteenth century, the principal determinants of
urban and other man-made developments were mainly strategic
and defensive: Iron Age hill forts; the road network and settlement
pattern of the occupying Roman army; castles and new towns
built by the Norman conquerors; the strategic fortified towns
of Edward I in North Wales. The day-do-day affairs of the
man in the street have left fewer physical traces for us to see
today. Houses and farms were constructed of less durable
materials than castles and town walls. The influence of the
Anglo-Saxon agricultural colonisation of Britain is perpetuated
more in the pattern of settlements and place names than in
physical remains.

After the fifteenth century the 'evidence in the stones' is much more apparent. Vernacular styles of architecture and building methods were influenced by Continental Renaissance architects, especially Palladio (1518-80). This new tradition, introduced into Britain by Inigo Jones in the early seventeenth century, led via architects such as Wren, Vanbrugh and Hawksmoor to the great urban planning schemes of the eighteenth century, such as Bath, Edinburgh New Town and the London squares, as well as to innumerable smaller urban developments and elegant country houses and parks all over the United Kingdom. This was a golden age of good taste in urban and countryside planning and a great deal survives to the present day.

Later, in the eighteenth century, the impact of the agricultural and industrial revolutions on land and townscape began to be felt. Three characteristic developments of the industrial era might be picked out: the working class town shaped by public health bylaws; the extensive development of transport systems, especially railways and ports; and the squalor of the coal mine, steel works and railway yard — dominating adjoining workers' houses and covering them with smoke and dirt. Men, women — even children — were hands to be exploited for profit and then discarded. The towns grew up and the foundations of the modern city were laid. It was a deadening place and a dreary heritage to pass on. Civic pride was materialistic; the new city parks were not meant for carefree pleasure but were ostentatious imitations of the eighteenth century gardens of the gentry. But a few men rebelled against this civic materialism and squalor and founded the garden city movement out of a desire to escape from the suffocation of industrial towns and create an atmosphere that was half urban, half rural. Enlightened employers such as the Cadburys and W.H. Lever built 'garden villages' for their workers at Bournville and Port Sunlight. The writings of Sir Ebenezer Howard led directly to the founding of the first true garden city at Letchworth in 1902, followed by Welwyn in 1919. The same principle of *rus in urbe* was applied to countless garden suburbs from Hampstead to New Earswick in York. The same movement led to campaigns to save common land for the enjoyment of townspeople and the struggles for access to mountains and moorlands began. Education slowly became available to all. Board schools, public baths and libraries were built. Democracy and bureaucracy advanced: the masterpieces of the Victorian town halls were designed by architectural competitions and constructed with pride.

The first Housing and Planning Act was passed in 1909. Considerably influenced by the garden city movement, it was a sign of the increasing concern of Parliament, some enlightened local authorities such as Manchester and Birmingham, and philanthropists such as the Cadburys, for sensitive public control of the shape, structure and quality of urban areas; many could no longer be called 'towns'. This Act was the first of a large family which grew quickly after the Second World War.

They included legislation to guide the distribution of jobs into areas of economic decline, to construct new towns as contributions to the development of city regions, to make and manage national parks and local country parks, to build houses and schools as parts of comprehensive social policies, to cope with the ever growing problem of motor traffic — and, more generally, to create an urban and regional planning system which can exercise control over the structure and quality of the environment of this industrial society, and can shape its future. Nearly half the fixed investment of the United Kingdom is either in the public sector or is constrained by public policies; most fixed investment is 'development' as defined by the planning acts. The latest examples in the Guide are indicative of the importance of the planning processes of today in helping the development of the economy and the achievement of social aims.

William Ogden

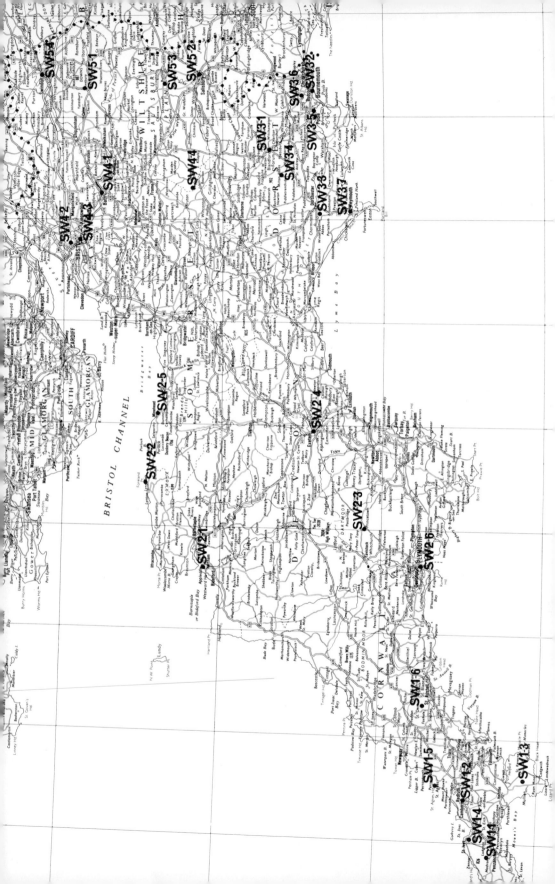

The South West

The South West, with its long coastline of 675 miles from Bristol to Land's End and along the Channel coast as far as Poole, is inevitably linked with British maritime history, and many coastal towns contain traces of very old port and harbour development. Indeed, it was the settlement of immigrants from the continent in search of tin that almost certainly introduced the languages which evolved into the Celtic tongues of historic times: an immigration that started perhaps twenty-five centuries ago.

From the first century B.C. to the fifth century A.D. these settlers established court-house villages that might well be the earliest evolution of planning in the far South West of England. Notable examples are at Chysauster three miles north of Penzance, where eight courtyard houses are ranged in pairs along a village street, and at Bant's Carn on the north coast of the island of St Mary's in Scilly, dating from about the second or third century A.D.

Even earlier are the great monuments of the Neolithic and Bronze Ages: Stonehenge and Avebury in Wiltshire, and Maiden Castle near Dorchester in Dorset, generally considered to be one of the finest Neolithic and Iron Age forts in England.

The establishment of the spa of Aquae Sulis at the town now known as Bath, is a significant example of early civic building. The warm springs were revived early in the eighteenth century but the Roman remains can still be seen.

The English heritage of Saxon town planning is exemplified in the oldest town in Dorset, Wareham, on the northern border of the Purbeck peninsula. A port developed late in the ninth century and the town still retains its characteristic ramparts and grid iron street plan with a later motte and bailey castle.

Military fortifications sprang up after the conquest of England by the Normans in the eleventh century. The finest examples are the castles of Dunheved at Launceston, and Restormel near Lostwithiel, both in Cornwall, and the gatehouse of Rougemont Castle in the centre of Exeter. Later castles were erected as part of Henry VIII's coastal defences of the region: at Falmouth, Pendennis Castle on a prehistoric hill fort, and St Mawes Castle on the eastern side of the Carrick Roads.

The cathedrals and their precincts at Salisbury and Exeter are classic examples of the Medieval English 'minster close'. Edward III licensed the building of a wall round Salisbury and the houses of the people who served the cathedral, resulting in the Close of today, entered via Medieval gateways, but with its houses refronted in Georgian times.

There can be little doubt that the eighteenth century and the early nineteenth century were a golden age for the South West, with fine examples of town and country house building, commercial enterprise, and port and harbour construction. Tremendous impetus was given to the development of deep mining in Cornwall by the new technology of the steam pumping engine. The Roman spa at Bath was revived in this age of splendid civic planning, and its Georgian architecture is well worth seeing: particularly the great sweep of thirty houses forming the Royal Crescent; Queen's Square; the Pump Room and Poulteney Bridge. The prosperity of the port of Bristol is also reflected in its fine Georgian terraces and the wealth of the mineral landowners and entrepreneurs in Cornish mining interests brought about the construction of many elegant streets such as Lemon Street in Truro, a broad ascent of houses still retaining much Georgian detail.

Great country houses reflected this economic prosperity and were an inspiration to landscape architects. The fine parks of Longleat and Wardour Castle in Wiltshire, were laid out by the notable English landscape architect, Lancelot 'Capability' Brown. Other superb examples are at Stourhead in the same county and at Trelissick, near Truro in Cornwall, both now owned by the National Trust.

Despite the isolation of the region from the coalfields, town building was given its greatest impetus by the industrial revolution and nineteenth century technological developments. Exeter, Plymouth, Truro and Penzance contain many terraces, squares, and crescents associated with the town planning of the period.

The development of the Cornish china clay industry after 1770 caused the growth of new ports to ship the clay to Runcorn, and then down the Trent and Mersey Canal to the Potteries. The railway age in the South West commenced when the Great Western Railway, conceived by Bristol merchants in 1832, opened its line to London in 1841. By 1948 the rails had been laid as far west as Plymouth. In 1859 Brunel's Royal Albert Bridge across the Tamar at Saltash near Plymouth was completed and through trains began to run from London to Penzance. The railway company comissioned a design for a complete new settlement in Wiltshire and, by the mid nineteenth century, the railway town of Swindon developed, with 300 dwellings and shops, a Mechanics' Institute and other buildings — a fascinating example of an early railway town.

With the completion of the railway line from London to Penzance, about twenty branch lines fed and nurtured small seaside towns such as Minehead, Bude, Newquay, Lyme Regis and Swanage. Many are worth visiting to see how the Victorian and Edwardian entrepreneurs developed their potential. The huge hotels, terraces of boarding houses and iron piers are particularly characteristic of the era.

During the present century the south and west of the peninsula, with its long stretches of spectacular coastline and its unspoiled farmsteads and moorland hinterland, has become a magnet for the holiday maker. The blessings and benefits are matched by attendant problems. The summer visitors pump cash into the economy but, at the same time, create traffic congestion in the narrow lanes and inlets and mar the peace of some of the old fishing villages. Planners are doing their utmost to balance the conflicting pressures. One solution has been to house visitors in holiday villages such as Little Orchard Village at St Agnes in Cornwall — an attractively landscaped chalet village developed in 1950 on a derelict mining site. Elsewhere ownership of coastal land by the National Trust and others has ensured its permanent protection from the worst excesses of tourist development.

Apart from holiday centres, development during this century has been concentrated in the main urban centres of Bournemouth/Poole, Bristol, Exeter, Plymouth and Torbay. Bristol, Exeter and Plymouth all suffered extensive war damage and show contrasting solutions to the problems of rebuilding their central areas. Plymouth became the only city in Britain to replan its centre on truly monumental lines and now possesses wide landscaped streets flanked with shops and civic buildings. Bristol created a new shopping centre at Broadmead which has now been updated as a pedestrian precinct. Exeter was rebuilt on basically its former plan. By contrast, the Arndale Centre in Poole and the Hampshire Centre on the outskirts of Bournemouth represent the two principal trends in shopping provision for the 1970s — enclosed town centre precincts incorporating leisure, civic and commercial functions; and out of town shopping centres dependent upon lower land values and extensive free car parking.

In spite of the summer crowds, the South West has a quality of life which attracts those who, for work, retirement or leisure, seek rural peace, majestic scenery or a gentle climate. It remains the nation's foremost holiday and retirement region but, with the prospect of oil discoveries in the Celtic Sea, the completion of the M5 motorway to Exeter, and ever increasing demands on home mineral resources, without continued vigilance and action the South West may lose that quality which it holds so dear.

Peter Laws

Chysauster Iron Age Village, showing the eight courtyard houses arranged in pairs along a 'village street'. *Crown copyright — reproduced with the permission of the Controller of Her Majesty's Stationery Office.*

4

Chysauster, near Penzance SW 1/1
OS Sheet 203   GR SW 4735

An Iron Age and Roman (100 B.C.-200 A.D.) agricultural village
on an attractive moorland site with fine views. The village is an
Ancient Monument under the care of the Department of the
Environment and is in a good state of preservation. Four pairs of
houses front the village street, each of which has the unusual
feature of a stone fenced back garden. Although unplanned,
Chysauster is one of the earliest and best preserved agricultural
settlements in the country.

East Pool Mine, near Redruth SW 1/2
OS Sheet 203   GR SW 6741

Tin mining was for centuries one of the most important industries
in Cornwall, but declined in the later nineteenth and twentieth
centuries. The landscape of parts of Cornwall is still, however,
dramatically affected by the remains of the tin mining industry.
The two Cornish beam engines at this mine were saved from the
scrapheap, one of 1887 raised miners and ore from 1,300 feet,
and another of 1892, erected at the mine in 1924, pumped water
from 1,700 feet. Both are now owned and managed by the
National Trust.

Taylor's 90″ pumping
engine at East Pool
Mine as it was when
working.
C.E.P.S.

Goonhilly Downs, The Lizard SW 1/3
OS Sheet 204   GR SW 7220

In the same way as the Post Office Tower in London (q.v.),
Goonhilly illustrates the recent dramatic and continuing growth
in telecommunications. It was Britain's first Post Office satellite
transmitting and receiving station. The site was taken over by the
Post Office in 1961 and the station was in operation in time for
the first transatlantic satellite communications to be transmitted
via Telstar in 1963. The large dish aerials of the station are
prominent on the surrounding downs.

Goonhilly satellite
communication aerial.
Post Office.

Halsetown, near St Ives SW 1/4
OS Sheet 203   GR SW 5038

A model mining village built about 1830 by James Halse, a
solicitor and MP for St Ives. The interesting original pattern of
development is still easily discernible, and consists of back to
back and side to side dwellings in blocks of four, each with its
own garden. The village, which is a conservation area, is reached
from the St Ives to Penzance Road.

Little Orchard Village, St Agnes

SW 1/5

OS Sheet 203   GR SW 7151

A chalet holiday village, built in 1950 on reclaimed derelict mine workings. The chalets have been attractively designed and carefully sited in the valley and the site has been landscaped. An uncharacteristically attractive example of speculative coastal tourist development.

Little Orchard Holiday Village near St. Agnes. *Cornwall County Planning Officer.*

China clay pits, St Austell

SW 1/6

OS Sheet 200   GR SW 9957 (Hensbarrow Downs)

A representative example of Cornish china clay extraction as carried out by English China Clays Ltd. With the decline of the tin mining industry, china clay extraction is now Cornwall's chief mineral industry. Unfortunately it invariably constitutes an unpleasant although often dramatic visual intrusion in the landscape.

Appledore Shipyard

SW 2/1

OS Sheet 180   GR SS 4630

Appledore, ideally sited at the confluence of the Rivers Taw and Torridge, was an important ship building centre for centuries, although it has declined in importance. However the local shipbuilding industry gained considerable momentum in 1970 with the opening of the largest covered shipbuilding dock in Europe. This development is typical of a modern industrial building, sited in an area of economic decline and serving both the primary purpose of building ships and the secondary purpose of creating employment.

Waste quartz tips from china clay workings near St. Austell. *English China Clays Ltd.*

Old and new shipyards at Appledore. *Devon County Planning Officer.*

Countisbury Hill and
Foreland Point, Exmoor
National Park.
Waverley Photographic.

Countisbury Hill and the Foreland   SW 2/2
OS Sheet 180   GR SS 7550

To protect the best remaining stretches of coastline in England,
Wales and Northern Ireland the National Trust launched
Enterprise Neptune in 1965. By 1973 they had raised two
million pounds and added a further 127½ miles of coastline to
their already substantial holding of 175 miles. One property
acquired under this scheme was Countisbury Hill and the
Foreland extending to 700 acres and 2½ miles of dramatic
coastline east of Lynmouth and within the Exmoor National
Park. Of exceptional beauty, the steep slopes down on the
rivers and parts of the cliff face are softened by hanging oak
woods. West of Foreland Point the landscape is bleaker, rising to
993 feet at Countisbury where the cliffs are among the highest
in England.

New Bridge; one of the
starting points for
guided walks for visitors
to Dartmoor.
*Dartmoor National
Park Officer.*

Dartmoor   SW 2/3
OS Sheet 191   GR SX 5874 (Princetown)

Dartmoor National Park, covering 365 square miles, accommodates
many conflicting uses and activities. Its recreational attraction
draws about 4½ million visitors a year with over 65,000 visiting on
a peak day. Military training takes place over 27,000 acres of
moorland and the Forestry Commission has planted about 5,000
acres, mainly with coniferous softwoods. Since 1806 Princetown
Gaol has dominated the centre of the moor and the need for
water to supply surrounding towns has created several proposals
to construct reservoirs on the moor. This illustrates that, in an
island as crowded as Britain, single land uses or activities can
rarely take precedence. To preserve the 'special character' of the
Park, the planning authority have defined areas for recreation
facilities on a scale appropriate to the conservation of the natural

features. Elsewhere voluntary agreements have defined those areas which can or cannot be planted with trees. To encourage visitors to leave their cars and learn more about the Park, guided walks are arranged during the summer.

Exeter   SW 2/4
OS Sheet 192   GR SX 9292

Originally a Roman settlement, Exeter later became the capital of the West Saxon kingdom and during the Middle Ages was the westernmost city in England. The city walls date back to Roman times and much of the Medieval defences can still be seen. The walls can best be viewed in Post Office Street, Southernhay West and Northernhay Gardens. Rougemont Castle dates from 1068 and its gatehouse is one of the finest pieces of Norman military architecture in England. The fine cathedral dating from 1275 was built on part of the site of the Roman city.

Princesshay Shopping Centre, Exeter. Rebuilt as a traffic street after war-time bombing but now reserved for pedestrians. *Nigel Heard, Exeter City Council.*

Exeter continued to be an important trading centre throughout the Tudor and Stuart periods. In 1566 a 1¾ mile canal containing the first pound locks in Britain was dug to enable ships to continue to reach the city, thus predating Brindley's Bridgewater Canal by 200 years (see Castlefields Canal Basin [NW 4/3]). The Guildhall in the High Street is reputed to be the oldest municipal building in the country and dates from the fifteenth century. Development continued during the Georgian period and Southernhay is an outstanding example of late eighteenth century urban planning.

Exeter suffered considerable damage during the last war and much of the central area has since been rebuilt — in particular the Princesshay Shopping Centre, completed in 1956. It is also a university town and the campus has expanded rapidly in recent years on a 300 acre parkland site which was once a private estate. The impressive modern buildings have been integrated with the original eighteenth and nineteenth century private buildings.

Exeter's importance lies in the continuity of its development. The city has stood on this site since Roman times — unlike Salisbury, for example, which has occupied four sites. Prosperity has been more or less continuous since the city's foundation and it has always been considered by many to be the capital of the South West.

Minehead, Butlin's Holiday Camp   SW 2/5
OS Sheet 181   GR SS 4698

The organised holiday camp, in which accommodation and entertainment are supplied on the same site, has been one of the main growth areas in British tourism since 1945. Some early camps were converted from ex-army depots, but such was their growth in popularity that these were soon replaced by purpose-built accommodation. Butlins at Minehead is a typical example of a modern holiday camp, built to a very formal plan and located on the coast in open countryside, but close to both road and rail communications.

Butlins Holiday Camp
at Minehead.
Aerofilms.

Plymouth

OS Sheet 201   GR SX 4754

SW 2/6

Plymouth has long been a major naval port because of its fine natural harbour. The old town incorporating the Barbican area and Sutton Harbour survived, as the commercial centre moved westwards, and largely maintains its narrow sixteenth century street pattern. It is now a designated conservation area. In the early nineteenth century the town's importance as a naval dockyard was emphasised by the construction of impressive civic buildings at Devonport such as the Guildhall in Grecian/ Doric style, and the Library in Egyptian style. An obvious target for enemy bombing in World War Two, the town centre has been almost totally rebuilt to the plans of Sir Patrick Abercrombie and J. Paton Watson. Unlike Exeter and Southampton, which were rebuilt on virtually the existing street plan, Plymouth is one of the best examples in Britain of the monumental formality of town centre planning favoured until the 1960s, with wide tree lined streets and expanses of grass and gardens.

The new city centre
of Plymouth
Aerofilms

9

Blandford Forum

OS Sheets 194   GR ST 8906

The town of Blandford has had a most unlucky history. It was
burned down in 1570, 1677, 1713 and finally in 1731. After the
fire of 1731, which destroyed almost all the town, Blandford
was rebuilt to a comprehensive plan, mainly by the local
brothers John and William Bastard. Much of the rebuilding
survives and gives Blandford a special distinction as a fine example
of mid-eighteenth century urban planning. Before the Georgian
era, the abundant use of timber for building meant that towns
quite often suffered disastrous fires, such as the Great Fire of
London of 1666. Since then the increasing use of relatively
fireproof brick has resulted in a fine heritage of Georgian
buildings in many country towns.

Bournemouth

OS Sheet 195   GR SZ 0890

A Victorian new town, developed as a resort from 1835 onwards,
through the enterprise of local landowners. The town was to
consist of detached villas set among pinewoods, and as a complete
contrast to previous (Georgian) tradition, terraces and other
urban forms of development were to be strictly avoided. The
population rose rapidly from 695 in 1851 to 5,896 in 1871,
37,650 in 1891 and 59,762 in 1901. On the advice of Decimus
Burton, the architect, the valley of the River Bourne was laid out
as public gardens, to constitute the town's central feature. This
important example of Victorian landscaping, over two miles long,
is still intact. In 1972, the Town Centre by-pass was carried
over the gardens on a bridge which received a design award from
the Civic Trust. At the sea end of the gardens, the Pier Approach
has been pedestrianised, and traffic diverted on to a flyover.

   In recent years many of the original villas have been
redeveloped as mostly undistinguished blocks of flats. However,
an impression of the town's Victorian flavour can still be
gained from the gardens and Old Christchurch Road, one of the
principal shopping streets.

Maiden Castle

OS Sheet 194   GR SY 6788

The largest and one of the best preserved ancient British hill forts.

Maiden Castle with
Dorchester in the
background.
Aerofilms.

The site was occupied from Neolithic times, and during the Iron Age was the chief settlement of the Durotriges. After the Roman invasion of A.D. 43, the fort was besieged and taken by the Second Legion under Vespasian. The Romans then built Durnovaria (modern Dorchester) in the valley below. This became the tribal centre and the hill fort was abandoned. A comparable shift in location of settlements at this time is seen from the Iron Age Trundle, Goodwood, to Roman Chichester.

Milton Abbas   SW 3/4
OS Sheet 194   GR ST 8001

An attractive late eighteenth century model village laid out by Capability Brown, the landscape architect. The present village replaced the earlier market town of Milton Abbas, which was demolished by Lord Milton, Earl of Dorchester. He employed Sir William Chambers to rebuild the present mansion and the village was moved in order to improve the view from the house. It remains largely intact to the present day and has been designated a conservation area. Some planning permissions for infilling have been revoked in order to preserve the village's outstanding character.

Milton Abbas.
B.T.A.

Poole   SW 3/5
OS Sheet 195   GR SZ 0190

In existence by the twelfth century, Poole reached the peak of its prosperity in the eighteenth century. This prosperity was based on trade with Newfoundland, and once it declined the town stagnated, so that even in 1960 the street pattern and development in the town centre was largely that of 1800. But postwar prosperity and the growth of traffic led to great pressures on the town centre. To save the most valuable historic area the Old Town CDA Map of 1960 proposed a 'Special Precinct'

The Harbour Office and Customs House, Poole.
B.T.A.

within which the preservation and improvement of the existing environment was to be paramount. Outside this prototype conservation area (which predated the Civic Amenities Act by seven years) the remainder of the central area has been largely rebuilt. A most notable achievement is the Arndale Complex consisting of a sports centre, library, bus station, multistorey car park and indoor shopping centre. This major town centre shopping precinct is in contrast to the Hampshire Centre, ten miles away on the northern outskirts of Bournemouth. These two sites offer a comparison between the principal trends in new shopping provision today — town centre redevelopment and out of town shopping centres.

Talbot Village, Bournemouth SW 3/6
OS Sheet 195   GR SZ 0794

A mid-nineteenth century model village, developed between 1845 and 1875 through the philanthropy of Georgina and Mary Anne Talbot. The land enclosures of the early nineteenth century had created extreme poverty among the local population, and the sisters sought to alleviate this by creating the village and the six farms which originally surrounded it. A free school was established and free medical treatment was made available. Almshouses and a church were built, but no shop or public house was permitted. The village is administered by a board of trustees and is comparatively unchanged, although it has long since been surrounded by later suburban development. It is significant both in terms of its physical appearance, and its social importance as an example of Victorian philanthropy surviving intact to the present day. There are current proposals to bring the village up to date with 'a balanced scheme of conservation and development'.

Talbot Village, Bournemouth. *Architects' Journal.*

Weymouth sea front.
B.T.A.

Weymouth   SW 3/7
OS Sheet 194   GR SY 6879

Weymouth is the Georgian seaside resort par excellence with an
impressive seafront. It first became popular through the patronage
of George III who visited it regularly for sea bathing from 1789.
Founded in Roman times, it has always been a substantial port
and is currently the main departure point for the Channel
Islands. A number of Tudor buildings still survive, notably
3 Trinity Street, an early seventeenth century pair of
semidetached houses (not common before the late nineteenth
century). They have been restored as a museum.

Rapid speculative expansion up to about 1830 left Weymouth
architecturally much richer than almost any other resort except
Brighton. It is therefore a fine example of late Georgian and
Regency town development and planning.

Lansdown Crescent,
Bath.
*Bath City Planning
Officer.*

Bath   SW 4/1
OS Sheet 172   GR ST 7565

The earliest (A.D. 44) and most famous of all British spas and
holiday resorts, Bath is now the most complete and best
preserved Georgian city in Britain. The substantial remains of
the Roman Baths can still be seen. In the Middle Ages, the town
was famous for its waters and its wool, but during the sixteenth
and seventeenth centuries the wool industry declined and a full
scale 'entertainment' industry grew up, based on the waters.
Bath therefore became a social and medicinal centre, and during
the eighteenth century enjoyed a period of great expansion and
popularity. The Corporation appointed Richard (Beau) Nash as
'Director of Tourism' in 1705 and over the next forty years he
'virtually invented the holiday industry'. Much of the impressive
architecture and urban design of Georgian Bath was the work of
the two John Woods, father and son.

The popularity of spas declined in the nineteenth century,
but by virtue of its unique townscape, Bath has remained popular
with tourists. In recent years it has suffered from the
redevelopment of its lesser Georgian areas, and from traffic.
Because of these problems, it was the subject of one of the
'four towns'* studies in the late 1960s. The emphasis now is
heavily on the conservation of *all* Bath's remaining Georgian
development.

                                        *See glossary.

Blaise Hamlet, Bristol

OS Sheet 172   GR ST 5679

Blaise Hamlet (1811) is a product of pure aristocratic indulgence.
J.S. Harford, the owner of Blaise Castle, wished to provide the
castle grounds with a rustic village, and commissioned John Nash
to create Blaise Hamlet — ten picturesque cottages set round
an oval village green, complete with pump and sundial. The
style is 'rural-gothic' with thatched roofs and tiles, and looks
forward not only to much Victorian fantasy building, but also to
Port Sunlight and the garden suburb movement.

John Nash's Blaise
Hamlet, Bristol.
*Bristol City Planning
Officer.*

Bristol

OS Sheet 172   GR ST 5933

Bristol is of Saxon origin and became a town of great importance
in the Middle Ages. Early voyages to America were made from
the city and, after the sixteenth century, Bristol became the
centre of British mercantile capitalism, with much of its wealth
derived from the slave trade. The prosperity of the eighteenth
century can be seen in the suburb of Clifton, developed between
1740 and 1840 as a residential area for rich merchants, and
containing some outstanding Georgian terraces and squares.
·In 1840-64 the impressive Clifton Suspension Bridge was built
by I.K. Brunel to link the suburb with the opposite side of the
Avon gorge. Nineteenth century development included the
moving of the docks to Avonmouth, since the river was too
shallow to take the larger vessels. But Bristol has remained an
important commercial centre — the biggest city in the West of
England.

Clifton Suspension
Bridge and Terraces,
above the river Avon,
Bristol.
West Air Photography.

Stourhead Gardens

OS Sheet 183   GR ST 7734

One of the first attempts to create a natural and picturesque style
of English landscape gardening, to replace formal geometrical

Stourhead Gardens.
*Wiltshire County
Planning Officer.*

French designs. The gardens were laid out between 1740-50 by
Henry Flitcroft for the banker Henry Hoare. A series of lakes
were created in the bleak valley and the banks laid out with trees
and rare species of shrubs, and dotted with Greek temples and
other architectural features. To ensure their survival, the gardens
are owned by the National Trust.

Avebury   SW 5/1

OS Sheet 173   GR SU 1070

This is the largest prehistoric stone circle in the country (and
probably also in the world), measuring some 450 yards across. At
its centre lies Avebury village. The main date of building was
circa 1800 B.C., 200 years earlier than the main phase of
Stonehenge. A long avenue of megaliths leads to a bank and
ditch, which enclose three concentric stone circles. The
organisation necessary to plan and build this monument must
have been prodigious for the time, and its use was probably
religious or ritualistic.

Avebury Stone Circle,
enclosing the later
village.
Aerofilms.

Salisbury   SW 5/2

OS Sheet 184   GR SU 1429

Modern Salisbury is a 'Medieval new town' dating from 1219.
Three previous cities in the locality were all on different sites.
The original shire capital at Wilton was three miles to the west;
the Saxon town of Searisbyrig has not yet been satisfactorily
located; and a Norman settlement, castle and cathedral have been
extensively excavated at Old Sarum. Finally, in 1219, after
difficulties with the civil authorities, the Bishop began the
construction of a new cathedral and associated new town. A
charter was granted by Henry III in 1227 and the cathedral at
Old Sarum was abandoned in the same year.

   The grid pattern of the city's streets is still plainly discernible, although later developments have encroached on the market place. The cathedral and grounds originally occupied about the same amount of land as the new town itself.

New town plantations* were very common in the Middle Ages: the bishops of Salisbury had already created Devizes and Sherbone Newland. Salisbury is a particularly good example, since it reflects the original development in its street pattern today. The new town can also be compared with the remains of the older settlement at Old Sarum to the north.

The city expanded considerably in the last century, but has conserved its historic character, even in its new building. A new shopping precinct, the Old George Mall, built on 'back land' has been successfully integrated with the surrounding older buildings with access gained through the Tudor facade of The Old George Inn. Nearby, the Victorian Market Hall in the market square is being converted into a new library.

Aerial view showing the Medieval street pattern of Salisbury. *Wiltshire County Planning Officer.*

Stonehenge SW 5/3
OS Sheet 184   GR SU 1242

Probably the most well known Ancient Monument in Britain. Built in five phases between *c* 1800 and *c* 1400 B.C., it represents an outstanding achievement considering the constructional techniques of the time. The bluestones which form the outer circles were brought from Pembrokeshire by sea and land, while the Sarsen stones comprising the inner circle came from the Marlborough Downs, some thirty miles away. The layout of the monument, particularly the way in which the sun rises in a direct line over the Altar and Heelstones on Midsummer Day, has led to suggestions that it was connected with sun worship. However, this is still uncertain, although its original use may well have been religious.

Swindon SW 5/4
OS Sheet 173   GR SU 1485

Stonehenge. *Wiltshire County Planning Officer.*

New Swindon was the creation of the Great Western Railway Co. between 1842 and 1860. The site was chosen for the company's

*See glossary

16

main railway works which were opened in 1843. The station and works were appropriately magnificent in design. The railway company built a new town of workmen's cottages for the works, 243 of which had been completed by 1853. The company also provided shops, a church, a school, a Mechanics' Institution and other amenities. But the planning and layout of the new town was undistinguished and tasteless, the station hotel failed, and property values went down. Despite this, Swindon demonstrates the general nature of mid-Victorian company towns and the original core has lately been improved under the 1969 Housing Act. A railway museum has been established in what was originally a hostel for Irish navvies building the railway.

The running down of the railway workshops in the 1950s resulted in the institution of a town expansion scheme under the 1952 Town Development Act, so that the town could take overspill population from London. This injection of people and jobs has helped to ensure the continued prosperity of the area.

The original railway
village at Swindon.
Beatrice Bollard.

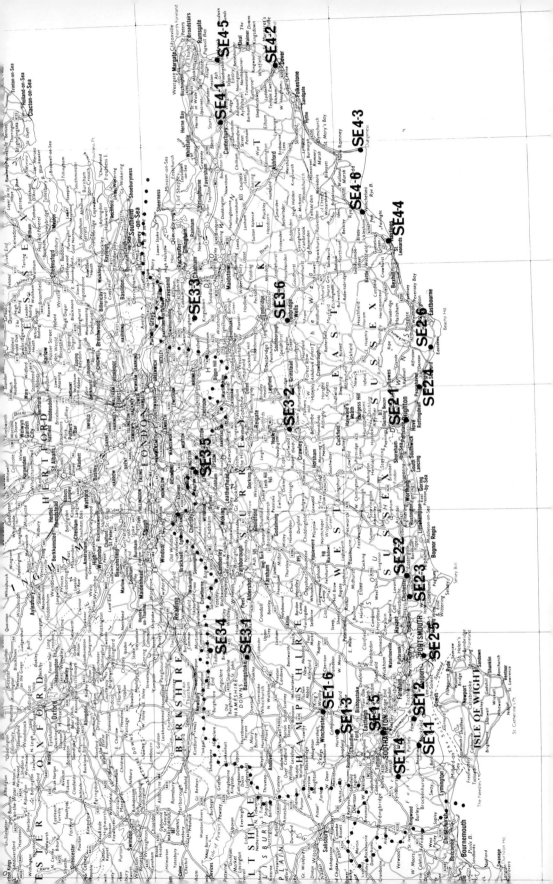

South East England

South East England is a topographically distinct area, bounded on the north by Greater London and the Thames Estuary, and on the south and east by the Channel and the North Sea. Only to the west is its boundary less clear. Geographically, there are four main types of country: chalk downs; sandy heaths and sandstone hills; claylands; coastal flats and estuarine marshes.

London's influence is strong throughout the region. All Surrey, much of East and West Sussex (including coastal towns such as Brighton), western Kent and, to a lesser extent, north east Hampshire is 'commuter country', thanks to the intensively developed electric train services of the Southern Region of British Rail. But suburban sprawl, although extensive, is more limited than many people imagine, and is sporadic more than twenty-five miles from the centre of London. The containment of suburban areas is due very largely to the firmness of planning authorities and the existence of the Metropolitan Green Belt — which existed in embryonic form before the Second World War, was fully established in the late 1940s, and has since been much extended.

The part of the region most independent of London is southern Hampshire. Here are the region's two largest cities, Southampton and Portsmouth, each having a population of about half a million. Both have a long history: Southampton as a mercantile port, Portsmouth as a naval base. Southampton has impressive remains of its Medieval city walls, currently being restored under a long-term conservation programme by the City Council. The shopping centre was almost entirely destroyed by bombing in the Second World War, and was rebuilt in the 1950s in an architecturally insipid manner typical of the period, perpetuating its old linear form. Only a few of the later buildings (from the 1960s and early 1970s) in the commercial area are architecturally impressive. The high/medium rise housing scheme at Northam (1959-65) designed by the city architect, Lewis Berger, is one of the best of its kind and period, with exceptionally good landscape treatment of the spaces between the buildings. Southampton's heyday as a passenger port was from 1920 to 1955, when it was the terminus of the Atlantic run. Now that passenger transit has declined the port has increased greatly as a cargo terminal, and has container berths. Portsmouth's naval dockyard contains Nelson's Victory, one of the great tourist attractions of the south, dry berthed in a dock constructed shortly before Trafalgar. Portsmouth is a complex city on an island site; its Old Town, still physically distinct, was heavily bombed, but the surviving historic buildings are well conserved, many as private residences. The remaining sixteenth to nineteenth century town defences are being systematically restored by the City Council. The present city centre, first developed in the later nineteenth century, was heavily bombed, and partly rebuilt in the 1950s, but this part has been much improved through pedestrianisation and tree planting.

The Portsmouth-Southampton area was first suggested as an area for major urban growth in the *South East Study* published in 1964. Colin Buchanan and Partners were commissioned soon afterwards to study the feasibility of accommodating an extra ¼ million population in the region and their outline plan formed the basis for the Draft Structure Plan for South Hampshire in 1972, recommending development in the hinterland of the two cities to accommodate an increased population of up to one-third million. Following an exercise in public participation and consultation, this is still being considered.

Along the coast of West and East Sussex is a series of sizeable seaside resorts, including Worthing, Brighton, Eastbourne and Hastings, with long stretches of suburban sprawl. The coastal area is favoured for retirement, with consequently growing pressures on the available building land. Of the Sussex coastal towns, Brighton is the largest and most complex, and has the most pressing planning problems. Originally a fishing town, it developed in the early nineteenth century as a fashionable resort, largely under the stimulus of the Prince Regent, later George IV. After the coming of the railway, Brighton became a favourite place for day trips by Londoners, but it did not cease to be fashionable while becoming popular, and is now at the same time both sophisticated and boisterous. There are miles of 'Regency' streets, many of which have recently been 'improved' as fashionable residential localities, and two areas (Kemp Town and Brunswick Town) of particularly grand-scale urban planning of the 1820s.

Brighton has developed into a regional subcentre for much of Sussex, and has the first of the newly founded postwar universities. The Greater Brighton Structure Plan, published in 1973, concludes that any further expansion of urban development would be quite unacceptable, since it would take place in the scenically splendid South Downs which form the backcloth to the built up area.

East Kent, and particularly the area round Dover and Folkestone Folkestone, has a problematic future. At present the two ports are flourishing, with increasing loads of cross channel traffic using the still inadequate roads leading to London. Now that the Channel Tunnel project has been shelved, both ports will probably be developed, and there will be a continuing need for better transport links with the rest of the country which do the minimum of damage to the environments through which they pass.

The inland towns of South East England, apart from those which are near to Greater London, are medium to small in size. The largest is Crawley, one of a series of new towns established round London in the late 1940s and the only designated new

town in the region. In the last of the series of regional plans
for London and the South East, the area from Crawley to
Burgess Hill has been suggested as an area for major growth. This
suggestion is justified partly by the existence of Gatwick Airport;
partly by the economic success and buoyancy of Crawley itself;
and partly by the fast expanding population in other parts of the
area. West Sussex County Council is now preparing a Structure
Plan for the area.

Several town expansion schemes have been undertaken by the
Greater London Council in conjunction with the local authorities,
notably at Basingstoke, Andover, Hastings and Ashford. The
major expansion of Basingstoke from a population of about
20,000 to about 80,000 and the smaller expansion of Andover,
from about 15,000 to about 45,000 were promoted as alternatives
to a proposal for a complete new town at Hook. Basingstoke
now has a partially renewed and greatly expanded town centre,
with a decked shopping area integrated with several layers of
parking space, and with offices, and an interesting variety of
high density, low rise housing schemes. At Andover the old, and
pleasant market town shopping centre has been substantially
expanded in a way that has not seriously affected its established
character, nor challenged the visual dominance of the town's
two notable nineteenth century buildings, the Classical Guildhall
and the Gothic parish church.

The region has three major 'heritage cities': Canterbury,
Winchester and Chichester. They were Roman towns, and their
main streets follow Roman lines. Each has a great cathedral —
that at Canterbury being the mother church of the Anglican
Communion. Both Winchester and Canterbury were Medieval
cities of major importance, and all three, especially Chichester,
were prosperous in the eighteenth century. But all are thriving
modern shopping centres of sub regional importance, and
Canterbury has the recently founded University of Kent.
Winchester and Chichester have well-preserved historic centres
with a wealth of notable buildings. Canterbury's historic centre
was partly destroyed by bombing and the devastated area was,
in parts, rebuilt with some imagination when (Sir) Hugh Wilson,
later famous as the master planner of Cumbernauld, was city
architect; but not all the postwar planning there is good. The
planning authorities for the 'heritage cities' appreciate the
immense value of the historic environments and are at pains to
conserve them. Much of Winchester High Street has been visibly
improved in the last few years through the action of property
owners and occupiers in restoring or outwardly improving their
buildings, in cooperation with the city and county councils.
Chichester was one of the four historic cities selected for study
in the 1960s; as a result, detailed recommendations were made
for the improvement of the whole of the historic city centre,
including the rerouting of traffic, the pedestrianisation of some
of the main streets, and the improvement of existing buildings
and spaces.

There are many other historic towns of great and varied

interest and charm, including Lewes, Arundel, Faversham,
Farnham, Tunbridge Wells, Sandwich, Rye and Winchelsea.
Tunbridge Wells became a sophisticated rural spa following the
discovery of a medicinal spring in 1606. It very gradually
developed into a small town, centred on what is now known as
The Pantiles — an urban space entirely enclosed by buildings,
of varying dates from the seventeenth to the twentieth century,
with a covered colonnaded walk set within the buildings on one
side. As a 'shopping precinct' it is more attractive than most
of its modern counterparts, possibly because it developed
gradually, and hence has a subtle atmosphere that is difficult
to obtain in a centre created all at once.

Largely due to the firm conservationist policies of the planning
authorities the region retains an amazing amount of unspoiled
countryside, much of it of great beauty. Apart from the
Metropolitan Green Belt, and areas held by the Crown such as the
New Forest, large parts of the region are protected by being
designated Areas of Outstanding Natural Beauty. For anyone
who doubts that so much of the region is unspoiled and attractive,
three areas are recommended in particular. First, the country
between Tunbridge Wells and Ashford, including villages which
are full of examples of the rich vernacular tradition of the Weald,
in timber, sandstone, brick and tile. Secondly, the country
between Haslemere and Chichester, partly sandstone hills and
partly chalk downs, including two charming small country towns,
Midhurst and Petworth. Thirdly, the country centred on Leith
Hill, in Surrey (which, rising to just under 1,000 feet, is the
highest point in South East England). This is varied and unspoiled,
though visited by thousands during summer weekends. The
recreational value of areas such as these increases as the population
of the South East grows, and their preservation, by and large,
is one of the greatest postwar achievements of planning
authorities in the South East region.

David W. Lloyd

Beaulieu and Bucklers Hard   SE 1/1

OS Sheet 196   GR SV 4000

Bucklers Hard, with
Beaulieu River and
the New Forest beyond.
*National Motor
Museum.*

Beaulieu, originally an abbey and manor house, is now well
known as the site of the National Motor Museum. Remains of

the abbey can still be seen, and the new museum has been well
integrated with the older development, and includes a large car
park hidden among trees. A few miles down the Beaulieu
River is the hamlet of Bucklers Hard, where many eighteenth
century warships were built of oak from the nearby New Forest.
The development of the ironclad warship meant the decline
of the shipbuilding industry, but the hamlet has recently been
restored and opened up for tourism by Lord Montagu, in
association with the motor museum at Beaulieu. It remains an
attractive example of Georgian waterside development. The
Beaulieu Estate was one of the first private estates in Britain
to be the subject of a comprehensive management plan based on
recreation and tourism. It was prepared by Leonard Manasseh
and Partners and forms the basis for all recent development.

Fawley Oil Refinery and Power Station   SE 1/2
OS Sheet 196   GR SU 4603

Prominently situated on Southampton Water, Fawley refinery
was begun in 1947 and is a good example of the national
need for oil over-riding environmental considerations at that time —
the refinery is only a few miles from the New Forest and Beaulieu —
but the need for a deep water location dictated its siting.
However, the refinery, which covers 2,000 acres, has been
landscaped to reduce the impact on local amenities.

The power station was built in the 1960s to take advantage of
the oil from the nearby refinery and the availability of cooling
water.

Casual visitors are not admitted to the refinery for security
reasons, but guided tours can be arranged.

Fawley Oil Refinery
on Southampton Water.
An Esso Photograph.

The I.B.M. Research
Centre based on
Hursley Park.
I.B.M.

Hursley, IBM Research Centre   SE 1/3
OS Sheet 185   GR SU 4225

The growth of research and development in industry has led to
the establishment of campus office sites often based on country
estates. Employing large numbers of highly paid and mobile
professional and technical workers, these complexes depend
extensively on private cars for travel to work, and on road
transport for servicing. Such sites as the IBM computer centre at
Hursley, employing 2,000 workers, bring about a complete
reorientation of journey to work patterns.

Bolderwood Picnic
Site in the New Forest.
*Hampshire County
Planning Officer.*

New Forest   SE 1/4
OS Sheets 195 and 196   GR SU 3008 (Lyndhurst)

Originally established in 1079 as a Royal Hunting Forest by
William I, the Forest is now a popular tourist and camping area.
It is managed by the Forestry Commission. Recently, the
pressure of visitors, and in particular their cars, has become so
great that restrictions have been introduced so that, for example,
camping is now only allowed on specified sites and the movement
of cars has been curtailed. A comprehensive programme of multi-
land use incorporating protection of the environment and
recreation development is being carried out by the Forestry
Commission.

　　The Forest consists of large areas of woodland, interspersed
with open moorland. The woodlands are divided into the original
'Ancient and Ornamental' areas and the specially planted
Forestry Commission conifer enclosures.

Southampton   SE 1/5
OS Sheet 196   GR SU 4111

There has been a settlement in the Southampton area since Roman times, but like Salisbury, the site has been changed. The Roman settlement Clausentum was on the east bank of the River Itchen; the Saxon village of Hamwih lay to the east of the Norman town and forms the basis of the modern city.

The Medieval defences dating from 1200-1500 A.D. are considered to be third in importance only to York and Chester. The Bargate is a particularly important feature, and there are many other sites of interest in the Old Town area.

An important port in the Middle Ages, Southampton declined in the seventeenth century, only to prosper again in the late eighteenth and early nineteenth centuries as a spa. Its modern development dates from the opening of the docks and the railway to London in the 1840s. The docks were extended in the 1890s and 1920s, and a new complex is currently being constructed to handle container traffic. During the spa period the most important urban planning scheme was Carlton Crescent to the north of the centre.

The area around Orchard Street is fairly typical of building associated with the early modern port. Between 1920 and 1940 the most notable urban design achievement was the building of the Civic Centre, the setting of which was improved in 1971 with the laying out of Guildhall Square.

Southampton suffered heavily during the 1939-45 war, and the main shopping area (Above Bar Street) has been completely rebuilt. Unfortunately no attempt was made to introduce precinct shopping as in Coventry, and it was only in 1971 that a part of Above Bar was closed to traffic. As in many other cities, a desire to rebuild quickly, and 'get back to normality' was the main reason for the retention of the old street pattern and the lack of a radical approach to reconstruction.

An important feature of Southampton's central area is its Victorian Parks which flank the main shopping centre on the north and east sides, giving it a most attractive setting.

Southampton West Docks and container port.
British Transport Docks Board.

Winchester
SE 1/6

OS Sheet 185   GR SU 4928

Winchester's importance, like that of Exeter, lies in its continuity, which dates back to its Iron Age origins as a tribal capital. This continuity, due partly to its defensive position and partly to its strategic location at the intersection of important routes, is shown in the Roman and Saxon street pattern which forms the basis of the modern town centre. The capital of England until the twelfth century it retains parts of its Medieval walls with remains of the Norman Castle and Henry III's Great Hall. There were three previous Minsters in the town before the present very fine Norman cathedral was begun in 1079, and much Medieval and Tudor development remains.

Modern Winchester has had to face up to the pressures of modern development and motor traffic without allowing damage to the historic character of the city. There is therefore a great

Winchester's Norman Cathedral.
B.T.A.

26

emphasis on conservation and the Roman High Street is now a
pedestrian precinct.

The Royal Pavilion,
Brighton.
*Brighton Resort and
Conference Services
Department.*

Brighton   SE 2/1
OS Sheet 198   GR TQ 2904

Royal patronage created Brighton as a fashionable seaside resort,
epitomised by the Royal Pavilion built for the Prince Regent in
1787 but remodelled into its present fantastic form by John
Nash between 1815 and 1820. Its status was reflected in the
formal planning of its urban development. Houses in Brunswick
Town, Hove, for instance, are uniformly painted, and controlled
by Act of Parliament.

In contrast to this formality the Lanes, a quarter of narrow
winding alleys following the plan of part of the old fishing
port, have now become a fashionable shopping centre. Recent
repaving and the addition of The Square — new shops with an
al fresco cafe — illustrates how, by careful attention to scale,
colour, materials and texture, modern buildings can be happily
integrated into an historical context.

On the outskirts of Brighton, GR 3409, the modern University
of Sussex shows similar sensitivity of design in its master plan by
Sir Basil Spence. Height of buildings, materials and design are
sensitively inflected to the fine downland setting.

The dramatic increase in the popularity of boating, the
natural inhospitability of this coast and the existence of dynamic
entrepreneurs has inspired the present construction of a large
marina.

Chichester

OS Sheet 197   GR SU 8604

A Roman town, on the site of a previous tribal settlement, the
principal streets of Roman Chichester radiated from a carfax to
four gates in the city walls whose lines can still be traced in the
Medieval reconstruction of the town. Easily accessible from its
hinterland, Chichester has a history of continuous prosperity,
reflected in its twelfth century cathedral, St Mary's Hospital and
monastic remains, and in the fine Georgian houses in the Pallants
and cathedral precinct. But its current prosperity as a shopping
centre and its busy road traffic have created sharp conflicts with
its historic character. Chichester was one of the four towns
chosen for study by the Government in 1967 to determine the
physical and financial implications of conservation policies in
the town. The Study Report recommended the exclusion of all
through traffic from within the city walls, the closure to traffic
of long stretches of the main shopping streets and the careful
provision of car parks and shop servicing facilities.

Medieval town wall and
spire of Chichester
Cathedral.
B.T.A.

Chichester Harbour, AONB

OS Sheet 197   GR SU 8004

Chichester Harbour, designated an Area of Outstanding Natural
Beauty, covers the creeks and inlets between Hayling Island and
the Selsey peninsula. It has very great natural history interest and
is a popular sailing centre. There are many competing demands
on the area. Until 1972 management and planning control was
divided between two planning authorities and other interests. The
Chichester Harbour Conservancy was then established in an
attempt to coordinate administration and to act as an advisory
committee on planning matters, thereby integrating the various
land and water interests. This area illustrates the all too common
physical and administrative conflicts present in fragile
environments and is one example of an attempt to overcome them.

Peacehaven

OS Sheet 198   GR TQ 4001

Originally proposed in 1916 as a garden city by the sea to be
named Anzac-on-Sea, Peacehaven has become known as a

Peacehaven.
Aerofilms.

28

settlement built with scant regard for social or environmental concern. The monotonous grid iron plan and lack of services and amenities are only now being alleviated. Its uncontrolled development in a prominent clifftop location led to widespread concern which contributed to a public acceptance of the need for comprehensive planning control.

Portsmouth SE 2/5

OS Sheet 196   GR SU 4200

Although Porchester Castle was originally a Roman fort, considerably extended in the eleventh century, modern Portsmouth dates from a charter of Richard I in 1194. The port was subordinate to Southampton for several centuries, and substantial defences were constructed in the Middle Ages, for example, the Square Tower of Henry VII and the Round Tower of 1417. The defences were continuously improved throughout the sixteenth, seventeenth and eighteenth centuries. They have largely survived and they are gradually being restored and opened to the public. The last of Portsmouth's defences, the ring of forts built on the downs outside the city in 1860, can also still be seen. In general, Portsmouth's defences form a continuous system dating from Roman times to the present day. The city's primary purpose has always been as a naval base, and many of the early, eighteenth century, naval dockyard buildings are included in the Naval Base Conservation Area in the south west corner of the present dockyard, where H.M.S. Victory, Nelson's flagship, can also be seen.

The city suffered considerable bomb damage during the last war. In 1964 a 'Master Plan' for the reconstruction of fifty acres in the city centre was drawn up. Much of this redevelopment, including Guildhall Square as a traffic free area, has been completed.

Opposite Porchester Castle, between Portsea Island and the mainland, an area of land being reclaimed as a leisure park, contains a marina, golf course, horse riding centre, sports centre and general recreational area.

Seven Sisters, Cuckmere Haven and Beachy Head SE 2/6

OS Sheet 199   GR TV 5895/5298/5798

Chalk cliffs below the Seven Sisters Country Park.
East Sussex County Planning Officer.

Between Eastbourne and Seaford lies one of the most majestic and unspoiled stretches of coast in the south of England. Designated as an Area of Outstanding Natural Beauty and a

Heritage Coast, with part of it a country park, it is now almost wholly in public ownership. However, its location and accessibility coupled to its beauty and the unusually varied plant and bird life have necessitated the introduction of a management policy based on inland 'activity zones' and a coastal 'remote zone' separated by a buffer zone.

Basingstoke   SE 3/1
OS Sheet 185   GR SU 6452

Sports centre and car park integrated into the new Basingstoke Shopping Centre. *E.N. Lane.*

Under an expansion scheme initiated through the 1952 Town Development Act, Basingstoke, which had a population of 25,000 in 1961, will grow to 89,000 by the late 1970s. Over 10,000 new houses have been built to take London overspill population, and of these, 75 per cent are municipally owned. A new town centre has been built, with 450,000 square feet of pedestrianised shopping space. The town has excellent communications to London, via the M3 and the main railway line, and has become a centre for the decentralisation of offices from London including the Civil Service Commission and the Automobile Association.

While helping to alleviate the housing problems of the conurbations, town expansion schemes such as that at Basingstoke inevitably lead to problems involving the social absorption of the newcomers in the existing community.

Crawley New Town and Gatwick Airport   SE 3/2
OS Sheet 187   GR TQ 2636

The designation of Crawley New Town and the establishment in 1958 of Gatwick as London's second international airport has created a growth zone of regional importance. The new town has substantially exceeded its target population (50,000, which it passed in 1959). The abandonment of the Maplin airport project may put greater stress on Gatwick. The compound effect of two growth poles in close proximity creates strong competition for labour and physical pressures on nearby towns such as Horsham.

New Ash Green   SE 3/3
OS Sheet 177   GR TQ 6065

New Ash Green – the shopping centre. *Bovis Homes.*

New Ash Green is a new village created on a green field site about eight miles east of Orpington (Greater London). The original design sought to encourage a strong sense of community through localised grouping of dwellings, and an emphasis on communal open space with a high standard of landscaping. As with a number of comparable schemes, after a promising start the village has undergone a change of designers and builders and it remains to be seen how the scheme will be fulfilled.

Silchester

OS Sheet 175   GR SU 6462

An extensive Roman Town (Calleva Atrebatum) and the only one in Britain to have been completely excavated. It was already an important tribal centre (the Atrebates) before the Roman invasion of A.D. 43, and was subsequently developed on the standard Roman grid pattern. Its prosperity, based on wool, lasted until about A.D. 400. The town stood at an important road junction between London and Salisbury.

Physical remains standing include a two mile long section of the east wall, and the outlines of many buildings can be traced. There is a small site museum but most finds are exhibited at Reading Museum. Unlike most Roman towns in Britain no subsequent development has destroyed its structure and atmosphere.

The Site of Roman 'Calleva Atrebatum', Silchester.
Aerofilms.

Surrey Green Belt and Ribbon Development   SE 3/5

OS Sheet 187   GR TQ 0851

'Ribbon development' along the newly built main roads out of London and other cities was one of the undesirable byproducts of the increase in motor traffic after 1920. In 1927, the Greater London Regional Planning Committee, with Raymond Unwin as technical adviser, recommended the control of sporadic development in the countryside round London and the provision of adequate recreational facilities. The Surrey County Council also secured a private Act of Parliament in 1931 which

gave them powers to control ribbon development. The Kingston Bypass (A3) at Hinchley Way is an example of the use of these powers. In 1935 the powers were extended nationally in the Restriction of Ribbon Development Act. To safeguard recreational facilities from development, the Green Belt Act of 1938 authorised local authorities to buy land for recreational use. Nearly 3,900 acres (e.g. the Sheepleas Estate, East Horsley) were acquired by Surrey County Council and various district councils, backed by the London County Council.

A service road at Hinchley Way on the Kingston By-pass provided under the 1931 Surrey County Council Act to prevent direct access onto the main road.
Surrey County Planning Officer.

Tunbridge Wells   SE 3/6
OS Sheet 188   GR TQ 5839

Tunbridge Wells developed following the fortuitous discovery of medicinal waters in 1606. Its patronage by royalty and the prevailing fashion for taking the waters led to its rapid expansion, including the construction in 1638 of the Pantiles as a raised promenade bounded by fashionable shops. The rustic character of the Pantiles was reflected in subsequent development and the town today retains much of its earlier informal atmosphere. The survival of the Pantiles is now assisted by the Grade One listing of most of its buildings and the designation of the area as a conservation area.

The Pantiles Shopping Arcade, Tunbridge Wells.
Kent County Planning Officer.

Canterbury   SE 4/1
OS Sheet 179   GR TR 1457

With its fine cathedral, and over 900 buildings listed as of historic interest, Canterbury is one of England's finest 'heritage' cities, and conservation and restoration are vital to its planning policies. As a market town it also serves a large part of East Kent and is therefore subject to development pressures for offices, shopping, education (it has a large modern university), service industries and transportation. The varied success with which these pressures have been accommodated within the historic fabric can best be seen by visiting the town.

Restored 14th century properties in Sun Yard, Canterbury.
Ben May.

The Roman lighthouse
at Dover Castle.
B.T.A.

Dover   SE 4/2
OS Sheet 179   GR TR 3241

Throughout its history the development of Dover has been
dominated by its strategic position facing the narrowest point
of the English Channel and Europe. The Roman, Norman and
Medieval remains all emphasise the significance of its location.
The wartime devastation and postwar growth in cross channel
ferry traffic illustrate the problems inherent in such a strategic
position. The Roman lighthouse near the Castle Keep dates
from the first century A.D. and is the earliest in Britain, while
the Castle itself was built during the twelfth and thirteenth
centuries.

The two nuclear power
stations built on the
shingle banks of
Dungeness.
Handford Photography.

Dungeness   SE 4/3
OS Sheet 189   GR TR 0816

Dungeness is noted for its nuclear power stations, its nature
reserve and its coast protection works. The two power stations
were built as part of the UKAEA's programme of increasing the
amount of nuclear generated electricity. Both stations contained
equipment which was very advanced for the time. As a contrast,
the whole of the Dungeness foreland (6,300 acres) is zoned as a
Site of Special Scientific Interest by the Nature Conservancy, and
contains the Dungeness Bird Observatory (1952) and the Hoppen
Pits, a group of natural freshwater lakes containing many species
of flora and fauna. The Dungeness coast is particularly subject to
erosion. The Southern Water Authority maintains an
embankment and seawall from Hythe to Fairlight (thirty miles)
and replenishes lost shingle from the southern side of Dungeness
with material excavated from areas east of the Point.

Hastings and St Leonards   SE 4/4
OS Sheet 199   GR TQ 2809

Now one urban area, Hastings and St Leonards have different
origins. The old town of Hastings, constricted by hills to the east

St. Leonards, with
terrace housing
overlooking the sea
and villas in the wooded
valleys behind.
Aerofilms.

and the west, retains its Medieval plan form of parallel streets with connecting footpaths and still has over 400 'listed' buildings. Its original function as a fishing port is still actively continued. By contrast, St Leonards, GR 2909, was developed in 1828 as a speculative resort by James Burton and his son Decimus. Like Regents Park, London, on which James had worked with John Nash, St Leonards was planned with terraces, colonnades and individual villas set in a carefully landscaped valley. Most of the original layout is still intact and the landscaping is now mature.

Sandwich
SE 4/5

OS Sheet 179   GR TR 3358

Sandwich, one of the leading Medieval ports in the country, is remarkable for the preservation of its original Medieval form and for the concentration within it of buildings of architectural or historical interest. Its situation today on the River Stour, with the encirclement of earthen ramparts and open fields beyond, greatly facilitates a recollection of the historic role and character of this early town. The whole area has been designated a conservation area and the County Council has produced a conservation plan to resolve modern day pressures and further an overall policy of conservation.

Sandwich Old Town.
Kent County Planning Officer.

Winchelsea
SE 4/6

OS Sheet 189   GR TQ 9017

Throughout much of the thirteenth century the former site of Winchelsea was eroded by the sea. As a Cinque Port its survival was of national importance and in 1282 King Edward I lent funds to rebuild it on a safer site. The site was divided in the form of a French bastide into thirty-nine rectangular blocks for development, with blocks for churches, a market square and the monastery of the Grey Friars. The subsequent retreat of the sea caused Winchelsea's decline as a port and few of the blocks were ever built up. Its decline has ensured the survival of the rectilinear street plan which makes it one of the best examples in England of Edward I's town planning skills.

Winchelsea.
Aerofilms.

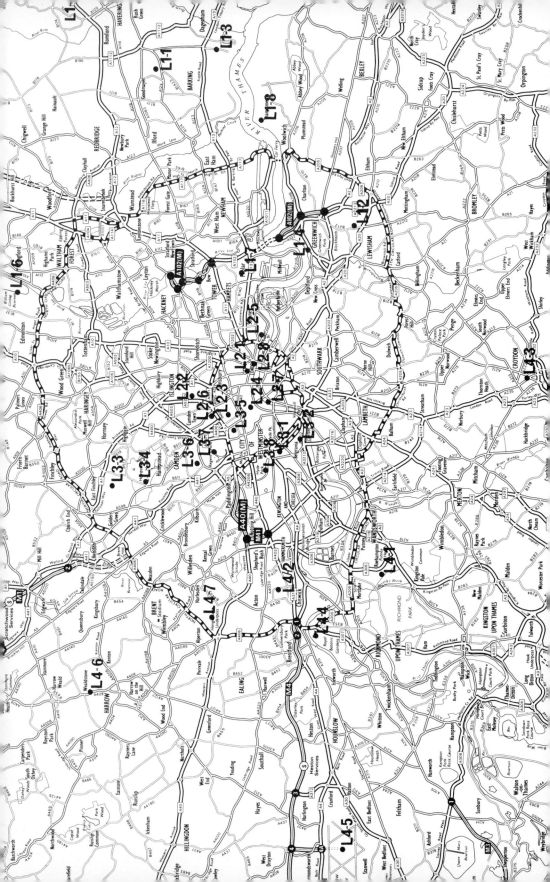

London

There have been plans and rumours of plans for London ever
since the Romans left. Sir Christopher Wren made plans, Sir John
Evelyn made plans. In his book *London Redivivum* Evelyn
declared that his aim was not mere restoration but to create a
London of 'a far greater beauty, commodiousness, and
magnificence'. He asked for a scale map showing 'all the
declivities, eminences, water courses and cetra of the whole
area'. This, surely, must have been the first time it was proposed
to make a land use map of London. Both Sir Christopher and
Sir John were defeated by vested interests. Even so, much planning
was later carried out by gifted individuals with wealthy clients.
From the sixteenth century, landed gentry built up their estates
in London and, in general, these were not only well planned
but models of good estate management.

In the early nineteenth century John Nash laid out Regent's Park
and built his famous terraces. The concept of a grand promenade
from Regent's Park to St. James's Park was not to be, but there
was the Regent Street Arcade which, earlier this century, was
pulled down. Nash's housing needs no introduction here except,
in passing, a wry smile that in those days many accused him
of 'jerry building'.

Early in the same century Thomas Cubitt, master builder,
reclaimed a clay swamp traversed by the river Westbourne. The
swamp, called Five Fields, was the haunt of 'snipe, fog and
footpads'. However, Cubitt's mansions eventually stood on a
gravel stratum, for the clay was removed to make bricks on the
site. This was ingenious planning which, combined with
magnificent building technique, became the Belgravia of today.

In 1860 Sir Charles Barry completed the Houses of
Parliament. Barry's plan for 'rearranging the Whitehall area'
would have extended to Northumberland Avenue, with a road
bridge connecting a redeveloped south bank. This was not
adopted, probably through lack of finance and the need for
extensive land reclamation of the foul Thames banks. Many
years later, similar proposals for the removal of Hungerford
railway bridge and its replacement by a road and pedestrian
structure appeared in the County of London Plan, 1943.
Unfortunately, Hungerford Bridge, noisy with trains, is still
with us.

Bridging the end of the nineteenth and early years of the
twentieth century came Sir Raymond Unwin's Hampstead
Garden Suburb, just north of Hampstead Heath, and Professor
Adshead's housing for the Duchy of Cornwall Estate in
Kennington. Adshead designed small housing schemes ahead of

their time in quality of design and layout. Today the development, in its intimate nature, reveals care and thought in contrast with its often shabby surroundings.

The First World War brought to an end vast and uninspired suburban developments, particularly in Ilford, Walthamstow, Leytonstone and Edmonton, which provided homes for low paid white and blue collar workers. The cheaper houses, many without bathrooms, were constructed by builders who were encouraged by cheap railway fares to stretch out into unspoilt countryside.

Immediately after the war, Topham Forest, architect to the London County Council, built the working class suburbs of Dagenham and Beacontree. Good in their way but lacking in imaginative layout, these estates later created the 'sons and daughters' problem. When families grew up, there were not enough houses for them and also not enough one and two bedroom houses for parents to move into when their families had left.

The great pre-1939 building boom was in moderately priced private housing for the professional and administrative classes. Again, the lure was a cheap season ticket, coupled with the promise of a 'good life' in the country. But as the suburban crawl spread ever outwards, the 'country' vanished. North of London, tube railways emerged from their tunnels, trekking out to Edgware and pushing well into the unspoiled country.

The eastern suburbs were extended still further. But in the late twenties and thirties, active planning became a reality, beginning in London with a tiny scheme to protect part of Streatham Common and a large ornamental garden. Further statutory schemes included the Highgate and Hampstead Scheme for the protection of Highgate village and Hampstead Heath.

The Town and Country Planning Act, 1932, permitted schemes to be implemented where redevelopment which would alter the character of an area was taking place. Almost entirely intended to protect threatened amenities, most of the schemes were based on London's major open spaces. But the London County Council, aware of the fast pace of residential redevelopment in inner London, quickly drafted eighteen statutory schemes covering over a third of the county and, by 1935, had been granted powers to prepare a scheme covering the whole county. The flood of housing still continued, however. Massive blocks of flats appeared in central London and flats were erected in the hitherto exclusive areas of single family houses in Putney, Wimbledon and Streatham.

One great event saved London, Greater London and much of the home counties from becoming an unbroken mass of buildings. This was the creation by Herbert Morrison of the Green Belt, the area around a town in which development is strictly controlled. The outward march of housing was also halted by the Second World War.

In 1941, the LCC was asked to prepare an ideal plan, regardless of possible cost, for postwar London. The County of London Plan, 1943, was the result. The plan had an impact almost greater than bombing. It was an act of faith, and the greatest step forward in comprehensive planning in London's history. It summarised London's malaise as: congestion of traffic; depressed housing; intermingling of housing and industry, and lack or maldistribution of open space. The plan received great publicity – exhibitions, a film, 'The Proud City', and a Penguin special publication. One of its aims was to increase London's open space and 2.5 acres per thousand population was adopted as the interim standard. The former Boroughs of Stepney and Poplar (now Tower Hamlets) were to be areas of major construction, since they had suffered extensively from bombing. The South Bank between Westminster and Blackfriars Bridge was to be reconstructed, and a system of ring and radial roads was to ease traffic congestion.

The 1943 plan was advisory; the London Development Plan which followed in 1950 reflected as much of the earlier plan as was financially possible. By 1960 the major policies were being implemented, with housing as first priority. In twenty years, the LCC built 114,000 permanent homes and repaired 3,000 after war damage. Boroughs, housing associations and private developers built a total of 224,000 houses and, in the same twenty years, 31,000 slum houses were cleared, and 39,700 families rehoused.

Housing development changed the face of large parts of London; the office bonanza in the mid-1950s changed the face of the West End, and the high buildings policy in the middle of the fifties changed it still more.

The target of 2.5 acres of open space per thousand was not reached, and only 300 acres had been added up to 1965 – a significant amount, however, when seen on the ground. Existing private parks acquired were the grounds of Holland House, Hurlingham polo and sports grounds and a modest extension to Hampstead Heath. A start was made on the planned 120 acre 'Hyde Park of South London' in Camberwell and a sports ground, 'King George's Fields', was laid out on the site of former slums. The remaining open spaces were a small, but valuable, contribution to areas lacking any form of open air recreation. Government finance for road schemes began to flow after 1955. Two of the most important schemes were the Marble Arch to Hyde Park Corner dual carriageway and the Cromwell Road extension leading to the M4 and London Airport.

And so the intent of the 1943 Plan was implemented, though the reality fell short of the ideals.

In 1965 when the Greater London Council and the new London boroughs were established, the planning process changed and became more complex. Nine years later, the planning situation remains fluid. The three ring road system which was to have been the basis of much of London's replanning has been abandoned, partly for political reasons and partly because of its destructive effect on London's fabric.

In the last ten years, the Port of London has entirely changed. Docks and warehouses are at present deserted, but St Katherine's

Dock has been partly redeveloped and plans are afoot for developing a huge area of former dockland in the East End. The south bank of the Thames from Nine Elms to Blackfriars Bridge has changed spectacularly and, before long, will enjoy the same prestige as its north bank counterpart. What is involved in much of London, however, is nothing less than clearing up the gigantic debris of the first industrial revolution.

John Craig

Becontree Estate, Barking   L 1/1
OS Sheet 177   GR TQ 4683

Becontree housing estate was constructed by the London County Council on the edge of the then built up area between 1921 and 1932. The estate covers some 2,000 acres and at its peak housed over 100,000 people. A brave early attempt at comprehensive planning, it lacked social and community facilities and made no attempt to create community groupings. The lack of local job opportunities was apparent until the growth of nearby Dagenham as a major industrial centre. Noted for its sheer size and apparent uniformity of house types (although there were in fact 91 different designs) this estate is characteristic of many other developments which followed it during the interwar period.

Becontree Estate (shortly after completion). *G.L.C.*

Blackheath, Span Developments
L 1/2
OS Sheet 177   GR TQ 3975 (The Priory)
TQ 4075 (The Hall)

A number of small estates, concentrated in the Blackheath area, were built by the Span Development Company between 1956 and 1965. Designed by Eric Lyons they showed an outstanding advance in the design and layout of speculative housing. The landscaping, which has reached a certain maturity at The Hall and The Priory, is of high quality. The properties are leasehold and each estate has a residents' association which collects an annual maintenance charge and is responsible for the upkeep of communal areas. This ensures a greater degree of personal concern for the environment than exists on most freehold owner occupied or council estates.

Blackheath – The Hall Estate.
Snoek-Westwood.

Ford Motor Co. Estate, Dagenham
L 1/3
OS Sheet 177   GR TQ 4982

The Ford Motor Company's estate at Dagenham represents a fine example of industrial integration from the arrival of iron ore at the wharf to the output of some 1,300 completed cars per working day. The complex began operations in 1931, providing welcome employment for the nearby Becontree Estate. It now employs 25,000 workers and covers 665 acres, and has expanded partly by the reclamation of Thames marshes. In contrast to the highly organised and automated manufacturing complex, the approach roads to the plant are inadequate for the loads put on them and are frequently congested at peak arrival and departure times.

The Ford Motor Company Estate by the Thames at Dagenham.
Ford Motor Company.

Greenwich Park and Royal Naval College
L 1/4
OS Sheet 177   GR TQ 3877

The Royal Naval College on the Thames at Greenwich is a superb complex of Renaissance buildings, comprehensively planned and designed by Sir Christopher Wren and completed in 1705. Wren incorporated as his central feature the earlier Queen's House by Inigo Jones and two magnificent colonnades therefore focus attention on this earlier building. As an example of formal Renaissance architecture in the grand design, Greenwich College is unsurpassed in Britain. It was originally built as a hospital, but since 1873 has been the home of the Royal Naval College.

Greenwich – Wren's Royal Naval College and Inigo Jones' Queens House, with Royal Observatory beyond.
B.T.A.

40

Harold Hill, Havering L 1/5
OS Sheet 177   GR TQ 5492

Harold Hill is a good example of the ring of 'out county' housing estates built by the London County Council after 1945. The estates were intended to relieve areas of housing stress in Inner London. Although designed and constructed to the currently prevailing styles and space standards, the estate suffers the same social problems as the earlier Becontree Estate. Occupied in the early 1950s by predominantly young families, this imbalance shows itself today in an excess of school places, a preponderance of people in the forty to fifty age group, and the certainty of a large proportion of retired residents in twenty year's time.

Lea Valley Regional Park, Waltham Forest L 1/6
OS Sheet 177   GR TQ 3895 (Pole Hill)

The Lea Valley Regional Park was the first and, to date, only park stretching through a number of local authorities and requiring special legislation for its implementation (Lea Valley Regional Park Act 1966). Stretching for twenty-three miles from Stratford (east London) to Ware (Herts) the park is planned to regenerate an area of industrial dereliction and provide much needed recreation facilities in east London. Park activities will include walking, riding, most water sports, nature study and industrial archaeology, as well as more concentrated sport and recreation activities. Although difficult to appreciate from any one view the scale of the scheme can be grasped from Pole Hill, north of Chingford.

Lansbury Estate, Tower Hamlets L 1/7
OS Sheet 177   GR TQ 3871

The east end of London suffered considerable bomb damage in the war and the LCC was faced with a large-scale reconstruction problem. The Lansbury Estate, a residential development with allied shopping and community facilities, was one of the early areas to be developed from 1951. It also constituted the live Architectural Exhibition of the 1951 Festival of Britain.

Housing in the Lansbury Estate (shortly after completion). *G.L.C.*

Thamesmead, Greenwich L 1/8
OS Sheet 177   GR TQ 4779

In contrast to Becontree and Harold Hill, Thamesmead, a modern
housing development, has been conceived within the
existing builtup area of London, on reclaimed marshes at Erith.
With an ultimate population of 50,000, the development also
provides community facilities and employment opportunities.
Advantage has been taken of a technically difficult site by
combining land drainage with the provision of a 350 vessel
marina and waterside landscaped areas. However, the extensive
use of site cast concrete, and high rise flat development, has
depersonalised the housing at a time when 'domestic' proportions
in housing are becoming increasingly important.

Thamesmead housing
on the banks of the
Thames.
Pace.

Paternoster and Barbican L 2/1
OS Sheet 177   GR TQ 3281

The great Fire of London of 1666 provided an opportunity to
restructure the heart of the capital. The opportunity was not
taken and again, after the blitz of the Second World War,
reconstruction was piecemeal rather than fundamental. In the
City of London, however, higher densities demanded by
intensified commercial activity led to developments, such as
Paternoster Square, north of St Paul's, comprising high rise
offices and shops designed by Lord Holford in 1956 round
major pedestrian spaces of differing character. The intention
was to create a cathedral precinct of informal nature (witness the
partial obscuring of the west front of St Paul's) in contrast to the
formal layout envisaged three centuries earlier by Christopher
Wren.

   An even larger scheme is the exciting Barbican development
on a sixty-two acre site owned and financed by the City
Corporation. To curb the outward flow of residents from central
London, forty acres of the site comprises new housing for
7,000 people and associated public buildings. Despite earlier
setbacks the scheme is now nearing completion and provides
total segregation between vehicles and pedestrians and extensive
use of differing levels. The site is dominated by major office
blocks and three residential tower blocks more than 400 feet high.
Undoubtedly a 'prestige' scheme by the City, the high demand for
the flats emphasises the social value of city centre living.

Flats in the Barbican
Development.
John Maltby.

Barnsbury, Islington L 2/2
OS Sheet 177   GR TQ 3083

Beyond the eighteenth century New Road (now Euston Road)
and the ring of railway termini grew a series of residential
estates in the early and mid-nineteenth century. These are
characterised by the Barnsbury area of Islington. In addition to

the fairly conventional villas and terraces, three features of note are Milner Square, *c.* 1841, a daunting late classical design; Lonsdale Square, 1838-41, in the neo-Tudor style and Thornhill Square *c* 1850. After a period of decline when this and similar areas provided relatively cheap housing for the capital's essential workers it has recently been rediscovered as a pleasant housing environment with a consequent rise in property values forcing out the lower paid residents.

Thornhill Square, Barnsbury.
G.L.C.

Bloomsbury — Bedford Square in the foreground, London University Senate House and the British Museum in the centre, with Russell Square beyond.
Aerofilms.

Bloomsbury   L 2/3
OS Sheet 176   GR TQ 3082

Bloomsbury was developed speculatively between 1775 and 1860 as a residential area (through traffic was originally excluded by gates). In its later phases (*c* 1820 onwards) other uses crept in — University College (1828), the British Museum (1822-47), and various hotels. The area was laid out in the classic eighteenth century English urban manner as a series of squares. Bedford Square is now the last remaining complete Georgian square in London, while Woburn Walk has the best sequence of eighteenth century shop fronts in London. Social changes in the twentieth century, and the expansion of the University, have considerably eroded the area's original character. Residential uses have been replaced by offices and institutions, and part of the area near the British Museum has been blighted for the last twenty years by the proposed National Library. The University continues to expand.

Covent Garden   L 2/4
OS Sheet 176   GR TQ 3080

Covent Garden, the market centre of London until 1974, can be claimed as the first Renaissance piazza in Britain. Designed for the fourth Earl of Bedford by Inigo Jones, it was built between 1631 and 1635 as the centre piece of a speculative housing development approved by King Charles I. Its residential appeal was limited by the establishment of its market functions. Virtually nothing remains of the original buildings but the area is worthy of seeing since it heralded the 'new classicism' of the Renaissance which influenced British town development for the next two centuries. Today the Covent Garden area, with a large — and vocal —

residential population is a focus of debate on town centre redevelopment and on who, in fact, should be the beneficiaries.

St Katherine's Dock, Tower Hamlets L 2/5
OS Sheet 177   GR TQ 3480

The original docks were constructed in the 1820s to the designs of Thomas Telford and were the first of London's modern docks. During recent years, the movement of trade down river to new docks at Tilbury led to the decline of St Katherine's Dock, which finally closed in the 1960s. The area is now being redeveloped as a complex including a marina, hotel, offices, a trade centre, flats and other uses, but some of Telford's original warehouses are being restored and will be integrated with the new development.

St. Katherine's Docks undergoing restoration and redevelopment. *G.L.C.*

St Pancras and Euston Stations L 2/6
OS Sheet 176   GR TQ 3083 (St. Pancras)

St Pancras, Euston and Kings Cross form the great trio of railway stations north of Central London. When it was built in 1865, St Pancras lay on the outskirts of the capital. The extent of development in London by about 1850 can in fact be seen by the location of the great railway termini, (from Waterloo, via Paddington, Euston, St Pancras and Kings Cross, to Liverpool Street and London Bridge), because the railways were able, in general, to penetrate only as far as the edge of the built up area.

The magnificent train shed of W.H. Barlow was hidden behind the grandiose Gothic revival hotel of Sir Gilbert Scott. This building has lately become a symbol of the rebirth of public interest in Victorian architecture, and plans for its demolition now seem to have been permanently shelved. Unhappily, however, this rebirth came too late to save the Euston 'Arch' by Philip Hardwicke (1838), which was demolished in the early 1960s. Euston was the first of the London termini to be rebuilt in modern times, and makes an interesting contrast to the older Victorian Kings Cross and St Pancras, which are both nearby.

St. Pancras Station. *B.T.A.*

44

South Bank L 2/7

OS Sheet 176   GR TQ 3080

The clearance of the site of the 1951 Festival of Britain on the south bank of the Thames opposite Charing Cross provided an opportunity for comprehensive redevelopment. The cultural functions performed by the Royal Festival Hall have been emphasised by the construction of the Queen Elizabeth Hall, the Purcell Room and Hayward Gallery, the National Film Theatre and the new National Theatre. This concentration of cultural facilities removes the spontaneity of a variety of activities but it has provided the opportunity to open up the river frontage to pedestrians with comprehensive walkways segregated from vehicular traffic. However, except for the short periods of the day when pedestrian traffic is heavy, the area suffers a rather sterile, bleak and windswept appearance.

Royal Festival Hall and Queen Elizabeth Hall on the South Bank of the Thames. *Fox Photos.*

St Paul's and Wren's City Churches L 2/8

OS Sheet 176   GR TQ 3281 (St Paul's)

The Great Fire of London in 1666 provided the first opportunity to replan the formerly anarchic layout of the City. Within ten days John Evelyn and Christopher Wren had each presented plans for the new London, both based on contemporary Italian and French models of broad straight streets, vistas centred on public buildings and piazzas. The complex pattern of land ownership and the need for immediate action prevented the adoption of either scheme. However, Wren rebuilt St Paul's Cathedral and fifty-five new City churches (including the most significant survivors, St Brides, Fleet St, St Mary-le-Bow, Cheapside, St Stephen, Walbrook and St Vedast, Foster Land) which dominated London's skyline for 250 years and illustrate what might have been.

Belgravia, Westminster L 3/1

OS Sheet 176   GR TQ 2879

Belgravia is the largest and most complete urban architectural

composition in the City of Westminster. Designed and largely
constructed by Thomas Cubitt in the first half of the nineteenth
century, it represents a characteristic speculation of the period.
Echoing the earlier estate development of Bloomsbury etc.,
Belgravia includes Belgrave and Eaton Squares and most of the
development is in the form of terraces, predominantly of
white-painted stucco. Today, thanks to its locality and its
continued ownership by the Grosvenor Estates, it remains
largely residential with some embassy and institutional uses.
Although retained in good condition the area has been
designated a Conservation Area by Westminster City Council
under the 1967 Civic Amenities Act. This gives protection not
just to individual buildings of merit but to whole areas of
architectural or historic interest.

Churchill Gardens and Lillington Gardens,   L 3/2   Westminster

OS Sheet 176   GR TQ 2978

In addition to containing the principal home of the Sovereign,
the Houses of Parliament and the government offices of Whitehall,
the City of Westminster is the home of some 237,000 people.
The City Council, therefore, has considerable housing
responsibilities, owning about 16,000 dwellings and building
an average of 500-600 each year. To ensure high standards of
development the Council has encouraged architectural
competitions for some of its housing schemes. Churchill Gardens,
fronting Grosvenor Road and the River Thames, comprises
1,661 flats at a maximum of nine storeys, built to the 1946 award
winning design of Powell and Moya. In contrast to many
contemporary schemes elsewhere Churchill Gardens includes
within its bounds a community centre, church, schools, garage,
public houses, shops, playgrounds and gardens. Further emphasis
of the enlightened nature of this scheme is provided by the
incorporation of a district heating scheme to use waste heat from
the nearby Battersea Power Station for space heating and domestic
hot water. Not only does this reduce atmospheric pollution, it is

Lillington Gardens
Housing Estate.
Brecht-Einzig.

46

cheap, saves labour and improves living conditions. Lillington Gardens, off Vauxhall Bridge Road, resulted from a competition in 1961 and provides 722 dwellings at a comparatively high density in excess of 200 persons per acre. The buildings, varying from three to eight storeys, are clad in facing bricks and enclose the site, subdividing it into well proportioned interlinking squares. The development thus creates a domestic scale so often lacking in comparable schemes. Parking for 327 cars is provided underground and the scheme also includes an old peoples' home, three public houses, two doctors' surgeries, one library and nine shops — continuing the tradition of social provision set at Churchill Gardens.

Hampstead Garden Suburb L 3/3
OS Sheet 176   GR TQ 2588

Hampstead Garden Suburb — Hill Close. *Barnet Borough Planning Officer.*

Hampstead Heath, looking towards the centre of London. *B.T.A.*

Hampstead Garden Suburb, a semirural residential enclave just north of Hampstead Heath, was founded in 1906 through the inspiration of Dame Henrietta Barnet, who wanted to prevent the kind of urban mediocrity that followed the extension of the London tube. Parker and Unwin, the planners of Letchworth, prepared the fine layout and Sir Edwin Lutyens designed certain buildings. The 800 acres of the Suburb now contain over 5,000 houses. Originally intended to provide houses for all classes of the community, more expensive houses were built in greater numbers and the area soon acquired its present middle class character. Despite this, the Suburb represented the planning of the period and, by 1914, at least fifty-two similar schemes were underway. Apart from the interest of its domestic architecture and mature landscaping, its carefully planned layout is a good example of differentiation between traffic streets and access roads. Much of the housing is in small closes, culs-de-sac and squares, and the charm of the Suburb is still preserved in its tree lined streets, its network of small footpaths, and its hedges. It received public transport in 1974, when a discreet, dial-a-bus service was introduced by London Transport.

Hampstead Heath L 3/4
OS Sheet 176   GR TQ 2686

Hampstead Heath, like Epping Forest, has survived attempts to enclose its common land for building. The obstinate Lord of the Manor, Sir Thomas Wilson, tried from 1818 until his death in 1868 to obtain power to enclose the Heath but, shortly afterwards, it was sold by his descendant to the Metropolitan Board of Works. Its 800 acres of heathland and trees, intersected by rambling paths, are now preserved for all time — a tribute, in particular, to the founders in 1865 of the Commons, Open Spaces and Footpaths Preservation Society whose persistent efforts have brought about the preservation of so many of London's open spaces.

Post Office Tower
L 3/5

OS Sheet 176   GR TQ 2981

From the Roman roads to the railway network of the nineteenth century communications have played a vital role in the development of this country, with an equally significant impact on the landscape. Today the need for contact is greater than ever with telephone trunk calls alone increasing at about 17 per cent a year. This increase encouraged the development of a microwave system of telecommunication based on London and covering the country. As line-of-sight contact was needed. a network of towers was constructed by 1970 spanning the country and radiating from the 620 ft high Post Office Tower in Maple Street. The system avoids a proliferation of cables and is capable of carrying 150,000 simultaneous telephone conversations or 100 two way television channels.

The Post Office Tower.
Post Office.

Regent's Canal
L 3/6

OS Sheet 176   GR TQ 3083

The Regent's Canal, built in 1816 and linking the Thames with the Grand Union Canal in West London, was one of the first inland waterways to receive a new lease of life for recreation and amenity purposes following its decline for commercial use. It was originally taken through Regent's Park to provide an ornamental landscape feature, but only in the last ten years have the British Waterways Board and the various London boroughs through which it runs looked at ways of turning this forgotten asset into a major recreation and amenity feature. From Little Venice to the Zoo, trip boats carry summer visitors and many trees have been planted on the banks and the towpath opened to the public. The London Borough of Camden have opened two Towpath Walks, one of which won a Civic Trust Award in 1973.

Regent's Canal.
*Camden Borough
Planning Officer.*

Regent's Park and Regent St
L 3/7

OS Sheet 176   GR TQ 2882

In 1809 John Nash, then a Crown architect, produced a proposal for the development of Marylebone Farm (now Regent's Park). In contrast to the prevailing fashion for squares he proposed a grand avenue linking the park with Carlton House overlooking St James's Park. Regent's Park was to remain semirural, containing many villas and surrounded by majestic terraces with housing for artisans and tradesmen beyond. The scheme was never completed in its entirety but Regent Street, Portland Place, Park Crescent, the terraces surrounding Regent's Park (for example Sussex Place and Cumberland Terrace), the eight parkland villas and the Park Villages to the east provide ample illustration of the most dramatic town planning scheme of its time.

Cumberland Terrace,
one of Nash's housing
developments
surrounding Regent's
Park.
B.T.A.

The Serpentine Lake in Hyde Park, with a backcloth provided by Westminster Abbey and the Houses of Parliament.
B.T.A.

The Royal Parks

L 3/8

OS Sheet 176   GR TQ 2780 (Hyde Park)

The Royal Parks consist of Kensington Gardens, Hyde Park, Green Park and St James's Park, and stretch from Bayswater past Buckingham Palace to Westminster, thus forming a welcome swathe of green in the midst of London. The largest, Kensington Gardens/Hyde Park, originally belonged to Westminster Abbey, but like many other ecclesiastical lands, was appropriated by Henry VIII and used as a Royal Deer Park for 100 years, until opened to the public by Charles I in 1635.

Alton Estate, Roehampton.
G.L.C.

Alton Estate, Roehampton

L 4/1

OS Sheet 176   GR TQ 2173

On the edge of Richmond Park, this estate, built between 1952 and 1956 by the then London County Council, is still an excellent example of a fairly high density mixed housing development. Given an assured start by its already superbly landscaped setting it uses a wide range of dwelling sizes and types (up to eleven storey point blocks) to accommodate nearly 10,000 people on 128 acres. The tallest blocks are sited on the highest ground and the landscape sweeps down the slope around and beneath the lower blocks. Despite wide acclaim for its visual and landscape quality and construction techniques, the estate is criticised for the same defects as other predominantly highrise developments: a lack of social and shopping facilities and of community spirit.

Bedford Park, Ealing

L 4/2

OS Sheet 176   GR TQ 2179

Chiefly remarkable for its unity, Bedford Park was an embryo garden suburb, the first of its kind, predating Hampstead Garden Suburb. Built mainly between 1876 and 1890, the architectural ideas first expressed here can be found in later garden suburbs and cities. The attractive house designs are the work of R. Norman Shaw (architect of 'Old' New Scotland Yard) and others. These buildings are chiefly constructed in red brick and many feature Dutch shaped gables, large bay windows and balustraded balconies. These details produce a distinctive Bedford Park style which is enhanced by the abundance of trees and shrubs and makes the area worthy of its conservation under the 1967 Civic Amenities Act.

Croydon Town Centre

L 4/3

OS Sheet 176   GR TQ 3266 (Whitgift Centre)

The development of Croydon centre started in the early 1950s when the County Borough Council evolved a policy of

encouraging offices to decentralise from London. This approach
is epitomised by the Whitgift Centre, developed between 1965
and 1969, on the eleven acre site of the former Whitgift School.
The development, financially most successful for the school,
comprises 200 shop units in two-level pedestrian shopping malls
surmounted by 500,000 square feet of offices in five blocks, all
serviced from below and linked to extensive multistorey car parks.
With the centre of Croydon an undoubted commercial success,
it must be questioned whether this was achieved to the sacrifice
of aesthetic and environmental quality.

Royal Botanical Gardens, Kew L 4/4
OS Sheet 176   GR TQ 1877

The site of Kew Gardens came into the ownership of the Royal
Family in the eighteenth century, and a botanic garden of nine
acres was begun in 1759. They became famous during the reign
of George III when the estate as a whole was landscaped by
Sir William Chambers. The gardens were taken into state control
in 1841 and have since been increased to over 200 acres. They
are now vitally important, not just as a public park, but also as a
scientific institution where plants and plant material from all
over the world can be identified and catalogued. The Gardens
also distribute plant material to other parts of the country,
serve as a Quarantine Station, and train about sixty gardeners a
year.

The Pagoda in Kew
Gardens; built in 1761
to the design of
William Chambers.
B.T.A.

London Airport (Heathrow) L 4/5
OS Sheet 176   GR TQ 0775

Developed from a wartime air force base and now almost totally
surrounded by urban development, London Airport (Heathrow)
is the world's busiest international airport. During the 1960s, the
growth in air travel and the increasing noise of jet aircraft led to
the search for a site for a major new airport (see Cublington
TC 3/2). However, the development of larger and quieter
second generation jets has caused the abandonment of these
plans with the inevitable further growth in passenger and freight
handling capacity at existing airports, especially Heathrow.

Central terminal area
of Heathrow Airport.
Handford Photography.

50

Metropolitan Railway Development

L 4/6

OS Sheet 176

As the suburban railways of London pushed outwards from the old builtup area, so suburban development followed them. A classic example is the extension of the Northern underground line to Edgware in the 1920s when Edgware Station was built among green fields and development followed later. The earliest and most celebrated railway linked suburban expansion was the development of 'Metroland' during the Edwardian period, when the Metropolitan Railway, whose line ran from Baker Street via Harrow to Aylesbury, actively promoted suburban development along its route, at such places as Neasden, Willesden, Wembley and Harrow. The best way to view this development is by taking the Metropolitan Line train from Baker Street to Harrow, or on to Amersham.

Park Royal

L 4/7

OS Sheet 176   GR TQ 1982

Park Royal, built at the beginning of the First World War, is a huge industrial complex with employment for some 40,000 workers. It is mainly serviced from the interwar arterial roads of Western Avenue and the North Circular Road, and suffers all the problems, particularly in transportation, of such a large concentration of unplanned industries. It represents the growth of London's industries at that time based on the market demands of the metropolis rather than the demands of power and raw materials which up till then had concentrated major industries on the coalfields.

The Thames and Chilterns

To the north west of London lies a varied and delightful part of
Britain. Major transport arteries traverse the area along which the
traveller passes from London to the further north and west. Yet,
in the counties of Bedford, Buckingham, Hertford, Oxford and
the Royal County of Berkshire, diligent planning policies have
sought to preserve the region's character and still accommodate
the economic activity needed to sustain the people who live there.
The very nearness to London has brought strong conflict of
demands for land on which to work, live and gain recreation. The
area nearest to London has absorbed a great increase in population
from the capital in 'out county' estates built by the London
County Council just after the last war at Oxhey and Borehamwood
in Hertfordshire and at Slough in Berkshire. The garden city
movement, influenced by Ebenezer Howard, had established
Letchworth in Hertfordshire in 1904 and Welwyn Garden City
in 1920. Here, the ideals of the movement were put into practice
with results that are well worth seeing today. The concept inspired
planners in other parts of the country but was also taken up by
speculative builders who plagiarised it in the interwar suburbs of
the London fringe. A large area of land was purchased under the
Green Belt Act of 1938 by the councils of counties adjoining
London to protect it from speculative development. This included
the 1,000 acres of Langley Park and Black Park near Slough. The
passing of the 1947 and subsequent Town and Country Planning
Acts has introduced total control over land use, although the
pressure for development remains strong.

The Thames, from earliest times both an asset and a hindrance
to communication, winds above Maidenhead, with steeply wooded
banks forming the edge of the Chiltern Hills. The river turns
northward through the Goring Gap which separates the Berkshire
Downs from the Chilterns through Wallingford and Oxford to
its source near Cirencester. Navigable as far as Lechlade, the
river is a much used source of recreation, with attendant
problems of congestion and demands for marinas. The valley
provides large reserves of sand and gravel for construction
purposes, and careful planning has ensured the minimum of
damage to the landscape, with additional gains for recreation
on water filled excavations.

Vigorous planning policies have also been needed to protect
the Chiltern Hills from conflicting demands — as a residential
area, as a source of timber for the High Wycombe area, and
for recreation. The open chalk downland of the Berkshire
Downs overlooking the Vale of the White Horse, and the wooded
chalk hills of The Chilterns to the east of the Goring Gap have
been designated as Areas of Outstanding Natural Beauty. Much

of the remaining land between the hills and the builtup area of London is Green Belt with an additional ten mile Green Belt round Oxford. In these areas, development is strictly controlled and directed towards the limited expansion of existing settlements and the first generation of new towns — Bracknell, Hemel Hempstead, Hatfield, Welwyn Garden City and Stevenage. A second generation new town at Milton Keynes in North Buckinghamshire has been started to help to relieve the pressures on the Chilterns. Pre-Roman trackways such as The Ridgeway and Icknield Way have provided guidelines for a network of long distance footpaths with fine and ever changing views. Access by walkers to the Chilterns and Downs is encouraged, and carefully sited picnic and car parking areas are provided for the less energetic.

The region provides a recreational outlet for Londoners but is also a backcloth for settlements with an industrial base. Many of the older market towns have become centres of industries. In the mid-nineteenth century, Oxford successfully repelled the Great Western Railway's intention to place its works there. Nevertheless, the growth of the car industry at Cowley has brought problems of congestion, and pressures on the historic core of the university city. The manufacture of motor vehicles is also an important industry in Luton and Abingdon. At Slough a First World War military site was transformed into one of the earliest privately planned trading estates.

The new towns have brought new industry and prosperity to the area. Because of its good communications, it is attractive to commuters to London, and there is pressure for new development of all kinds.

In siting the new motorways, great care has been taken to avoid damage to the landscape. The route of the M4 was the subject of considerable investigation, and the crossing of the Chilterns scarp by the M40 at Stokenchurch is a splendid example of cooperation between the roadbuilder and landscape architect. The older town centres have been improved by reducing central area traffic and by initiating pedestrianisation schemes, in particular at Abingdon (famous, also, for the successful battle to prevent the erection of a large gasholder which would have dominated the town), Aylesbury, High Wycombe, Oxford and Watford.

This is a prosperous agricultural region, with sheep farming on the open downlands, mixed farming in the Oxfordshire plains and predominantly arable farming on the eastern Chilterns. The beechwoods of the Chilterns which provide the timber for the furniture industry contrast with the hedgerows, scattered woodlands and isolated trees dating from the Enclosure Acts and Awards of the seventeenth and eighteenth century. The economics of the arable farming industry have wrought changes in the landscape through the creation of ever larger fields but, scattered throughout the region, are large and small estates illustrating the English genius for landscape gardening, with especially fine examples at Ashridge, Blenheim, Hatfield, Woburn, Stowe and

Luton Hoo, all contributing to a picturesque scenery and fine architecture. Conservation of woodlands has been achieved by outright purchase by the local planning authorities and by the making of Tree Preservation Orders. Most of the historic town centres and villages of character have been designated Conservation Areas — there are now more than 450 of them in the five counties. Abingdon, for example, has been declared a Town Scheme under the Historic Buildings Act, and in Oxford a great deal of restoration and enhancement of the university buildings has been carried out. Much has also been achieved in the careful control of new buildings in the smaller settlements. The demand for new, large office blocks and supermarkets brings particular problems of scale. Building materials reflecting the local geology contribute largely to the differing character of the settlements — limestone at the edge of the Cotswolds, red sandstone in North Oxfordshire, warm, red brick in South Buckinghamshire and flint and brick buildings in the Chilterns.

David Overton and Gordon Sibthorpe

High Wycombe   TC 1/1
OS Sheet 175   GR SU 8693

The restricted site of High Wycombe has been both a blessing and a curse. In the eighteenth century it became a major coaching centre and many fine Georgian buildings remain. The inevitable congestion created by motor transport was alleviated by the construction of the M40 motorway bypass and an inner relief road. In conjunction with the latter, a covered shopping centre was completed in 1970 with the largest shops occupying the space under the road and the main pedestrian routes remaining at ground level. This represents the first major scheme to make full commercial use of the space beneath an elevated urban motorway and integrates shops, offices, a bus station, a multistorey car park and a retail market. The principal feature of the scheme is a two storey vaulted arcade of shops opening into an octagonal concourse roofed by a glazed dome.

Reading   TC 1/2
OS Sheet 175   GR SU 7173

A flourishing industrial and commercial town of about 135,000 inhabitants, Reading's importance in planning terms stems from its attempts to deal with its severe central area traffic problem. A standard ring road solution had long been proposed, but in the mid 1960s traffic management experiments sponsored by the Ministry of Transport gave priority to buses and pedestrians. Bus-only lanes, both with and against the flow of traffic, were introduced, buses were given priority at junctions and through traffic was excluded from some streets. These measures were generally successful and were later adopted by many other towns. The western half of the ring road has also been completed.

Reading town centre and inner distribution road.
Aerofilms.

Slough Trading Estate   TC 1/3
OS Sheet 175   GR SU 9581

In 1920, a former army transport repair depot on 600 acres of land was purchased by the Slough Trading Company. Since then, new industrial premises have been built to rent and a phased development programme has continued virtually uninterrupted. By 1970, the Company's Golden Jubilee year, the estate had become the largest industrial leasing organisation in the world with 850 buildings aggregating 6½ million square feet and providing employment for 30,000 people.

West Wycombe High Street.
The National Trust.

West Wycombe   TC 1/4
OS Sheet 175   GR SU 8394

West Wycombe village at first sight appears to exhibit little evidence of planning. Predominantly disposed along the main A40 road with no front gardens the houses represent the simplest form of unplanned village growth. Some of the attractive brick and half-timbered houses date from the fifteenth and sixteenth centuries and many from the seventeenth and eighteenth. However, their sheer survival has been due to their protective ownership since 1934 by the National Trust.

Windsor and Eton

OS Sheet 175   GR SU 9677

These two towns face each other across the River Thames.
Windsor, with its royal castle, is a mecca for tourists, while Eton
is famous for its college. The relationship between the
distinguished historic buildings of Eton college, the picturesque
old High Street, the river and the backdrop of Windsor Castle,
make Eton a most attractive small town. Windsor owes everything
to the presence of the castle, and the tourism which it now brings.
The Great Park of 4,800 acres surrounds the castle and town.
Ward Royal, a new housing scheme in Windsor, has received an
architectural award.

Windsor Castle,
dominating the town –
physically and
economically.
B.T.A.

Oxford

OS Sheet 164   GR SP 5106

With the High Street described by Thomas Sharp as 'the greatest
and most typical work of art England possesses', the heart of the
oldest university city in England is of outstanding architectural
and historic value. The conservation of this national heritage has
become the cornerstone on which the city's planning policies are
based. They are aimed at: restricting the physical growth of the
city by restraining the growth of employment and defining a
tightly drawn urban threshold (or Green Belt); reducing traffic
movement in the town centre with the help of a framework of ring
roads and rigorous traffic management, including the closure of
Queen Street and Cornmarket to all except essential service
traffic and buses; developing a vigorous policy of decentralising
non-essential functions from the city centre, and limiting the
height of new buildings, thus protecting the view of 'dreaming
spires'. The growth of shopping and other commercial activity is
now concentrated in a new Westgate complex, peripheral to the
historic centre, and to be served by an inner traffic relief road.

The struggle to save the famous Christchurch Meadow from
the relief road, is a classic case study in the preservation of
historic towns.

St. Mary's Church
(left) and the Radcliffe
Camera (right) from
the Tower of Magdalen
College, Oxford.
B.T.A.

Rousham Park

OS Sheet 164   GR SP 4724

At Rousham Park, William Kent 'revolutionised the whole
conception of garden design' (Miles Hadfield) by creating a series
of landscape 'paintings' through which one could walk, an
ideal which led to the larger scale works of Capability Brown and
Humphrey Repton. Rousham was laid out between 1720 and
1725, making use of the bends in the River Cherwell and the
natural shape of the land. The grounds, with classical temples,
cascades and statues, survive largely as Kent intended and visitors
can still stroll through the Glade of Venus and admire the
Temple of the Mill.

Looking across 'Venus's
Vale' towards the
'Upper Cascade' at
Rousham Park.
Country Life.

The House at Stowe, now used as a school. *B.T.A.*

Stowe   TC 2/3
OS Sheet 152   GR SP 6737

William Kent began to lay out the 200 acres of parkland at Stowe in the picturesque manner about 1730. As at nearby Rousham, he made use of cascades, grottoes, pavilions and classical temples, most of which survive and are being restored. Kent's work was later incorporated into the larger parkland improvements of Capability Brown (who started his career in the kitchen garden at Stowe) making Stowe one of the most impressive landscaped parks in England. The house features work by Vanburgh and Robert Adam, but now a public school it is also flanked by twentieth century educational buildings.

Wallingford, showing the regular street pattern of the Saxon 'new town', *Aerofilms.*

Wallingford   TC 2/4
OS Sheet 175   GR SU 6089

Wallingford was founded by the Saxons to defend an important crossing of the River Thames. The Saxon earth ramparts are still visible on the northern, western and southern sides of the present town, especially at Kine Croft. The town was given a standard 'cross grid' street pattern which it retains today. The castle at the north east corner was rebuilt in the thirteenth century. Wallingford is therefore a typical example of a Saxon 'burgh' or fortress town, which has survived without appreciable expansion.

Blenheim Palace and Woodstock   TC 2/5
OS Sheet 164   GR SP 4416

Blenheim is the grandest Baroque palace or country house in Britain. It was built by the nation for the first Duke of Marlborough as a reward for his victory over the French at Blenheim in 1704. Sir John Vanbrugh was the architect of the house, but the park was remodelled some fifty years later in the picturesque style by 'Capability' Brown. The lake he created by damming the River Glynne is considered to be his masterpiece.

The total composition of house and park is most impressive.

The neighbouring village of Woodstock was, until recently, one of the most pleasant small towns in the country, and still retains much of its eighteenth century elegance. Although it existed prior to the building of Blenheim, it owes most of its fortunes to the existence of the palace, whose grounds directly adjoin the town.

Blenheim Palace designed by Sir John Vanbrugh, and the Park laid out by 'Capability' Brown. *Aerofilms.*

Aylesbury   TC 3/1
OS Sheet 165   GR SP 8213

Friars Square, Aylesbury, was completed in 1969 as a pedestrian shopping precinct adjacent to the old Market Square. Its 300,000 square feet of shopping floor space with associated car parks, market square, market hall and bus station has shifted the centre of gravity of the town to the west. The total decline of the old shopping streets has only been averted by the growth in population and spending power of the town and its surrounding catchment area. Surmounting the Friars Square development are the new county offices of Buckinghamshire County Council, reminiscent in the dominance of their territory of the great town halls of the last century.

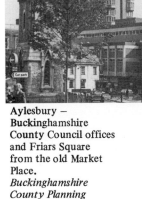

Aylesbury – Buckinghamshire County Council offices and Friars Square from the old Market Place.
Buckinghamshire County Planning Officer.

Cublington   TC 3/2
OS Sheet 165   GR SP 8526

The search for a site for a third London Airport has lasted for at least fifteen years. Stansted was the first choice, but after a vigorous public protest campaign, the Government set up a

Cublington Spinney —
bearing the legend:
'This spinney was
planted by the
Buckinghamshire
County Council in
gratitude to all those
who supported the
campaign against the
recommendation that
London's third airport
should be at
Cublington. Parish
councils, organisations,
societies and many
individuals contributed
towards the cost of the
spinney. This point
is the centre of the
area proposed for the
airport'.
*Buckinghamshire
County Planning
Officer.*

The Open University
headquarters, Walton
Hall, Milton Keynes.
*Milton Keynes
Development
Corporation.*

Planning Commission Inquiry under Lord Justice Roskill to examine alternatives and select a site. After hearing evidence from interested parties, Roskill short listed four sites, of which three were inland, north of London and one, Foulness, was on the coast east of the capital. The Commission eventually recommended Cublington, but after more rigorous protest from the local inhabitants, the Government selected Foulness (renamed Maplin) for environmental reasons. However, in July 1974, it was decided not to continue with the project, but to develop various existing regional airports instead.

Milton Keynes TC 3/3
OS Sheet 152   GR SP 8837 (Walton Hall)

Perhaps the most celebrated of the latest group of new towns, and the first London new town since 1949, Milton Keynes was designated in 1967 and covers an area of 22,000 acres, including several existing settlements. The target population is 250,000 by A.D. 2000. The site was chosen for its excellent communications (it lies on the M1, the main London — Birmingham railway, and the Grand Union Canal). Another pioneering feature is the intention of attracting half the total investment in building from private developers. Internally, the city is served by a grid of primary roads, allowing for greater car usage, but creating difficulties for public transport. One of the main aims in developing Milton Keynes was flexibility, enabling the city to change as it develops and adapt to new technologies and social habits. The city is also the home of the Open University.

Whipsnade Zoo TC 3/4
OS Sheet 166   GR TL 0017

Whipsnade was originally conceived, not as a conventional zoo, but as a breeding and conservation establishment. However, for economic reasons it has been commercially exploited. It was originally opened to the public in 1931 and the aim was to display the animals in an atmosphere as close as possible to their natural habitat. In this respect it was a forerunner of such animal parks as Longleat and Woburn. The zoo covers 460 acres on a downland site and most of it is accessible by car.

Woburn TC 3/5
OS Sheet 166   GR SP 9433

Like many other country estates Woburn Abbey came into private hands after the Dissolution of the Monasteries when Henry VIII granted it to the Russell family (subsequently the Dukes of Bedford). The continuing single ownership of the park and most of the village has resulted in a unity of design, with one arm of the village crossroads forming a landscaped approach to the Park. The village was substantially rebuilt after a fire in the eighteenth century and gives the impression of a small Georgian town allied to later nineteenth century estate cottages. The changing fortunes of estate owners encouraged the Duke of Bedford after the war to develop his estate for recreational use, and Woburn has become synonymous with the Wild Animal Kingdom and amusement park — leisure uses compatible with an estate originally laid out for the recreation of a wealthy minority.

Woburn Abbey and deer park.
B.T.A.

Letchworth Garden City   TC 4/1
OS Sheet 166   GR TL 2230

The first garden city, inspired by Ebenezer Howard and founded in 1903, Letchworth was conceived as an independent and selfcontained unit with a controlled social and architectural structure. It has a wide range of prosperous industries, homes and gardens with ample well landscaped open spaces, now reaching maturity. It 'is a demonstration of the technique of organic town planning under the system of unified estate ownership and leasehold, and the compatibility of that system with the freedom of industrial and business enterprises and the democratic conduct of a town's affairs' (F. J. Osborn [1945], preface to *Garden Cities of Tomorrow*). The fact that the planning and architectural vocabulary of Letchworth have become so acceptable in twentieth century planning leads one to forget the enormous step forward taken by Howard and his followers, and its impact on later population dispersal and new towns policy.

Garden city housing at Letchworth.
Hertfordshire County Planning Officer.

Old Warden   TC 4/2
OS Sheet 153   GR TL 1243

To the south east of Bedford, an area of contiguous country estates and estate villages illustrates the importance of this form of landholding and development in some parts of Britain, even to this day. Old Warden village was created by Lord Ongley in the late nineteenth century and reflected the Victorian desire to evoke a rustic Medieval atmosphere by use of irregular, loosely

Old Warden estate village.
Bedfordshire County Planning Officer.

spaced building groups in 'Gothic' and 'Elizabethan' styles, surrounded by a picturesque setting of trees and slopes. Many of these cottages seem to have come straight out of Victorian architectural pattern books — everybody's idea of a rustic cottage. Adjacent are Old Warden Park, Southill Park and estate village and Ickwell Green village. All three villages are characterised by the use of yellow ochre colouring for the buildings, and their informal style is in contrast to the classical formality of such earlier estate villages as Lowther and Harewood.

Cardington   TC 4/3
OS Sheet 153   GR TL 0646

Cardington airship hangars.
Bedfordshire County Planning Officer.

The giant hangars at Cardington are a reminder of the short-lived existence of airships for commercial and military use. Originally built between 1917 and 1921 by Short Brothers (who also created the nearby Shortstown garden village) the hangars were later extended to house the R 100 and R 101. The hangars were abandoned with the demise of airships after the R 101 crash in 1930. They passed to the RAF in 1939 and are now used only for inflating balloons for sport and parachute training.

Stevenage   TC 4/4
OS Sheet 166   GR TL 2324

Cycleway intersection at St. Martins Way, Stevenage.
Stevenage Development Corporation.

Designated in 1946 under the New Towns Act of that year, Stevenage was the first of the eight new towns established around London to decant people and jobs from the crowded metropolis in accordance with Abercrombie's 1944 proposals. Initial local hostility eventually diminished, and Stevenage has developed into a stable town of nearly 80,000 people with a wide range of industries. The town centre was the first in Britain to be planned for pedestrian use only, with an encircling service road providing access to car parks and shop loading bays. Throughout the residential neighbourhoods separate provision has been made for vehicles, cyclists and pedestrians and an extensive cycleway network intersects the town with underpasses at main road junctions.

Stewartby   TC 4/5
OS Sheet 153   GR TL 0042

The thick belt of Oxford Clay stretching from Oxfordshire to the Wash provides the raw material for brick manufacture on a large scale. Development at Stewartby near Bedford has continued since the house building boom of the 1920s when the London Brick Company's works became the largest in the world. Reclamation of worked-out pits has taken the form of infilling and restoration to agriculture and the creation of water areas for recreation use.   The growth of Stewartby village in the

shadow of the brickworks chimneys began in 1927 and has continued ever since with the provision by the LBC of a village hall, a club, a school, and homes for old people.

Welwyn Garden City   TC 4/6
OS Sheet 166   GR TL 2413

The success of Letchworth Garden City encouraged Ebenezer Howard to undertake a second development, and in 1920 he established Welwyn Garden City. With the master plan and many house designs by Louis de Soissons, the town has a more urban and formal character than Letchworth. The impressive central parkway is surrounded by public buildings and shops originally limited by Howard in their number and class of trade. In 1948 the Garden City became part of an enlarged New Town and the Development Corporation continued the work of the original development company. The town remains a pleasant environment in which to live and work and is a living tribute to the idealism of Ebenezer Howard, which has affected, directly or indirectly, the living conditions of millions of British people.

64

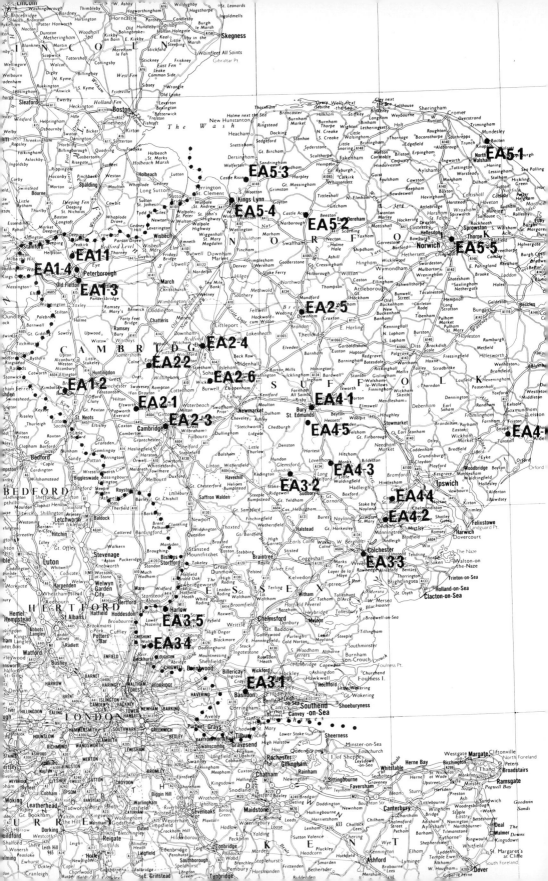

East Anglia

Thrusting out into the North Sea, East Anglia is off the main national routes and is not to be discovered on the way to other places. It is not surprising that it has an image of a rural backwater, of the idyllic 'thatched cottage' England.

On examination, this pastoral image fades into sepia: the nineteenth century was not a golden age for East Anglia. Industry passed it by, its farming was neglected and depressed, and many of its younger people migrated elsewhere. This completed its decline from the prosperity of earlier centuries, when the region played a forceful and active part in national life. But from a town planning point of view, the standstill of the last century preserved for present generations much of the tangible evidence of the region's previous prosperity. The best known examples are in the carefully preserved medieval Suffolk wool towns of Lavenham and Long Melford and the larger centres of King's Lynn, Bury St Edmunds and Norwich. Cambridge is, of course, a special case in which the old-established colleges continue to play a central role in the life of the modern city.

East Anglia began its climb back to prosperity in the thirties when the siting of industry became less dependent on coal and iron ore. As London has grown, the tentacles of its influence have rippled outwards over a widening area, and commuting and planned migration schemes have extended further into the region. Increasing affluence has provided opportunities for people to take environmental qualities into account when they decide where to live, both in their working lives and on retirement. All these factors have combined to make East Anglia one of the fastest growing regions in the postwar period.

The character of East Anglia is essentially agricultural, with fertile soils intensively cropped by arable farming. But the region's prosperity depends less and less on agriculture. Low wages in farming and capital investment in new industries have caused a substantial movement of workers to jobs in Norwich, Peterborough, Ipswich and Cambridge. Car ownership is high and growing and, for much of the region, the residual public transport service cannot support the frequency and speed of journeys people want. Many of the jobs have stemmed from town expansion schemes, which have regenerated small towns such as Huntingdon, St Neots, Haverhill and Thetford. Equally important, however, has been the establishment in the region of small firms whose owners prefer the unhurried pace of East Anglia's small towns to the pressures of London.

The dangers of redevelopment are becoming recognised, especially where commercial pressures can destroy the evidence of a town's past. In the same way, overuse can destroy

66

environmental charm outside the towns, in the Norfolk Broads and the Brecklands. On the coasts, the East Anglian resorts range from the brashness of Great Yarmouth and Southend to the period charm of Frinton, Aldeburgh and Hunstanton. But the Norfolk and Suffolk coasts still retain a quietude which could easily be lost. Even the essential countryside is not unchanging. Modern agriculture fits uneasily into enclosure landscapes, which are being redrawn into larger and larger fields. The oaks, beeches and elms of the hedgerows are ageing and often diseased, and are gradually being replaced by much smaller stands of commercial woodlands, with less familiar species. In the villages, the churches, which are a characteristic feature of the region, have become difficult to maintain, and estate development has spread around them.

The landmarks in this gazetteer must be related to the social and economic forces that produced them. A visit to Grimes Graves provides us with an impression of the scale of the prehistoric flint mining industry and the conditions experienced by the people who worked in it. What are the new landmarks replacing? And what will remain relevant in the future? We can visit the sites of the great fairs of England at St Faiths, St Ives, and Stourbridge in Cambridge, and trace the drovers' routes from Scotland and the north into East Anglia, where the cattle and sheep were fattened before sale at the fairs to the London merchants. It is important to understand how the advent of the railways ended their importance. The development of lorry traffic similarly ended the use of the Norfolk wherry and the Fen lighters, both designed for their waterways.

The clearest expression of the intervention of planning is provided by the new towns. Basildon and Harlow were both in the first round of new towns designated to give relief to London. They demonstrate how this brave idea has been translated into physical form, and indicate the degree to which it is possible to achieve the concept of selfcontained and balanced communities within a single town.

The extent to which this experience can be transferred to existing towns can be partially gauged by a comparison with Peterborough, where a new town is being grafted on to an existing industrial town. While this reduces the problem of the simultaneous transfer of jobs and people, much more effort has to be placed on the restricting of the existing core. The siting of Peterborough adds further distortions. The presence of brick clay workings to the south, and the Fens immediately to the east has thrown the emphasis of development to the north and west. In these circumstances, the success of this experiment has to be seen not only in the rate of growth achieved, but in the painstaking attention to the details of how it takes place. This is evident in many ways, including the recreational development of the Nene Valley, and the incorporation of cycleway systems into the structure of the new development.

While the new towns represent the achievements of planning on a grand scale, the expanded towns are significant for their encouragement of local initiative and the recognition by the local community of the benefits of the stimulus to be gained by assisting in the relief of London's difficulties. The effects of this expansion are most marked at Thetford, both in the size of the development which has taken place, and in the reconstruction of the town centre.

Further down the scale come the villages. The outstanding example of a new village is Bar Hill, to the west of Cambridge. This has been criticised as a piece of urban development imposed on the countryside, but it must be seen as part of the long tradition of village policy in the country. It not only reflects the effort to restrain the growth of Cambridge, but springs from the development of village colleges as part of the life of the people outside the city. One result of this is that the Cambridgeshire villages are larger and contain more modern development than in the region.

Whether the growth of Cambridge should be restrained in an effort to maintain the character of its centre is a debate which is likely to continue. The visitor should certainly see the Lion Yard development, which dominated much of the debate on the planning of the city in the fifties and sixties. It is perhaps too early to judge if this skilfully executed scheme has been successfully integrated into the heart of the city.

In contrast to Cambridge, Norwich and Colchester have been the sites of postwar universities, banished to parkland sites on the suburban fringes. Colchester is outstanding for its Roman ancestry, while Norwich holds a special place in the introduction of conservation policies which marry new development with old buildings and areas of character.

In many ways, the selection of large and self-evident landmarks does scant justice to East Anglia or to the achievements of planning in the region. For the character of the region lies in its diversity and in its retention of a human scale. The achievement of planning is that this can still be recognised, though the effort to achieve it has largely gone unsung. The eye that wishes to see deeply into East Anglia must look beyond landmarks to the day to day minutiae which are the substance and heart of planning.

Tony Bird

Car Dyke   EA 1/1
OS Sheet 142   GR TF 1704 (Werrington)

Far from originating with James Brindley in the mid-eighteenth century the first artificial navigations in Britain date from Roman times. Car Dyke is part of a formerly navigable canal system from the Humber to near Cambridge, believed to be of Roman origin. At Werrington, north of Peterborough, the Dyke is very well preserved with a ditch up to fifty feet wide and five feet deep to water level. The east bank along this stretch is a massive feature up to sixty feet wide and six feet high with a flat top some twelve feet wide. It now forms a water drainage channel, part of the drainage complex on the western side of the fens, and for considerable stretches is in generally good condition.

Grafham Water   EA 1/2
OS Sheet 153   GR TL 1568

The problem of water supply in lowland England is not always one of quantity but often of having the water in the right place at the right time. The water which would otherwise pass unused down the River Ouse to the Wash is pumped in times of excess flow (normally winter) up to the 600 acre Grafham Water reservoir. In times of shortage (normally summer) the flow is reversed and the water is returned for abstraction lower down. With less need for absolute purity of water, extensive recreation provision is made at the reservoir with sailing, fishing, picnicking and nature study encouraged.

Sailing and fishing close to the Aerator Tower of Grafham Water Reservoir.
Anglian Water Authority.

Old Fletton   EA 1/3
OS Sheet 142   GR TL 1895

On the same belt of Oxford Clay as the Stewartby brickworks near Bedford, brickmaking has been carried out around Old Fletton south of Peterborough since 1875. For the last ten years or so the London Brick Company, in conjunction with British Rail and the CEGB, have been operating a reclamation scheme on one thousand acres of brick clay pits to the east of the A15. The older workings are being filled — using pulverised fuel ash from the Trent Valley power stations — and then planted and landscaped. At present planted only with conifers, later possible uses are for land and water based recreation and industrial sites. The relative proximity of excavation and fill makes rail tranport economic, unlike the suggested large scale use of Cornish china clay waste for concrete aggregate.

Restoring 1,500 acres of brick pits with power station ash at Old Fletton, using a specially designed hovercraft.
C.E.G.B.

Peterborough   EA 1/4
OS Sheet 142   GR TL 1998

Like many English towns, Peterborough displays distinct periods of rapid growth followed by periods of relative stability. The present street pattern of the central area dates from 1154 when Abbot Martin de Bec moved the market place and associated buildings to its present higher site and laid out the town at the gates of the Minster. The coming of the Great Northern Railway in 1851 brought about a similar rapid expansion. Workshops and sidings were constructed with cottages and a school for the railway workers on a grid iron pattern parallel to the main railway line. As the railways prospered this pattern of development was extended over a wide area east of the railway and north of the city centre. The railway, school (now disused) and New England railway cottages (although mostly still occupied) are deteriorating, and consideration is now being given to improving and preserving some of them. The most recent period of expansion came with the designation of the city as a New Town in 1967 to accommodate an additional 90,000 population by 1985, mainly as overspill from the south east.

Great Northern Railway cottages, Lincoln Road, Peterborough.
Peterborough City Planning Officer.

Bar Hill   EA 2/1
OS Sheet 154   GR TL 3863

In 1950, town planning consultant William Holford drew up a policy to protect the city of Cambridge and restrict its growth. A 'necklace' of villages surrounding the city were to be expanded, but protected from loss of character due to excessive growth, by the building of new villages on virgin sites. Bar Hill, five miles north west of Cambridge, is the first and only one to be built. The village contains 1,250 houses, a shopping centre, social facilities and a light industrial estate. As at New Ash Green, however (q.v.), the cost of developing a totally new community overstretched the developers and the original enthusiasm for creating selfcontained new villages has waned.

Bedford Rivers and Fen reclamation   EA 2/2
OS Sheet 143   GR TL 3975

Until the seventeenth century drainage of the Fens had been small scale and piecemeal. In 1637 the Duke of Bedford employed the Dutch engineer Vermuyden to excavate a straight twenty mile long waterway to take the waters of the Ouse into the Wash. Fourteen years later with the parallel New Bedford River and the washlands between to absorb flood waters, the southern 'peat fens' were comprehensively drained although the drying out and shrinkage of the peat has necessitated continued pumping. The comprehensive nature of the initial drainage, in contrast to the Wash coast (q.v.), results in a characteristic landscape with straight drains and roads and widely scattered farm houses.

The Old and New Bedford Rivers with flooded washlands between.
Aerofilms.

Cambridge   EA 2/3
OS Sheet 154   GR TL 4458

An historic town which has been dominated, physically, economically and socially, by its university for the last 800 years. It was originally a Roman settlement and a busy commercial centre before the first college, Peterhouse, was founded in 1284. The present college buildings date from the fourteenth century onwards.

The influence of the university on the development of

Cambridge town centre hemmed in by land and buildings of the University. *Aerofilms.*

Cambridge has been considerable. Through the ownership of land, the colleges have, over the centuries, effectively prevented the expansion of the town to the west, so that the pattern of settlement appears lopsided, with the university to the west and the town spread out in an arc around it to the north and east. Some interesting experiments in built form and town structure are now going on. Their aim is to preserve historic Cambridge and at the same time to make the town efficient in meeting the urban demands of today, and tomorrow.

Ely, situated on higher land surrounded by reclaimed fenland. *Aerofilms.*

Ely   EA 2/4
OS Sheet 143   GR RL 5480

Ely has been for centuries the 'capital of the fens', but until the eighteenth century it was an island surrounded by water. As the largest island in the extensive fenland marshes, it was a natural settlement point for the Saxons and later the Normans, being almost completely safe from attack by invaders. It was the last area of resistance to the Norman invasion. It was also a natural ecclesiastical centre – a monastery was founded in the seventeenth century, and later the Normans built the present magnificent cathedral (1083). The unique crowning 'lantern' was added in the fourteenth century, and Ely with its cathedral now stands out as a prominent landmark in the midst of the flat fenlands.

Grimes Graves   EA 2/5
OS Sheet 144   GR TL 8189

Grimes Graves forms the largest and best known group of Neolithic flint mines and associated flint working sites in Britain. From the 700-800 pits in the area, some as deep as forty feet, flint was extracted from the chalk and fashioned into implements for export throughout Britain. The site is thought to have been worked from about 2330 B.C. to about 1740 B.C.

and the excavated pits, now preserved as an Ancient Monument, provide a vivid picture of this extensive and important mining industry.

Wicken Fen   EA 2/6
OS Sheet 154   GR TL 5570

At Wicken Fen the National Trust owns 730 acres of undrained fenland with a rich plant, bird and insect life. Whereas man has struggled with the forces of nature for centuries to reclaim the fenlands for agriculture, here extensive management practices are necessary to maintain the traditional fen conditions and prevent the land from drying out. In an island as intensively used as Britain even the most apparently natural landscape must be sensitively managed.

The pock-marked land surface of Grimes Graves, showing the infilled shafts of the flint mines. *Cambridge University Collection, copyright reserved.*

Wicken Fen Nature Reserve, surrounded by reclaimed fenland. *Aerofilms.*

Basildon   EA 3/1
OS Sheet 178   GR TQ 5718

Basildon New Town was established with the dual purpose of housing overspill population and industry from London and redeveloping unserviced and substandard shack developments which had become the permanent homes of about 25,000 people. Substantial areas of the town are nearing completion, including the Pipps Hill industrial area laid out by the Development Corporation but with some freeholds subsequently conveyed to occupiers: the Five Links housing area comprising nearly 1,600 dwellings ranged around courtyards with the total segregation of pedestrians from vehicles; and the Castlemayne estate built by the Development Corporation for sale to owner occupiers.

The Aquatels development adjacent to the A127 comprises an hotel with integral recreation area based on a lake created as part of the storm water regulating system. Material excavated from the lake will form a dry ski slope and earthmoulding for a golf course. The hotel and facilities will be used predominantly by business people during the week and holiday visitors at weekends. Access to the site is free with charges for the use of facilities. This development, financed by private capital, is an

Factory for Yardleys Ltd. on the Pipps Hill Industrial Area, Basildon New Town. *Stanland.*

interesting example of trends in coordinated recreation provision.

Cavendish   EA 3/2
OS Sheet 155   GR TL 8046

Church Cottages, Cavendish, form one of those often photographed little pieces of England which we take for granted. However, they only survive as a result of restoration in 1958 paid for by public subscription and grants. Burnt down in 1970 and rebuilt in 1972, they now provide homes for elderly villagers. Without conscious effort, this apparently unplanned development would long since have disappeared.

Church cottages, Cavendish, before restoration. *Richard Burn.*

Church cottages, Cavendish, after restoration. *B.T.A.*

73

Colchester

OS Sheet 168   GR TM 0025

Colchester was a tribal capital for several centuries before the
Roman conquest, but in A.D. 49 the first permanent Roman
colony in Britain was established here. The town was laid out on
a standard grid iron pattern, still discernable today. Although
sacked by Boadicea in A.D. 60, the town was rebuilt with a fine
wall, which ensured its continued existence as a major city and
administrative centre of Roman Britain. It remained an important
town under the Saxons, with an economy based on trade and
agriculture. During the Middle Ages it was the centre of a
flourishing cloth industry.

Colchester is a town that has survived for three thousand years
mainly because of its ability to adapt to changing circumstances.
Today, it is a tourist centre, a garrison town and important
market town.

Epping Forest

OS Sheet 177   GR TQ 4198

Epping Forest has been a resort for Londoners since the eighteenth
century, when the Land Revenue Commissioners declared that it
should remain unenclosed. In 1871, the Corporation of London
brought a lawsuit to prevent enclosure of common land and to
safeguard grazing rights, and in 1878 became Conservators of the
Forest. Today, they maintain, manage and finance its 6,000
acres of woods and common land for public recreation and the
conservation of wildlife. Without the guardianship of the
Corporation, this former Royal Forest of Essex would now
almost certainly be built up.

Harlow

OS Sheet 167   GR TL 4510

One of the ring of London's new towns recommended in
Sir Patrick Abercrombie's Greater London Plan of 1944, Harlow
was designated in 1947 with a target population of 80,000 later
raised to 120,000. The intention was to form a balanced and

Low density housing,
built between 1950
and 1954 at Broomfield,
Harlow New Town.
Wainwright.

selfcontained community, very much in the spirit of Ebenezer Howard's garden cities. One of the features of Harlow is the low housing density compared with later new towns (e.g. Cumbernauld), which has allowed much open space and a high quality of landscaping. The plan is based on the neighbourhood concept, with units grouped round the town centre. A pleasing variety of housing designs has been achieved by encouraging different architects to design residential areas.

Bury St Edmunds EA 4/1
OS Sheet 155   GR TL 8564

The Abbot of the Saxon abbey of St Edmundsbury at the time of the Norman conquest was a Frenchman, Baldwin, and perhaps for this reason the lands and power of the Abbey survived. Its importance rapidly grew and Baldwin laid out a chequer board development of streets with the central axis, Churchgate St, focused on to the high altar of the Abbey. Bury St Edmunds thus became one of the most important regularly laid out Norman towns in this country. Today the grid pattern of streets, with the ecclesiastical square of Angel Hill and the Great Market to the north, are clearly discernible: evidence of the strong continuity over centuries of street patterns.

Bury St. Edmunds. The grid layout of the Norman town can clearly be seen before the gates of the Abbey. *Aerofilms.*

Dedham Vale EA 4/2
OS Sheets 155 and 168/9   GR TM 0733

Dedham Vale was designated as an AONB as much for its connections with the painter Constable as for its outstanding natural beauty. Despite the industrial and technological changes of the last 150 years there are vistas in this area which are virtually unchanged since Constable painted them. Ownership of some properties by the National Trust, e.g. Flatford Mill, and protective designation by the Countryside Commission, attempt to ensure the survival of one of the best known landscapes in England.

Willy Lott's cottage, near Flatford Mill, protected for its connections with John Constable.
B.T.A.

Lavenham and Long Melford   EA 4/3
OS Sheet 155   GR TL 9149

The wealth of much of East Anglia in the Middle Ages was founded on the wool trade. Lavenham is architecturally the most magnificent of the Suffolk wool towns. It was built around the market square and a great many half-timbered Medieval buildings, as well as the beautiful church, still survive today.

Long Melford, nearby, has been called the 'stateliest small town in Suffolk', and consists of a single broad main street, a church and three great country houses. Both Lavenham and Long Melford dramatically illustrate the wealth and importance of this part of England during the Medieval and Tudor periods.

Long Melford Church and Green.
B.T.A.

Little Wenham   EA 4/4
OS Sheet 169   GR TL 0839

A unique Medieval village grouping of church, castle, moated hall and tithe barn, all dating from the thirteenth to fifteenth cenutries, and surviving intact to the present day. The castle is the dominating central feature.

The Medieval tythe barn at Little Wenham. *Suffolk County Planning Officer.*

Rushbrooke   EA 4/5
OS Sheet 155   GR TL 8961

The notable tradition of English agricultural estate villages has been continued into the twentieth century by the development in 1957 of Rushbrooke Village, designed by the architects Richard Llewelyn Davies and John Weeks. The simple building forms and materials based on an informal plan 'express themselves politely in accents that are recognisably regional and not harshly alien to an ancient and honourable tradition' (Clough Williams Ellis).

New housing in Rushbrooke Village. *Architectural Review.*

Snape Maltings   EA 4/6
OS Sheet 156   GR TM 3957

The changing scale of rural industries has made many buildings in the countryside obsolete. Some find new uses as holiday and retirement homes or antiques centres, etc. One of the early nineteenth century malthouses at Snape, restored after the

Snape Maltings, converted into a concert hall for the Aldborough Festival. *Suffolk County Planning Officer.*

initial conversion was badly damaged by fire, has become the main concert hall centre for the Aldeburgh Festival of Music. The remainder are still in commercial use. Such development illustrates the flexibility needed in making the best use of our environmental assets.

Bacton Gas Terminal   EA 5/1
OS Sheet 133   GR TG 3334

Since the discovery in the 1960s of commercial quantities of natural gas under the North Sea, the activity of the gas industry has rapidly changed from small scale local manufacture and distribution to a nationally integrated system of supply, the gas flow pattern now being from the coast into urban conurbations via a high pressure pipeline system.

Three reception terminals have been built to receive and process the gas and a fourth is in course of construction. The largest is at Bacton, on a 186 acre site, accommodating three producers and capable of supplying 15 per cent of Britain's total energy requirements.

The exposed nature of the cliff top site has demanded sensitive design and landscaping and a single architectural style has been used throughout. By placing the structures and boundary fence back from the cliff edge, users of the beach are visually unaware of the terminal's existence.

Bacton natural gas terminal. *British Gas Corporation.*

Castle Acre   EA 5/2
OS Sheet 132   GR TF 8115

The site of Castle Acre village is full of historical associations, and illustrates most vividly the continuity of settlement characteristic of English villages. The whole village lies within defensive earthworks, established shortly after the Roman conquest, and is dominated by the long neglected but currently being excavated castle ruins. These have been described as 'perhaps the finest castle earthworks in England' (E.S. Armitage). The Peddars Way Roman road passes through the village and may

Castle Acre, showing the rectangular Romano-British enclosure, the Norman castle, Medieval church and village and priory at top left. *Aerofilms.*

help to explain the regular grid iron street plan. To the south west, just outside the earthworks, stand the majestic ruins of the late eleventh century Cluniac Priory. The existing cottages crowd together around the market square and along the narrow streets on sites probably in continuous use since the twelfth century.

Castle Rising   EA 5/3
OS Sheet 132   GR TF 6624

Castle Rising, once a port from which the sea has long retreated, displays a grid iron street plan probably contemporary with its well preserved twelfth century castle and church. The many similarly planned villages evident throughout the country emphasise the ease and simplicity with which a rectilinear street pattern could be laid out. The extensive use in older buildings of 'Carrstone', a soft gingerbread coloured sandstone obtained only in the locality, illustrates the visual significance of local building styles. Local styles and the use of local materials decreased with the coming of the railways, and standardised building and highway regulations, building styles and materials are destroying the characteristic atmosphere of the place.

Kings Lynn   EA 5/4
OS Sheet 132   GR TF 6220

Kings Lynn is an ancient port whose importance throughout history is emphasised by its Medieval churches, two guildhalls, two market places, four Medieval friaries and abundance of fine Georgian houses. The town has received a more recent fillip by its decision to receive London overspill under the 1952 Town Development Act. To cater for expanded trade, the central shopping area is being pedestrianised with total segregation from

Elizabethan merchant's
lookout tower at
Clifton House, Queens
Street, Kings Lynn.
*Norfolk County
Planning Officer.*

vehicles, a degree still unusual in Britain. The comprehensive
scheme involves the provision of rear servicing, service roads
bridged over landscaped pedestrian streets and an integrated
bus station and car parking.

Norwich   EA 5/5
OS Sheet 134   GR TG 2308 (City Centre)

The site of Norwich was first settled by Saxon invaders in the fifth
and sixth centuries and it had become a borough before the
Norman Conquest. Its easily accessible — yet easily defended —
location at the heart of a well-populated and fertile farming area
led to inevitable development. The Cathedral was founded in 1094
and the Castle built on its prominent mound about 1130 to
defend the growing town and its important market. The city's
importance in Medieval times can be seen in the 32 pre-
Reformation churches which still remain within the two mile
circuit of the fourteenth century city walls.

 Largely by-passed by the Industrial Revolution the city
continued to prosper with the timely replacement of its
traditional woollen textile industry and the continued
development of its commercial and administrative functions.
Today it serves as the principal administrative, educational and
commercial centre for much of East Anglia, housing the new
University of East Anglia, Norfolk County Council
Headquarters and many major commercial concerns. However,
the prosperity which this brings threatens the historical and
architectural character of the city. With a Medieval street plan
evolved to serve pedestrians and horse-drawn vehicles the streets
are unable to cope with modern motor traffic. The present plan
for the central area therefore seeks to save the historic core of
the city by creating a ring road, mostly following the line of the
city walls, with loop roads to conveniently sited car parks and
carrying service traffic and buses. Within the core traffic is being
excluded; as in London Street where total closure to vehicles
(completed in 1969) set an example which many other towns
have since followed by dramatically improving the environment
and increasing shopping turnover.

 Norwich was the scene, in 1959, of the first Civic Trust
"face-lift" scheme — in Magdalen Street. Although quite
spectacular and emulated elsewhere the results were rather
shortlived by not solving the underlying economic problems
of the area. In contrast, as a major contribution to European
Architectural Heritage Year 1975 the City Council is
encouraging the rehabilitation of the nearby Colegate area
where new life, particularly new housing, is being injected into
an historic but run-down industrial area near the city centre.
A wide range of public and private agencies are being urged
to consider the various facets of conservation — traffic
management, building restoration, infill development (such as the
new housing at Friar's Quay), planting and paving etc.

London Street, Norwich.
Formerly a two-way
traffic street, now an
attractive foot street.
Norwich City Council.

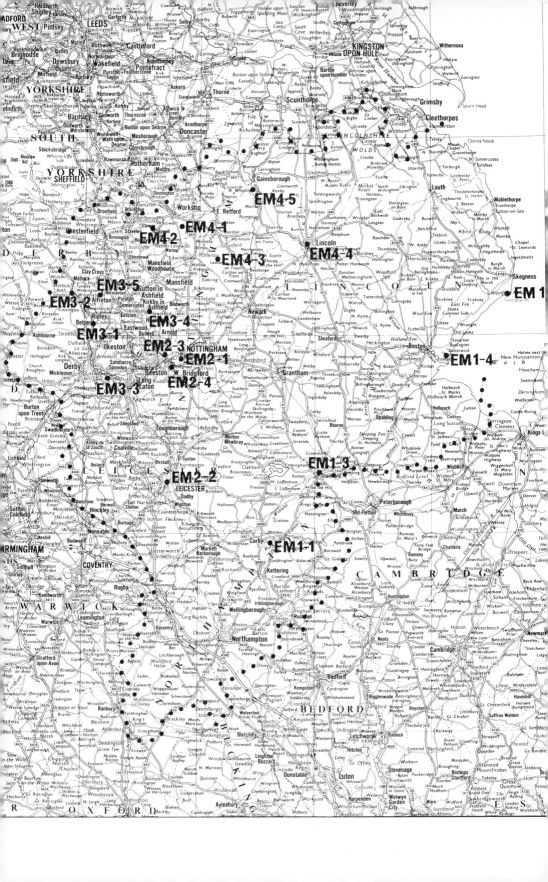

The East Midlands

Of all the regions of England the East Midlands must be the least easy to define. Even the chief river, the Trent, is shared with the West Midlands and Yorkshire and is regarded as the divide between the North and South of England instead of as a unifying feature. This lack of identity has a long history, for it was only during the ninth and tenth centuries, following the Danish invasions, that the East Midlands formed an administrative entity as the Danelaw. The Danes chose five boroughs as their military and commercial centres: Nottingham, Derby, Leicester, Lincoln and Stamford, and only the last has failed to retain its place in the regional economy. The region's five counties in the new patterns of local government can be traced back to the shires based on the boroughs of the Danelaw.

Over the centuries, the people of the region have become accustomed to watching great events taking place around them rather than among them. Armies marching northwards from the capital would pass through the region to deal with rebellious Scots or Northerners. The region has seen great routeways laid across its surface, almost always in a north-south direction: the first roads built by the Romans; Medieval roads; turnpike roads; canals; railways and, most recently, motorways.

Early man has left few extensive marks of his activities but at Arbor Low, in Derbyshire, one can still sense what a wild, dangerous place the world was to primitive man when he set up that ring of stones on its windswept plateau. In the same county, the Caves at Cresswell Crags have yielded evidence of a succession of prehistoric cultures and are now being made more accessible to the visitor.

With the Romans came their roads, towns and urban life. Leicester and Lincoln were their main centres and our knowledge of both would be greater were it not for the presence of modern cities on the same sites. As rebuilding takes place, work by archeologists enables us to learn a little more about our remote past. The need to integrate the work of archeological investigation into the town redevelopment programmes is not the least of the problems faced by local planners. There is a reassuring sense of the continuity of human life in such cities. At Lincoln one can see granite setts in the road surface which mark the bases of columns of Roman buildings before passing beneath a gateway of the Roman city which still survives. At Leicester, the Roman forum has been laid open for the visitor to see and both cities have fascinating displays of their Roman past in their museums.

The region is rich in Medieval towns. Pride of place must go to Stamford in Lincolnshire, surely one of the most beautiful towns in the country. Here, one can walk along street after street of Medieval stone buildings with hardly a jarring note. Newark in Nottinghamshire belongs to that strange category of planned Medieval towns, and nearby, at Southwell, is a Medieval cathedral set in a little town hardly larger than a village.

Lincoln is a cathedral city. Here the great building, still much the largest in the town, is set on the top of a hill for all the world to admire and around are narrow streets of graceful buildings acting as a foil to one of the great monuments of Western civilisation.

During the seventeenth and eighteenth centuries, prosperity came to the region for the first time and the face of innumerable towns and villages still show the effects of the rebuilding and refurbishing which went on during those centuries. Indeed, the typical picture of an East Midlands town is one mainly derived from that time: streets of well mannered brick houses, rather more imposing around the market place and with only the church as a reminder of the Medieval past. Such towns are Ashby-de-la-Zouch in Leicestershire, Ashbourne in Derbyshire and Louth in Lincolnshire.

The industrial revolution, while in no sense passing the region by, did not produce a great industrial conurbation. Yet the industrial revolution saw its beginnings here where the earliest phase of machine production of textiles utilised the power of the river Derwent and its tributaries in Derbyshire. This phase ended with the development of steam power, but one can still come across cotton mills and workers' housing now strangely out of place in remote settings of great beauty.

During the nineteenth century the region developed as the main centre of the footwear and knitwear industries. In the second half of the nineteenth century Leicester and Northampton became the principal industrial centres. By that time a few lessons had been learned in urban development and these towns are notably less congested than many less fortunate factory towns elsewhere.

The largest city in the region is Nottingham, until the nineteenth century a modest county town still gathered beneath the shadow of its castle and with the largest market place in England at its centre. First, canal and river navigation, then railways brought vast changes, but the surrounding common lands remained unenclosed until the middle of the nineteenth century. By then the population was rising rapidly and building densities rose to the highest in the country: Nottingham had the unenviable reputation of having the foulest slums in England. The modern city has much to commend it — a fine array of open spaces and attractive landscaping of the banks of the river Trent.

The East Midlands countryside is unspectacular but it is here, among the fields and woods and villages, that the heart of the region is to be found. Small villages with humble cottages cluster round the church and great house, the whole set in a carefully planned and satisfying landscape of maturing woodlands and meticulously tilled fields. The social structure of which this feudal countryside is the physical expression is changing but it is still possible to travel for miles through such a landscape.

Here and there one can experience very different landscapes. In the flat Fens of Lincolnshire, England seems to be trying to imitate Holland. Much of the Peak District National Park, with its high exposed plateaux and verdant dales, is within the region, as is Charnwood Forest in Leicestershire, an isolated area of steep, rocky hills — almost a pocked-sized Alps. Nottinghamshire and Derbyshire house the most important coalfield in the country, too recently developed to have created the vast, devastated landscape surrounding older coalfieds. Here, the collieries, villages and spoil tips are set in seemly surroundings and many of the colliery villages are carefully planned settlements of considerable interest.

The region has an oilfield on the Nottinghamshire border with Lincolnshire, tiny compared with other oilfields, yet producing oil in commercial quantities. To the east are the North Sea sources of oil and natural gas: the coast of Lincolnshire, long favoured for seaside recreation, now has a new role to play with its natural gas terminal at Theddlethorpe.

The production of coal near the Trent has also led to the development during the past quarter century of one of the two main centres of electricity generation in Europe. Only in the Ruhr Valley will the visitor find a comparable array of power stations.

Occasionally, modern planning in the East Midlands has produced spectacular results: the new towns of Corby and Northampton and the town development schemes at Daventry and Wellingborough are examples. Hardly less so is the different enterprise of creating the Peak District National Park, in many ways the most positive planning achievement of all British national parks.

The East Midlands is still a pleasant part of England. Even its principal cities are recognisable urban entities surrounded by largely unspoilt countryside rather than formless conurbations. It still has many attractive towns and villages; the countryside retains many of the trees and hedgerows which gives it its traditional charm and its coastline is still largely undeveloped. Not a little of the credit for this state of affairs must go to those who have been responsible for planning its town and villages and the countryside surrounding them.

John Anthony

Corby   EM 1/1
OS Sheet 141   GR SP 9377 (Cranford St John)

The growth of Corby has depended on the extraction of iron ore deposits and their conversion into iron and steel. Being low grade ore (20-30 per cent) extraction is by opencast methods over very

Cranford St. John
ironstone quarry —
before reclamation.
*Northamptonshire
County Planning
Officer.*

Cranford St John
ironstone quarry —
after reclamation.
*Northamptonshire
County Planning
Officer.*

Stamford — the first
conservation area in
England.
B.T.A.

large areas of land. Reclamation has been extensive and continuous, thanks to the provisions of the Mineral Workings Act 1951. Under this Act the Ironstone Restoration Fund finances reclamation of land with contributions from land owners, operators and central government — a scheme which could have parallels in other extractive industries. As a result of improved drainage and redistribution of top soil much of the land is now agriculturally superior to unmined land.

Gibraltar Point   EM 1/2
OS Sheet 122   GR TF 5659

Gibraltar Point is a coastal area of national importance for bird migration and the flora of coastal accretion. Designated as a nature reserve, the area attracts many visitors from nearby Skegness and further afield. To ensure the survival of the flora and fauna, facilities are being provided to encourage wildlife and control visitors. A freshwater mere is being enlarged to attract ducks and other water fowl, and a field study centre and visitor centre with nature trails and picnic sites are available to channel visitors to acceptable areas.

Stamford   EM 1/3
OS Sheet 141   GR TF 0307

One of the finest Medieval towns in Europe, Stamford was once

an important commercial and cultural centre. Originally a Roman town on the important Ermine Street, it was later expanded by the Saxons, Danes and Normans. It was given by Elizabeth I to her chief minister, Lord Burghley (who built the nearby Burghley House) and became a pocket borough. In the eighteenth century it became fashionable because of its position on the Great North Road. By means of their influence and patronage, Burghley's successors prevented the expansion of the town, and most important, prevented the railway from passing through. The resulting economic decline meant that the town has remained largely fossilised as it was in 1850, unsullied by later nineteenth and twentieth century development. It was the first conservation area to be designated under the 1967 Civic Amenities Act.

Wash Coast   EM 1/4
OS Sheet 131   GR Frieston Shore TF 3942, Lawyers Creek
                 TF 4033, Boatmere Creek TF 4728

Unlike the marshy swamps of the Southern Fens, which have been drained by massive engineering works such as the Bedford Rivers (q.v.) the Wash coast has been progressively pushed back by irregular small scale reclamation. Some 70,000 acres of first class arable land have been added in the last 300 years. Continuing progress with marsh reclamation can be measured by the succession of parallel sea banks whilst the need for drainage is emphasised by the abundance of surviving windmills. The settlement pattern reflects the story of reclamation — long narrow parishes stretching out from the old village centres with hamlets on the reclaimed land.

Land reclamation on the Wash coast. Each bank represents a successive stage of reclamation. *Aerofilms.*

Holme Pierrepont   EM 2/1
OS Sheet 129   GR SK 6138

The valuable sands and gravels of the Trent valley have been extracted in many places for constructional use. At Holme Pierrepont the resultant dereliction has been removed by creating the National Water Sports Centre. Here a 2,000 metre rowing course of international standard (the first in Britain) has been constructed, with supporting facilities and a country park and nature reserve. The cost of the project has been offset by grants from the Countryside Commission and Sports Council and by commercial sponsorship — even of a fishing lake.

Leicester, New Walk   EM 2/2
OS Sheet 140   GR SK 5804

The 2000 metre rowing course at Holme Pierrepont National Water Sports Centre. *Aerofilms.*

Many British towns show evidence of development influenced by the flourishing spa towns of the eighteenth century. One of

the best examples is New Walk, Leicester. Laid out in 1750 as
a tree lined promenade a mile long linking three squares and
faced with high class town houses, it has been declared a
conservation area and recently rehabilitated. Although many of
the buildings have been replaced and the function of others
changed for use as offices and institutions, New Walk retains
much of the gracious character envisaged by its creators.

Nottingham   EM 2/3
OS Sheet 129   GR SK 5739

Like most British towns, the centre of Nottingham suffers severe
traffic congestion. Unlike most towns solutions have been sought
without the need for major road construction. A free bus service
round the central area reduces shoppers' traffic and the proposed
'zone and collar' control represents an ambitious but locally
opposed attempt to control car commuting by regulating traffic
flows from residential areas onto the main roads. These controls
would be complemented by improved public transport with
bus-only lanes and a park and ride service. In the central area,
shopping streets have been closed to traffic and two major
covered shopping centres have been built. The Victoria Centre,
on the site of the old Victoria Station, is one of the best such
centres in the country, both commercially and environmentally.
However, its success has had repercussions on the existing
shopping areas of the town.

West Bridgford, Asda Shopping Centre   EM 2/4
OS Sheet 129   GR SK 5863

The Asda shopping centre at West Bridgford, built in 1963-4, was
one of the first out of town shopping centres in Britain, modelled
on American lines, with adjacent parking for 1,000 cars.
Floorspace was leased by the parent company to individual

traders in a wide range of goods. Interestingly, certain traders were unable to compete with city centre stores in Nottingham and, after a change of ownership, it has been developed as a conventional department store specialising in goods likely to be purchased on a weekly basis.

Belper   EM 3/1
OS Sheet 119   GR SK 3448

The increasing scale of industrial production permitted by the harnessing of water power led to the establishment or growth of villages and towns around the factory buildings. At Belper, the firm of Strutts housed 300 workers' families between 1792 and 1831 in houses such as the north and south Long Rows, providing social and community facilities worthy of the welfare state. These well-built, relatively spacious houses close to the cotton mills on the River Derwent survive to this day as a tribute to the humane ideals of at least some early industrialists.

East Mill, Belper, and the weir on the River Derwent which provided its original source of power. *Derbyshire County Planning Officer.*

Cromford   EM 3/2
OS Sheet 119   GR SK 2956

Richard Arkwright's second spinning factory driven by water power was established on the banks of the River Derwent in 1771. The mills can still be seen in the village, together with early industrial housing. Cromford illustrates the early stages of the industrial revolution, based on water power. The later development of steam power freed the factories from dependence on fast flowing rivers, and so Cromford never developed further and was soon overshadowed by the growth of industrial cities on the coalfields.

Elvaston Castle

EM 3/3

OS Sheet 129   GR SK 4033

Elvaston Castle, south east of Derby, was one of the first country parks to be designated under the 1968 Countryside Act. Owned and managed jointly by Derbyshire County Council and Derby Borough Council, it provides countryside recreation mainly for town dwellers. Based on a castle, largely rebuilt in 1817, and 200 acres of parkland, the park provides woodlands, riding areas, picnic and camping sites, formal gardens and nature trails. Such country parks, within easy reach of towns, ease the pressure on more remote and solitary places and reduce the risk of damage to the intensively farmed countryside.

Newstead

EM 3/4

OS Sheet 120   GR SK 5253

A late nineteenth century coalmine and colliery village, built by the mine owner to house his workers. Many such villages were built in mining areas throughout the country in the nineteenth and early twentieth centuries.

Nearby is Newstead Abbey, the home of Lord Byron until he was forced to sell it to pay his debts. It has been restored by Nottingham Corporation who now own the property. It contains a collection of Byronic relics. The park and gardens form pleasure grounds intended primarily for the citizens of Nottingham.

South Wingfield

EM 3/5

OS Sheet 120   GR SK 3755

With the contraction of the coalmining industry numerous pits have been abandoned, leaving local authorities, aided by

South Wingfield Colliery – before reclamation. *Raymonds, Photographer.*

South Wingfield
Colliery — after
reclamation.
*Raymonds,
Photographer.*

government grants, to clear up the mess. Unlike the ironstone
industry there is no standard procedure for reclaiming coal
remains and, alas, it often takes an 'Aberfan'* disaster to initiate
action. Derbyshire County Council, however, have been most
active in removing their unwanted heritage and the former
Wingfield Manor colliery, like a number of others, has now
become farmland and forest crossed by bridle ways and a
necessarily diverted stream.

*In 1966 a slag heap at Aberfan (South Wales) slipped, burying part of the
village in coal waste and killing 144 people, including 116 children at the
local school. This disaster prompted a fresh examination of the stability of
waste coal tips.

Clumber Park and Sherwood Forest   EM 4/1
OS Sheet 120   GR SK 6268 (Major Oak)

Sherwood Forest, despite its similar origins as a Royal hunting
forest, has lacked the unity of management apparent in the
New Forest. Through the years, land has been taken for
agriculture, commercial conifer planting, collieries, colliery
villages and military training. So many stately homes and
landscaped parks were established that a part of it became known
as 'the Dukeries'. One such park was Clumber Park, bought with
the help of public subscription for the National Trust in 1947.
Its recreational use since then has been extensive — up to
12,000 visitors a day — and its designation in 1971 as a country
park has ensured the development of the management and warden
service to cater for this scale of use.

Cresswell Crags, near Worksop   EM 4/2
OS Sheet 120   GR SK 5374

A Palaeolithic settlement, the home of 'Cresswellian Man' — the
attractive wooded limestone gorge contains caves (e.g. Church

Hole Cave), with early examples of primitive pictorial art. The site is not yet open to the public

Laxton EM 4/3
OS Sheet 120   GR SK 7267

Open fields at Laxton.
Aerofilms.

By historical accident Laxton remains the only village in England dependent on the continued cultivation of open fields. The system by which most of England was once farmed was finally killed by the General Enclosure Act of 1845 which permitted land owners to enclose their open fields and thus undertake more advanced and productive forms of agriculture. Laxton, however, escaped enclosure and in 1951 passed into the ownership of the Ministry of Agriculture as an historical curiosity. Since then its visual impact has declined as surrounding farmland has been reopened for large scale arable cultivation, but the existence of working farms within the village indicates its particular character.

Lincoln EM 4/4
OS Sheet 121   GR SK 9881

Originally an ancient British settlement, Lincoln was a major Roman fortress town at the junction of Ermine Street and the Fosse Way. Some Roman remains, such as the West Gate, survive. Because of its strategic location, the city was later chosen by William the Conqueror as the site for a castle. A good deal of Medieval Lincoln survives and the crowning glory is the cathedral, built between 1185 and 1280. The evolution of the original Roman grid plan to the later Medieval street pattern can be studied on the ground by the observant visitor.

Brayford Pool was an artificial inland dock, originally Roman, but expanded in the Middle Ages and later in the eighteenth and nineteenth centuries. It is now used for recreation.

Swanpool Garden Suburb (1928) is a fragment of an ambitious housing project on garden city lines. Although never finished it shows the influence of Hampstead Garden Suburb and Letchworth and is still very much in its original condition.

Brayford Pool, Lincoln: of Roman origin.
Lincoln City Planning Officer.

With the demand for electricity doubling every decade, the scale
and impact of power stations and transmission facilities is bound
to increase also. West Burton is one of a chain of power stations
along the River Trent making full use of the Trent's water for
cooling, and using coal from the nearby highly productive
Yorkshire and Nottinghamshire coalfield. To minimise the
impact of this 2,000 megawatt station extensive studies were
undertaken to establish the best grouping and colouring of
cooling towers and chimneys. The station subsequently received
a Civic Trust Award as 'an immense engineering work of great
style which, far from detracting from the visual scene, acts as a
magnet to the eye from many parts of the Trent Valley and from
several miles away' (Civic Trust citation).

West Burton Power
Station.
C.E.G.B.

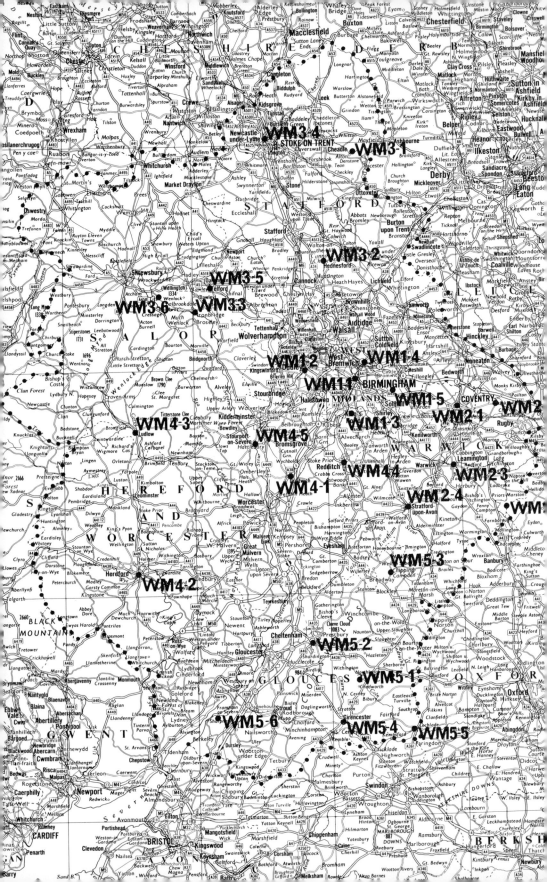

The West Midlands

As a generalisation, the West Midlands may be thought of today
as a region with an industrial heartland in an extensive agricultural
countryside setting. Urban life is concentrated in a polycentred
conurbation extending north west to south east from Wolverhampton
through the Black Country and Birmingham to Solihull, and
from north east to south west from Sutton Coldfield to
Stourbridge.

It has not always been so, for this Midland plateau area was
formerly the least inviting part of the region, crossed by few
routes. Until the end of the eighteenth century, economic power
was vested in peripheral centres such as Worcester, Coventry and
Lichfield. Over the last 200 years a revolution in geographical
values has made the plateau the centre of economic activity, based
initially on the exploitation of coal and iron, but soon developing
an array of metal based industries and engineering.

The history of town planning in the region reflects this
economic background. The West Midlands is rich in Medieval and
later instances of planning interest throughout the small towns
of the countryside areas. For the last two centuries, development
in the conurbation (and the Potteries — the exception to the simple
pattern just described) provides most of the interest. The distinction
between the two periods only blurs in the twentieth century
when the ripple of new industrial life has extended urban
tentacles well into the surrounding areas and provided old
centres with their own economic resurrection.

Before the second half of the eighteenth century the town
planner can refer to examples of Medieval new towns at Ludlow
and Stratford where typical grid iron street patterns are in evidence.
Compact Medieval townscapes with rich street architecture still
form the bases of many centres: North Gloucestershire settlements
in the Cotswolds, Herefordshire villages, towns in Warwickshire
and Worcestershire, the Welsh marches, Shrewsbury and other
towns such as Newport in Shropshire. Fine examples of landscape
gardening can be seen at country houses such as Compton
Wynyates and Charlecote Park. A special feature is the early
nineteenth century development of spa towns; Cheltenham,
Malvern and Leamington, in particular, provide a distinctive
character.

With the Industrial Revolution a whole new range of urban
developments affected the landscape. The spectacular and
epoch-making Ironbridge spanning the River Severn near
Coalbrookdale activated a period of rapid town building. For
good reason, many of these urban products have been derided
and the mythical 'Coketown' has been satirised as the product
of an unhappy age. The bitterness of past social conditions belongs

94

to much of what has been swept away in twentieth century improvements.

The West Midlands benefitted as much as any region from the canal age. Stourport was the first planned canal port, and a remarkable pattern of canals gave the region new outlets. Telford's 'new cut', the principal canal between Birmingham and Wolverhampton, was as much a nineteenth century monument as the Curzon Street railway terminus at Birmingham. With the decline of the canal, the railway reinforced the Black Country's centrality. In the twentieth century the motorway was yet again to make the West Midlands a national hub.

The nineteenth century gradually saw the development of an effective form of town government. The first improvements concerned public health, and the Victorians' great contributions to urban planning were underground – in the myriad new pipes and channels which sewered and watered and provided essential services to town populations of an unprecedented size.

The clearance of unfit dwellings and subsequent redevelopment began in Birmingham in the mayorality of Joseph Chamberlain, and the cutting of Corporation Street gave the city centre a new commercial feature. The building of town halls and libraries and the provision of parks dispelled much of the rawness of earlier urban life. The Victorians regarded their urban developments as 'progress' and were keen to invest their new institutional buildings with all the ornate trappings of the period. Birmingham's Council House is a fine example. But the essential feature was still poverty of living conditions and intense overcrowding. The Black Country, in particular, was a complex mass of extractive industry, metal working and congested houses.

The West Midlands provides a national example of innovatory thinking at the end of the nineteenth century which contributed so much to the development of town planning. This was the development of the Bournville estate by the Cadbury brothers to house the workers at their chocolate factory. It reflected the objectives of all housing and social reformers: air, space and sunlight in a low density layout. The garden city movement took up these themes, and a new form of residential architecture began to supercede the rigid monotony of the byelaw street. The Harborne Tenants Estate in Birmingham was an example of the new aim.

After the First World War, statutory town planning extended throughout the region, and the effect of schemes can be seen in many urban areas: new routes of communication, new highway designs (the dual carriageway and roundabout made their appearance), strict control of development in terms of space about buildings, zoning restrictions and residential densities. The Ribbon Development Act, 1935, had a noteworthy, though belated, effect on linear urban sprawl. These contributions of town planning were in suburban areas. But the developed parts of cities, and particularly city centres and the fringe zone of mixed industrial and commercial uses, remained problem areas which awaited new powers to facilitate comprehensive local authority action. There was, however, a start to slum clearance, and in the late 1930s local authority redevelopment schemes provided new features in the urban townscape.

Birmingham took Private Act powers in 1946 to begin its inner ring road, mooted since 1919, but the city made use of the 'blight' provisions of the Town and Country Planning Act 1944 to inaugurate a comprehensive attack on the obsolete development of its inner areas.

All the major urban areas of the region can point to striking examples of postwar planning activity. Coventry superimposed a new pattern of development on a Medieval street system devasted by war, with the innovation of a pedestrian shopping precinct, aligned on the ruined spire of St Michael's Cathedral. The city was in the forefront, too, of advanced residential layouts which segregated the pedestrian from the motorist: Willenhall Wood is an example from the late fifties. Since then, an elevated inner ring road has provided a frame to the city centre.

Wolverhampton is one of many towns in the region where a new shopping complex has been grafted on to an old urban centre. An old established industrial use was extinguished and the vacant site developed for an indoor shopping mall. But Birmingham can claim the most massive central redevelopment for shopping, as at the Bull Ring, where in the first phase 140 shops were provided under one roof and on different levels, in association with an improved railway station and bus station. In about fifteen years the centre of the city was transformed from its Victorian skyline. The office boom has provided more floor space than in any other provincial city.

Major planned residential units can be seen in the region's new towns (Telford and Redditch), town expansion schemes (Droitwich and Tamworth) and peripheral estates (the largest at Chelmsley Wood). The effect of control over land use is shown in the clearly demarcated urban boundaries; Green Belts and rigid control policies have prevented the urban sprawl of the interwar years. This can be seen very sharply on the south west side of Birmingham where the necessity to protect areas of high landscape value around the Lickey and Clent Hills now provides an amenity and recreation area close to the city.

Planning efforts to enhance the visual amenities of the region can be seen in the determined schemes of reclamation of derelict land; the Central Forest Park at Stoke on Trent is a noteworthy example. Meanwhile, a new interest in conservation is rescuing the vitality of the region's history. The rehabilitation of Brindley Walk has revived the canal area in central Birmingham, while at Spon End, Coventry, a Medieval environment is preserved. At Worcester, Shrewsbury, Lichfield and elsewhere the galloping process of postwar development has not destroyed old townscapes.

Perhaps it is natural for the West Midlands to be pre-empted in its road planning. The M6 and M5 motorways thread their way neatly through the conurbation and intersect at Gravelly Hill — dubbed, metaphorically, 'Spaghetti Junction' — an awe-inspiring monument to the internal combustion engine.

Other aspects of planning we can only touch on: industrial trading estates, the National Exhibition Centre, new university campuses at Keele, Warwick and Aston, country parks as at Coombe Abbey, Warwickshire, suburban shopping centres as at Solihull, countryside management (the restricted access policy in the Cannock Chase Area of Outstanding Natural Beauty), urban parks (the River Arrow scheme at Redditch), incremental urban management (the adaptation of the Colmore Estate, Birmingham from the eighteenth century onwards, and today, pedestrianisation of the city's shopping streets, and the city centre bus service), private sector redevelopment (the Calthorpe Estate, Birmingham), forest management (Forest of Dean) and restoration of historic towns (Cheltenham).

Gordon E. Cherry

Birmingham   WM 1/1
OS Sheet 139   GR SP 0787   (City Centre)

Birmingham first gained industrial prominence during the Civil War (1642-8) by supplying swords to the Parliamentary army. In the latter part of the eighteenth century the town, through the energies of manufacturers such as Boulton and Watt, became a spearhead of the Industrial Revolution. The greater part of the city's expansion occurred in the later nineteenth century, when it became the foremost metal manufacturing centre in the country. The legacy of this period of rapid growth was large areas of slum housing and at the end of the Second World War a massive programme of clearance and redevelopment was begun which is now nearing completion. Many of the former residents have returned to the principal redeveloped areas, ringing the city centre, but others have been rehoused in new estates on the edge of the city (such as the massive Chelmsley Wood) or in new and expanded towns such as Telford, Redditch and Droitwich.

At the same time plans were made for a new road system, the centrepiece of which was to be a city centre ring road. Approval for this was given in 1946 but, owing to financial restrictions, the road was not completed until 1971.

The last 25 years have also seen redevelopment of substantial parts of the city centre, including the Bull Ring covered shopping centre — one of the first in the country. In recent years however the City Council has made efforts to conserve the best of the central area's Victorian heritage, such as the commercial buildings around Colmore Row.

Black Country   WM 1/2
OS Sheet 139   GR SO 9490   (Dudley)

The Black Country comprises the area west of Birmingham whose industrial growth during the late eighteenth and nineteenth centuries depended on local supplies of coal, iron ore and limestone. These are little used today but the inherited skills and industrial shrewdness of the population have ensured the continued industrial affluence of the area. The original dispersed settlement pattern of the Black Country has survived in the many villages and small towns. Despite amalgamations of local authorities, local pride is strong and integrated planning for the overall improvement of the area is difficult. The Black Country can best be experienced in a 'village' pub, or by travelling on the Birmingham-Wolverhampton railway, the A4123 arterial road or on the extensive canal network.

Bournville, Birmingham WM 1/3
OS Sheet 139   GR SP 0481

A landmark in the history of the philanthropic industrial village which also presaged the garden city movement, Bournville originated in 1878, when Cadburys moved their factory out from Birmingham and also built twenty-four semidetached houses for essential workers. This embryonic settlement was expanded from 1893 onwards by the Bournville Village Trust, and there are now 6,600 houses. The standard of amenity was high, and a density of only six houses to the acre was decreed by George Cadbury. The architecture is 'archetypally suburban', and the street layout is flexible, based on the close, the cul-de-sac, and the crescent — all looking forward to the garden suburb and modern suburbia.

The village green, Bournville, Birmingham. *Bournville Village Trust.*

The Midlands Links Motorways WM 1/4
OS Sheet 139   GR SP 0990

Graveley Hill Interchange (Spaghetti Junction) — where the Aston Expressway (right) joins the M6 (top to bottom). *Aerofilms.*

The opening of the Midlands Links in 1972 completed the main network of motorways between London, the Midlands and the North, by connecting the M5, the M6 and the M1. The network contains two large interchanges; at Ray Hall, where the M6 and M5 meet in a triangular free flowing junction covering 150 acres, and at Gravelly Hill, in Birmingham, where the famous 'Spaghetti Junction' joins the M6 to the Aston Expressway and the local road network. The latter is extremely complex (a railway, canal and river pass through the site), yet occupies only thirty acres. However, because of its location in the midst of an urban area, it has been criticised for the disruption it causes through visual intrusion and pollution from motor vehicles.

Solihull National Exhibition Centre WM 1/5
OS Sheet 139   GR SP 1984

Most large exhibition centres in Britain have traditionally been situated in the London area — for example Olympia and Earls Court. The proposal, first made in 1969, to build a major new exhibition and conference centre near Birmingham was therefore greeted with some surprise, especially by trade organisations based in London. However, the proposal gained Government support, and work was begun in 1972. The Centre, which is one due to be opened in 1975, includes one million square feet of exhibition space, together with a hotel, conference centre, restaurants, bars, shops, car parking and other facilities. Despite the scepticism of Londoners, the site is ideally situated, lying in the centre of England, adjacent to Birmingham Airport, astride the main London to Birmingham railway line, for which a new station is being built, and adjacent to the new M42 motorway. It is thus within reasonably easy reach of most of England and Wales.

Coventry WM 2/1
OS Sheet 140   GR SP 3379

The Lower Precinct, Coventry, with the spire of the ruined cathedral in the distance.
Coventry City Planning Officer.

Enemy bombing in 1940 destroyed forty acres of the city centre of this ancient town (origin: Saxon), and a new central area has been created over the last twenty-five years. The new cathedral (1960) incorporates the ruins of the old, and a short distance to the west lies the revolutionary shopping precinct, begun in 1950. Coventry was one of the very few towns to rebuild its central shopping area on precinct lines after the war, and thereby set an example which other cities later sought to follow. More recently, the city has completed its inner ring road (1971-4), whose object is to provide access and circulation of traffic to and from the central area.

Fosse Way   WM 2/2
OS Sheet 140   GR SP 4372 (Brinklow) SP 4788 (Venonae)

Any large scale map will reveal the extent of the Roman road network of Britain — indicated by the straight routes oblivious of contours and largely lacking village settlements. From Moreton-in-Marsh (Gloucestershire) to Leicester, the Fosse Way follows an almost straight line for over fifty miles with only four later villages straddling its route. Between Nuneaton and Lutterworth, the Way, which runs from Lincoln to Exeter, intersects Watling Street, which runs from London to Chester (the modern A5). Eight miles south at Brinklow the Fosse Way can be viewed from the motte and bailey of the Norman castle built to guard this strategic route.

The Fosse Way (top to bottom) crossing Watling Street (now the dual carriageway A5) on the Warwickshire/Leicestershire boundary. *Aerofilms.*

Royal Leamington Spa   WM 2/3
OS Sheet 151   GR SP 3165

A Regency spa town, with the prefix 'Royal' granted by Queen Victoria in 1838, Leamington never achieved the pre-eminence or the architectural glories of Bath, but nevertheless contains some fine examples of Regency architecture, especially the terraces leading off the Parade. There were many inland spa towns in the eighteenth and nineteenth centuries, of which Bath, Tunbridge Wells, Leamington, Cheltenham and Harrogate are perhaps the most well-known examples. The popularity of inland spas declined, however, as that of the coastal resorts rose but, like all the above towns, Leamington retains much of its original character and is an attractive residential and shopping centre.

Lansdowne Crescent, Leamington Spa. *Warwickshire County Planning Officer.*

Stratford-upon-Avon and the Stratford Canal   WM 2/4

OS Sheet 151   GR SP 2055 (Stratford-upon-Avon)
SP 1052 (Bidford-on-Avon)

The birthplace of William Shakespeare, Stratford was established as a new town by King John for the Bishop of Worcester in 1196. It then consisted of a grid of three streets parallel to the river with three at right angles, and this is still the basis of the town centre today. The new town, strategically situated in the centre of the Midlands, became an important centre for the marketing of malt, with trade reaching as far as Wales and Lancashire. Its prosperity in Tudor times is reflected in the many half-timbered buildings. In later years, it has derived its prosperity from tourism, particularly associated with the 'Bard'.

The Stratford Canal originally completed a loop between the Rivers Avon and Severn and Birmingham, but the navigation rights were bought up and extinguished by the railway in the mid-nineteenth century. The railway line is now derelict, but the canal and River Avon have been restored to use over the last twenty years.

Wormleighton   WM 2/5

OS Sheet 151   GR SP 4554

At Wormleighton is the site of a deserted Medieval village. Towards the end of the Middle Ages landowners began to enclose the 'open fields' and turn arable land into pasture for sheep or cattle. In 1498, William Cope evicted the inhabitants of Wormleighton, destroyed the village and enclosed the open fields. Government resistance to the enclosure system, with its consequent rural depopulation, resulted in the next landowner, John Spencer, being ordered to rebuild the village and reinstate the open fields in 1522. This he did, and the new village of Wormleighton lies adjacent to the earlier site, the remains of which (e.g. the fishponds) are still easily visible. Amongst the many deserted villages of England Wormleighton stands out for the full documentation of its history.

Alton Towers   WM 3/1
OS Sheet 128   GR SK 0743

The picturesque movement in English landscape gardening lasted well into the nineteenth century. One of the best later examples is the 600 acre grounds of Alton Towers, laid out between 1814 and 1827, with rare trees and shrubs, lakes, fountains and a Chinese pagoda, by the fifteenth Earl of Shrewsbury. The grounds are now maintained as a public pleasure park. The house, a vast Gothic mansion dating from 1831, is now preserved only as a shell.

Cannock Chase   WM 3/2
OS Sheet 127   GR SK 0413 (Castle Ring)

Cannock Chase, the smallest AONB designated under the 1949 Act, covers twenty-six square miles. Being so small, and close to large centres of population, the area is under great pressures for recreation and other resource use. Coal mining from surrounding pits has undermined much of the area, resulting in subsidence (e.g. at the German War Cemetery), and sand and gravel is still extracted from surface pits on the Chase. Between 6,000 and 7,000 acres are now occupied by the Forestry Commission who permit extensive public access to their conifer fore~~sts where~~ they have laid out nature trails etc. Over 31,000 acres ~~are now in~~ public ownership and part of this has been decla~~red a motorless~~ zone by Staffordshire County Council. Such ac~~tion, initially~~ resented by some visitors, is becoming increasin~~gly necessary if~~ the countryside is not to be unacceptably damaged phys~~ically~~ and visually by motor vehicles.

Cannock Chase — area of outstanding natural beauty.
~~Staffo~~rdshire County ~~Council.~~

Coalbrookdale and Ironbridge   WM 3/3
OS Sheet 127   GR SJ 6703

Justifiably known as 'the cradle of the Industrial Revolution', the Coalbrookdale area provided the world's first iron bridge (crossing the River Severn at the point which took its name), first iron boat, first iron rails, the cylinders for the first steam engine, the first locomotive and the first iron aqueduct. In 1709 Abraham Darby first smelted iron with coke in the Coalbrookdale valley. The early industrial rise of the area also meant its early demise, and for nearly a century the area was in decline until incorporated into Telford new town. Now the industrial remains are being preserved as one of the most important industrial museums in the country, occupying a number of sites including Darby's original furnace, the Ironbridge, Coalport China Works and the Blists Hill site. Here the story of coal, iron, clay and

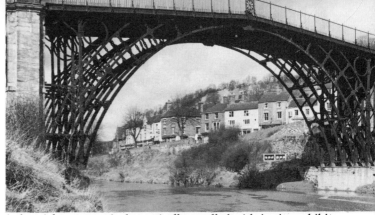

The World's first iron bridge, spanning the River Severn, near Coalbrookdale.
B.T.A.

industrial transport is dramatically recalled with *in situ* exhibits and reconstructed features, including coal mines, tile works, blast furnaces, working steam engines and a canal inclined plane.

Stoke-on-Trent   WM 3/4

OS Sheet 118   GR SJ 8848   (Hanley Forest Park)
                    SJ 8550   (Westport Lake)

Gladstone Pottery Museum – Stoke-on-Trent.
Stoke-on-Trent Director of Environmental Services.

Stoke-on-Trent, whose industrial development was based on coal, iron and pottery, has suffered 200 years of industrial exploitation, resulting in a legacy of dereliction from coal mining, clay marl extraction and obsolete transport routes (especially railways and canals). By 1969, 7.2 per cent of the city's land was classified as derelict. Since 1967, a crash reclamation programme aided by a Government grant has been under way, and many sites have been transformed into attractive open spaces. The 120 acres of Hanley Forest Park, a former colliery, and Westport Lake, formerly flooded waste land, are now in use for boating and other water activities. The city's heritage is also being preserved in a pottery factory and group of typical nineteenth century 'bottle ovens' at the Gladstone Pottery Museum.

Telford   WM 3/5

OS Sheet 127   GR SJ 6909   (Telford town centre)
                    SJ 6904   (Madeley)

First Phase of Telford new town centre. Note the large 'hypermarket' store (with white roof) and extensive car park to attract 'out-of-town' shoppers.
Star Journal Studios.

Dawley was designated a new town in 1963 as part of a regional plan to rehouse overspill population from Birmingham and the Black Country. The site was chosen primarily because of the need to reclaim the great amount of derelict land in the area, a legacy of the industrial revolution. The area of designation was later expanded and the new town renamed Telford. The target population is 220,000. Because it is based on three main existing communities (Dawley, Wellington and Oakengates), the new town has an essentially fragmented layout, but a ring motorway is being constructed to join these settlements together on a 'necklace and beads' principle. Similarly a new shopping centre is being built to give the town a focus and sense of coherence, while also acting as an 'out of town' shopping centre for the surrounding region.

Wroxeter   WM 3/6
OS Sheet 126   GR SJ 5608

Wroxeter was one of the first Roman fortresses to be established after the invasion of A.D. 43. Its purpose was to guard the western frontier with Wales, and act as a link with the River Trent frontier to the north east. Later, the Legion was moved north to Chester and Wroxeter became a cantonal town and tribal capital. Much of the site remains to be excavated, but it is still possible to see parts of the Roman town. The local church incorporates Roman masonry.

Droitwich   WM 4/1
OS Sheet 150   GR SO 9063

An ancient salt town and spa, whose brine springs were known to the Romans. Salinae (the Roman Town) was established in A.D. 43 and became well-known as a salt producing centre. The use of brine for healing developed after 1830 and Droitwich then developed as a spa (baths opened 1836 and 1887), and the town is still popular as a tourist and conference centre. In 1963 the town was chosen to receive overspill population from Birmingham and an expansion scheme was begun under the Town Development Act 1952. The target population is 30,000 by 1981 (i.e. 6,000 new houses.

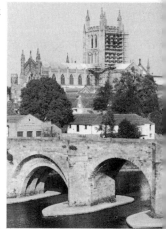

Hereford   WM 4/2
OS Sheet 149   GR SO 5140

Hereford is a cathedral city of Saxon origin. The site was 'chosen' because it commanded two fords over the River Wye and because it was easily defensible, lying between the river and marshland to the north. Henry III had a large castle here and the city developed in importance because of its strategic location close to the Welsh border. As with other similar towns, such as Shrewsbury, Ludlow and Chepstow, further growth largely passed Hereford by once the importance of the border declined after about A.D. 1400. As a result, the city still retains its Medieval street layout and ancient character.

Hereford Cathedral and
Wye Bridge.
B.T.A.

Ludlow   WM 4/3
OS Sheet 138   GR SO 5174

Ludlow was a Medieval fortress new town built to guard the

Ludlow, with the castle overlooking the River Teme and the grid street pattern of the town clearly showing beyond.
Aerofilms.

Welsh frontier or 'marches'. The castle was founded in 1085 and the town was later laid out on the standard grid pattern of the time. The town and castle remained an important defence throughout the Middle Ages and enjoyed royal patronage. The town still contains much evidence of its Medieval importance, in particular the castle ruins.

Redditch   WM 4/4
OS Sheet 150   GR SP 0467

The small town of Redditch was designated a new town in 1964 to help to relieve overcrowded conditions in the West Midlands conurbation by accepting population overspill (see also Telford and Droitwich). The target population is 90,000. The town is being developed as a series of selfcontained residential districts surrounding the town centre. Redditch's most significant feature is the large Arrow Valley Park (containing a twenty-eight acre lake), adjacent to the central area and surrounded by residential developments.

Stourport on Severn   WM 4/5
OS Sheet 138   GR SO 8171

The construction of the Staffordshire and Worcestershire Canal in 1766-71 by James Brindley and its rejection by nearby Bewdley caused the growth of Stourport as the only town in England founded in consequence of a canal. With the industrial development of the nearby Black Country it became the busiest inland port in the Midlands after Birmingham and many of its fine Georgian buildings survive. With the decline of the canals

Stourport's importance decreased, but it is now popular again as a leisure centre and the canal basin at the junction with the River Severn is full of cabin cruisers.

Chedworth   WM 5/1
OS Sheet 163   GR SP 0513

One of the best preserved Roman villas in Britain. Chedworth has been extensively excavated. Walls have been extended and roofs constructed so that the buildings can be entered and the mosaic floors inspected. In later Roman times the Cotswolds were an important wool area and wool was processed at Chedworth. Finds can be seen in the on site museum.

Cheltenham   WM 5/2
OS Sheet 163   GR SO 9422

One of the great inland spas that prospered in the eighteenth and nineteenth centuries before the rise in popularity of sea bathing and the coastal resorts. The town has Saxon origins and had a Medieval market but only rose to prominence after the discovery of spa water in 1716.

Its resort origins can be seen in the extensive parks and gardens and it still contains some fine Georgian and Regency architecture and urban planning, including the Pittville Pump Room, the Promenade and the Montpellier Rotunda. Continuing its resort function, Cheltenham has become something of a cultural centre, the Music Festival being founded in 1944.

Chipping Campden   WM 5/3
OS Sheet 151   GR SP 1539

An old Cotswold wool town. Like parts of East Anglia, the Cotswolds were an important wool centre in the Middle Ages and many local towns grew prosperous on the trade. This later declined, leaving us today with a number of attractive and still basically Medieval towns, including Chipping Campden. The outstanding townscape quality of Chipping Campden is due to its broad High Street, which is set on a fine curve and is flanked by a continuous line of fourteenth to seventeenth century houses of traditional Cotswold design and materials.

Cirencester   WM 5/4
OS Sheet 163   GR SP 0202

Cirencester was originally a Roman town, the second largest in
Britain by about A.D. 150. Throughout most of its history its
prosperity has been based on wool — particularly during the
Middle Ages. The town retains many reminders of this period,
especially the church (almost entirely rebuilt by 1530 out of
profits from the wool trade) with its detached south porch (1490)
facing the Market Place.

The Triangle development of 1966-9, between Coxwell, Dollar
and Thomas Streets, is a modern attempt to recreate the Cotswold
townscape tradition and shows how new development can be
integrated into the historic core of a town without loss of
traditional character. It received a medal from the Ministry of
Housing and Local Government for outstanding quality in
housing and also a Civic Trust Award in 1969.

Cirencester market
place and church, built
from the profits of the
Medieval wool trade.
B.T.A.

Cotswold Water Park,
created from worked
out gravel pits.
*Wiltshire County
Council.*

Cotswold Water Park   WM 5/5
OS Sheet 163   GR SU 2199 (Lechlade)

The Cotswold Water Park is an attempt to create a major water
sports centre using lakes created from worked-out gravel pits.
The park is intended for the use of aquatic sportsmen, naturalists
and others who wish to enjoy, in a general way, a stretch of inland
water. A master plan was published in 1967, and since then
considerable work has been done in reclaiming and landscaping
the area for a variety of uses, including sailing, canoeing, fishing,
water skiing, walking and riding. The park's ownership is divided
between the original gravel operators and the local county
councils and work on the park is overseen by a joint committee.

Slimbridge Wildfowl Trust   WM 5/6
OS Sheet 162   GR SO 7205

The area was set in Trust in 1946 for the conservation of wildfowl,
research and the application of research into wildfowl and the
education of the public about wildfowl. The Trust has been
considerably expanded since its opening and now incorporates
a comprehensive collection of wildfowl of international
importance. The Honorary Managing Director is Sir Peter Scott.
Slimbridge was a pioneering effort in natural wildfowl
conservation and research, and the area comprises a well-
landscaped series of pools and enclosures, with a chain of hides
overlooking the magnificent Severn estuary.

The Visitor Centre at
the Wildfowl Trust,
Slimbridge.
J.V. Beer.

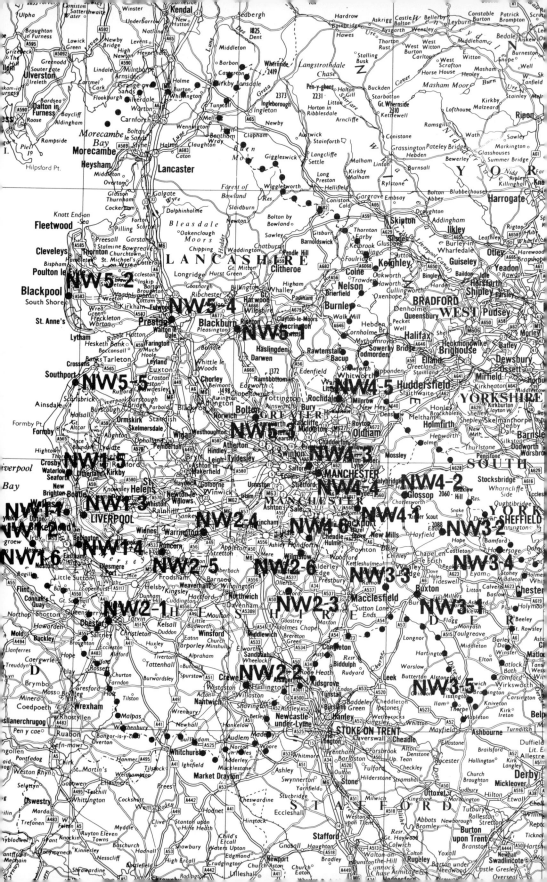

The North West

The North West Region is interesting to the person with a taste
for planning and architecture. Indeed, it would be disappointing
if the home of nearly seven million people and the birthplace of
the Industrial Revolution could not provide a variety of urban
developments that reflected the inventiveness of nearly 200 years.
But the region's history goes back much further and embraces the
Roman and medieval periods as well as more modern times. And
the interest is not confined to the urban areas. The region
abounds in excellent countryside and there are many fine country
houses and stately homes set in areas of great scenic beauty.
Stretching from the Pennines to the sea the North West of
England is, in effect, a cameo of the best of the country,
illustrating in a small compass that range of interrelated activities
and physical form that is uniquely British.

Throughout the Roman occupation the North West was the
scene of continuous activity. Melandra, near Glossop in Derbyshire,
is the site of a Roman fort and township which housed the
garrison army for over 400 years. Current excavations have
revealed the extent and nature of the encampment and the site
is open to visitors. The Romans remains at Chester have also been
well preserved and researched.

Medieval planning is illustrated in Chester, where the Rows —
the pavement arcades — provide shelter and add dignity to the
shops and houses round the cathedral. By a policy of restoration
and management, the local city council and an interested amenity
society have recently succeeded in restoring to Chester much of
its medieval charm.

Real planning landmarks began to appear in the eighteenth,
nineteenth and twentieth centuries. In the eighteenth century,
both Liverpool and Manchester boasted houses of great distinction
and, in Manchester, the area round St Ann's Church and King
Street suggests something of the gracious scale of those former
years. The terraces and squares above the Anglican
cathedral in Liverpool (although technically early nineteenth
century) reflect the high standard of living of the local merchants.

Relatively little known, but full of character and elegance,
is the Moravian Settlement at Fairfield in Droylsden, Manchester.
This group of houses, with the church and former theological
college, was established in the mid-eighteenth century and was for
a long time the largest Moravian community in Britain. The
cobbled streets, Georgian-style houses and subtle tree planting,
reflect an ordered life that contrasts vividly with the Victorian
artisans' dwellings surrounding the Settlement.

Buxton ranks high among the many watering places developed

during the eighteenth century. The great crescent, now being restored, is framed by elegant streets and terraces, many of which end in dramatic views of the surrounding countryside. In a much less formal way, and not planned in anything like the same detail, Knutsford is a typical Cheshire town of the period, and was the prototype for Mrs Gaskell's 'Cranford'.

In the North West, as elsewhere, the surge of industry and commerce in the nineteenth century led to the creation of docks, warehouses and canals, and to a new municipal grandeur which reflected this commercial dynamism. In Liverpool, the whole dock complex, starting with Hartley's Albert Dock, is still impressive, and the Hartley warehouses are now to be preserved by being adapted for use by the Liverpool Polytechnic. Functionally related, but physically and chronologically separate, is the great Manchester Ship Canal, thrusting into the heart of the city, and allowing it to grow in prosperity and size. During this time, the greatest opulence began to be reflected in individual buildings and, as they were placed in juxtaposition with each other, a sort of town planning was achieved. Castle Street, Liverpool and Upper King Street, Manchester are good examples of this. Meanwhile, the municipalities were not to be outdone, so the St George's Hall-Walker Art Gallery complex was developed giving distinction and grandeur to an otherwise mediocre part of the city of Liverpool. In Manchester the new town hall was erected and Albert Square became a place of distinction and pomp.

At the turn of the century, W.H. Lever (later Lord Leverhulme, the industrial magnate), decided to create suitable homes for his increasing numbers of Liverpool workers. He took an option on some land in New Ferry and began to develop Port Sunlight on the Wirral Peninsula, where he sought to combine a feeling for architecture and gardening in a pleasant residential development. Now that the houses have been given plumbing and the motor car has been accommodated, Port Sunlight continues to provide a visual setting that is rarely surpassed. This was housing for the people by private benevolence. In just over two decades, the responsibility fell to local government and, in Liverpool, the city architect, Lancelot Keay, began to develop an adaptation of the garden suburb/garden city concept in the suburbs, while in Manchester, Barry Parker was laying out a new town at Wythenshaw.

This was in the mid 1930s, when the creation of the Mersey Tunnel — basically an engineering feat — had tremendous planning implications. It made easy access to the Wirral a powerful force for the development of 'quality' housing. The building of the East Lancs road (one of the first trunk roads) made fuller exploitation of the land between Manchester and Liverpool inevitable.

After the Second World War, during which the region suffered considerable damage from air raids, little was done until the mid-1950s and early 1960s. Then Liverpool broke new ground by employing a planning consultant to recast the whole of its central area. The fruits of this programme are now being reaped as multilevel circulation, pedestrian precincts and new commercial developments come into use. Other cities have followed suit in various ways. Manchester has redeveloped the enormous inner housing areas of Hulme and Moss Side. Bolton has pioneered the successful conversion of streets to pedestrian precincts, and Blackburn has shown how a rather drab, undistinguished town may be transformed by a combination of new building and environmental improvement.

Two new towns in the region are well worth visiting. Skelmersdale, the earlier of the two, demonstrates many of the characteristics of the early new towns — lowish density neighbourhood developments, local shops and pedestrian precincts. Runcorn, designed for public transport rather than the private car, has a shopping centre with a dramatic use of different levels and extensive undercover shopping facilities.

The long programme of clearing derelict land is continuing. This work, carried out by the former Lancashire County Council, has secured the restoration of thousands of acres of industrial pit heaps to agricultural or recreational uses. Examples can be seen in the countryside immediately round Wigan and the former South Lancs coalfield. Some of the loveliest scenery in Britain is in the Peak District National Park, where the visual beauty attracts such numbers of visitors that there is a real danger of environmental damage from cars and coaches. So the Planning Board has devised a scheme in the Goyt Valley which provides ample car parks at the edge of the valley and a minibus service into the valley itself — a pioneering management technique likely to be copied elsewhere.

In trying to indicate the many planning landmarks of the North West it is difficult to pinpoint the most significant phenomenon of all: anyone travelling in the region for the first time can have no conception of the dirty buildings, treeless streets, grey grass and polluted atmosphere that existed even ten years ago. Credit for the great change that has taken place can be attributed to many: to government, to the Civic Trust for the North West and to the Council for the Protection of Rural England. These and many other agencies are helping to recreate an attractive and humane environment.

Graham Ashworth

Birkenhead, Hamilton Square   NW 1/1
OS Sheet 108   GR SJ 3289

A late Regency/early Victorian Square in the classic English tradition, built between 1826-50 by Gillespie Graham, who used Edinburgh Square as his model. The Town Hall was added in 1887. The central gardens were originally private, but have been a public park since 1903. The Square illustrates the solid provincial prosperity of the early Victorian era, based on the

Industrial Revolution. It is the only square outside London to be classified as A1 by the Department of the Environment.

Birkenhead Park   NW 1/2
OS Sheet 108   GR SJ 3089

An early Victorian city park laid out by Joseph Paxton in 1844. The death rate in industrial cities was rising due to poor living conditions. The city park was seen as a way of alleviating this situation although, in typical Victorian fashion it treated the symptom rather than the cause. Many of the parks paid for themselves — Birkenhead Park was financed by selling land around its perimeter for housing. The city parks had to be easily accessible to the urban populations and, significantly, the first street tramway in Britain ran between Birkenhead Park and the Liverpool Ferry.

Liverpool   NW 1/3
OS Sheet 108   GR SJ 3490 (City Centre)

Although an old town, with a charter granted by King John in the thirteenth century, Liverpool did not become prominent until the eighteenth century, when it became involved in the slave trade. The railway age saw Liverpool expand to become second only to London as a port for both passengers and goods. In recent years the city has undergone much slum clearance and there has been a great deal of population overspill to the new towns of Runcorn and Skelmersdale. The city is justifiably proud of its past — the traditional business centre round Castle Street has been designated a conservation area, and shopping streets in the city centre have been closed to traffic. In 1965 an area of worn out warehousing in the central area was rezoned as an office expansion area and over two million square feet had been built by 1974. Mid-Victorian middle class commuter housing can be seen in Grassendale and Cressington Park (six miles south east of the city centre), built as railway suburbs with their own station. Sefton

Park Conservation Area (four miles south east of the city centre) is one of the great parks laid out between 1860 and 1870 to act as 'green lungs' for the city (see Birkenhead Park, NW 1/2). The great docks complex along the Mersey contains the particularly fine Albert Dock — the first of Liverpool's 'modern' docks, opened in 1845 — the buildings of which may become the new Liverpool Polytechnic.

Philip Hardwick's Albert Docks, Liverpool — with the Liver Building on the left. John Mills Photography.

Port Sunlight   NW 1/4
OS Sheet 108   GR SJ 3384

One of the great late nineteenth century model estate villages, developed by philanthropic factory owners for their workers (see also Bournville and New Earswick). It was begun in 1888 by W.H. Lever when he moved his soap factory from Warrington. The ground plan, although varied and not at all a rigid grid, is formal in concept and 'suggestive of Versailles', with grand vistas and gardens. Lever himself played a major part in the design. A great number of different styles of architecture can be seen and the whole village is a unique residential development of unusual character.

W.H. Lever's 'model village' at Port Sunlight. Wirral Borough Director of Development.

114

The new Seaforth
container docks at
Sefton, north of
Liverpool.
Stewart Bale.

Seaforth Docks   NW 1/5
OS Sheet 108   GR SJ 3296

The growth in the size of ships and the increasing use of container
and bulk cargo carriers has brought about the development of
many new port facilities (e.g. Southampton and Tilbury) and the
running down of many traditional docks (e.g. St Katherine's
Dock, London, and Albert Dock, Liverpool). The Seaforth
Dock complex, in the Metropolitan District of Sefton, was
officially opened in 1973 to cater for container traffic and bulk
grain handling. The grain terminal is the largest in Britain and the
highly mechanised container terminal is computer controlled.
For security and safety reasons visitors are not permitted into the
docks although the Mersey Docks and Harbour Company
distribute explanatory leaflets.

Wirral Way Country Park   NW 1/6
OS Sheet 108   GR SJ 2383 (Thurstaston Station)

This linear country park is based on a disused railway line, which
ran along the south side of the Wirral peninsula. Opened in 1968,
it stretches for twelve miles from Hooton to West Kirby. Facilities
such as camp sites, picnic and fishing areas are provided, and there
is an information centre at Thurstaston. Country parks originated
in the 1968 Countryside Act and those so far opened are of widely
differing characters. The Wirral Way is unusual because of its origins
as a railway and its resulting linear form.

The Cross, Chester,
showing the Rows
shopping arcade,
designed in 1888 to
replace the original
Medieval buildings.
B.T.A.

Chester   NW 2/1
OS Sheet 117   GR SJ 4066

Now one of Britain's most important historic towns, Chester
was originally a Roman legionary camp guarding the Welsh border
and the north west. The walls, which almost complete, are
basically Roman, with medieval additions, and are regarded as
the best in the country. The Roman grid plan still forms the basis
of the central area. In medieval times, Chester was prosperous
as a port serving Ireland, France and Spain. Later the River Dee
silted up and the town declined. In the nineteenth century, it
became an important railway junction, and the central area was
extensively 'restored' in mock-medieval style. Modern pressures
of traffic and redevelopment led to the selection of Chester as
one of the 'four towns' to be the subject of a detailed
Government conservation study, whose recommendations are now
being implemented.
    Modern development is being successfully combined with the
older buildings — the new Grosvenor shopping centre is skilfully
integrated with the Rows, a two level shopping area of medieval
origin.

Crewe
OS Sheet 118   GR SJ 7055

The epitome of the important railway junction, works and
company town, Crewe was begun in 1842, but very little of the
original development remains — even the street lines have been
altered. The site was selected because here the Birmingham —
Liverpool, Birmingham — Manchester and Birkenhead — Crewe
lines met. The new town was designed by Locke and
Cunningham and was of a high environmental standard for the
time. A variety of housing types was provided, to suit all classes,
and there is no doubt that Crewe was one of the best of
Victorian industrial new towns.

Jodrell Bank Radio Telescope, near Knutsford   NW 2/3
OS Sheet 118   GR SJ 7971

A symbol of the new era of telecommunications and astronomical
research, and a prominent landmark on the Cheshire Plain,
Jodrell Bank Telescope (1957) was the first instrument of its
type and size in Europe. It is operated by the Manchester
University's Department of Radio Astronomy. The unit
concentrates on research, with a 'spin-off' in monitoring satellites
and other space probes. Because of the sensitivity of the apparatus,
there are restrictions on building and the use of some electrical
equipment within a specific distance of the site.

The main radio telescope
at Jodrell Bank.
*University of
Manchester, Dept. of
Radio Astronomy.*

Manchester Ship Canal (between Manchester   NW 2/4
and River Mersey)
OS Sheet 108 and 109   GR Between SJ 3881 and SJ 8197

Manchester was one of the centres of the industrial revolution, but
by the end of the nineteenth century the centre of industry was
shifting away from the city towards the port of Liverpool, and
the cost of shipping Manchester goods through Liverpool became
prohibitive. For these reasons, between 1887 and 1894,
Manchester industrialists built the Ship Canal which could
accommodate ships up to 14,000 tons. Manchester therefore
became an important inland port, restoring prosperity and
avoiding the high harbour dues of Liverpool. Tourist trips are
now run by the Canal Company from Manchester Docks.

Manchester Ship Canal
at Ellesmere Port.
Port of Manchester.

116

The Brow Estate, Runcorn New Town – housing and car parking successfully integrated. *John Mills Photography.*

Mill cottages at Styal, now owned by the National Trust. *Cheshire County Planning Officer.*

The Royal Crescent and former stables (with dome), Buxton. *B.T.A.*

Runcorn New Town NW 2/5
OS Sheet 108   GR SJ 5381 (Shopping City)

Designated in 1964, Runcorn is one of the new generation of new towns. Others, such as Milton Keynes or Washington, have concentrated on catering for private transport, but Runcorn has been devised round a comprehensive public transport system based on a figure eight bus-only road network. Housing areas are arranged around the figure eight – of these, Holton Brow is significant in that rigid road engineering standards were abandoned in its design. The town centre (called 'Shopping City') is a joint venture between the Development Corporation and a property company and attracts shoppers from much of Merseyside.

Styal Village and Mill, near Wilmslow NW 2/6
OS Sheet 109   GR SJ 8385

An early nineteenth century cotton mill and 'model' village, built to house the workers. The mill, set in the valley of the River Bollin, originally depended on water power, the availability of which was always the primary factor in the location of early cotton mills. The village and mill are now owned by the National Trust and the mill is to be restored as a museum of the textile industry.

Buxton NW 3/1
OS Sheet 119   GR SK 0573

The popularity of spas in the eighteenth century led to the creation of many smaller erstwhile competitors to Bath. Although its springs were well known to the Romans, Buxton was developed by the Duke of Devonshire after 1780 with the deliberate intention of rivalling Bath. Its popularity and development lasted well into the nineteenth century. Fine examples of architecture and urban design include the Crescent (1780), the Pavilion Gardens and the Devonshire Royal Hospital (1859). The town has retained its popularity by acting as a tourist centre for the Peak District.

Edale and the Pennine Way
OS Sheet 110   GR SK 1285

Edale is at the southern limit of the 250 mile Pennine Way, a long distance footpath stretching the length of the Pennine Hills to the Scottish border. Although initiated by the 1949 National Parks and Access to the Countryside Act the complete route was not opened until 1965. This end of the Pennine Way is close to large centres of population, and is extensively used. Some parts are suffering from physical erosion. At Fieldhead Edale the first purpose-built information centre in a British National Park was opened in 1966. It contains displays and information material to help visitors and offers a local weather forecast for the surrounding high moors.

Erosion on the Pennine Way near its southern end above Edale.
Peak Park Planning Board.

Goyt Valley
OS Sheet 119   GR SK 0173

NW 3/3

The Goyt Valley experiment was the first comprehensive rural traffic management scheme in this country, designed to see whether a 'park and ride' policy could cope with traffic problems at rural beauty spots. During summer weekends cars are restricted to peripheral car parks and tourists visit the valley on foot or by a minibus service. The removal of most of the traffic has brought a general air of peacefulness to the valley and lakes; visual intrusion by parked vehicles has been removed, traffic noise reduced and narrow roads, formerly badly congested with traffic, released for the almost exclusive use of pedestrians.

Goyt Valley – before the exclusion of cars.
Peak Park Planning Board.

Goyt Valley – after the exclusion of cars.
Peak Park Planning Board.

118

North Lees Hall and Estate   NW 3/4
OS Sheet 110   GR SK 2383

The Peak Park Planning Board has acquired the 1,265 acre North
Lees Estate as an experiment in the management of similar estates
where recreation, farming, forestry and conservation interests
need to be reconciled. Six miles from Sheffield, the estate contains
a variety of landscapes, the fifteenth century North Lees Hall and
Stanage Edge, the finest gritstone climbing edge in England. The
Board has implemented techniques to control access to the Estate
and to provide facilities and information. The most successful
techniques will be applied to similar estates in the Peak Park.

Tissington Trail   NW 3/5
OS Sheet 119   GR SK 1746 to SK 1167

The Tissington Trail and its adjoining section of the High Peak
Trail, provides a twenty-three mile stretch for walking, pony
trekking and cycling, completely segregated from vehicular
traffic and in spectacular Peak District scenery. On its
foundation in 1968, it formed the first comprehensive scheme
to reuse derelict railway lines for recreation and nature
conservation. Following soiling and seeding of the tracks, the
unsightly station buildings were demolished and car parks, toilets
and nature trails established. The former signal box at Hartington
has become a warden briefing centre and information point.

The Tissington Trail –
formerly a derelict
railway line.
*Peak Park Planning
Board*.

Compstall, Stockport   NW 4/1
OS Sheet 109   GR SJ 9690

An industrial tied village built between 1820 and 1870 to house
textile workers from the Andrews Mill (the names of members
of the Andrews family have been perpetuated in the streets). The
village consists of over 100 stone-built cottages, a 'company'
church and chapel, a Cooperative Society store and a worker's
Institute. The housing has been declared a General Improvement

Area, and it is intended to transform the surrounding valley and defunct mill ponds into a country park.

Glossop NW 4/2
OS Sheet 110   GR SK 0394

High up in the Pennines, Glossop was an early centre of the cotton industry in the North West, based first on water and then on steam power. The Wren Nest Mills and associated housing in High Street West date from 1800-10. Later, Howard Town and Norfolk Square were built (*c* 1838) to house workers at nearby Howard Town Mills. The Mills, together with the market hall, railway station (1845) and Norfolk Square itself can still be seen.

Manchester, Castlefield's Canal Basin and NW 4/3
Liverpool Road Railway Station
OS Sheet 109   GR SJ 8397

These nearby sites in the centre of Manchester illustrate the two successive transport systems of the Industrial Revolution – the canals and the railways. Castlefields Canal Basin was the Manchester terminus of the Bridgewater Canal – Britain's first 'modern' canal – built by the engineer James Brindley for the Duke of Bridgewater in the 1760s. The Basin was extended and additional warehousing was added up to about 1800, and these original Georgian warehouses can still be seen, although in a sadly derelict condition.

   The Liverpool and Manchester Railway was opened in 1830 – some sixty years after the Bridgewater Canal – and like the canal was a pioneer in its field. The Manchester terminus was at Liverpool Road and the original station buildings are still standing – the first passenger terminus station in the world. Like the nearby canal basin, however, they are in a derelict condition; but a plaque, unveiled in 1930 at the centenary celebrations, commemorates the opening of the railway age.

Castlefields canal basin at the Manchester end of James Brindley's Bridgewater Canal. *Manchester City Engineer & Surveyor.*

Manchester Town Hall, symbolic of the town's 19th century wealth. *Manchester City Engineer & Surveyor.*

Manchester

OS Sheet 109   GR SJ 9498 (Town Hall)

The construction of canals linking Manchester with Bolton, Bury and Rochdale between 1790 and 1805 marked the start of Manchester's growth as the main distribution centre for the booming Lancashire cotton industry. From then on growth was continuous and the prosperity of Victorian Manchester is vividly reflected in Alfred Waterhouse's grandiose gothic Town Hall of 1868. This now forms part of a comprehensively planned civic area which will incorporate law courts and other civic functions with pedestrian ways and piazzas. Redevelopment of the Victorian city centre has been largely piecemeal (c.f. Birmingham) but some projects, such as the District Bank and London Assurance Buildings in King Street, contribute a new element of townscape. To the south of the city centre an area of about 2,000 acres is undergoing redevelopment incorporating a further education complex where the University, Polytechnic and Institute of Science and Technology house about 25,000 students on a comprehensively planned campus. Within this same arc of redevelopment is the extensive municipal rehousing scheme at Hulme, covering some 400 acres, with its own district shopping centre.

Coming full circle from its historical origins the Rochdale Canal has now been converted into an award-winning landscaped linear park where the water, no deeper than ten inches, is no longer a hazard to safety.

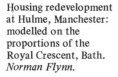

Housing redevelopment at Hulme, Manchester: modelled on the proportions of the Royal Crescent, Bath. *Norman Flynn.*

Rochdale, Deeplish

OS Sheet 109   GR SD 9012

When slum clearance schemes began in earnest after 1945 the emphasis was on redevelopment rather than improvement. This attitude was seriously questioned during the early 1960s and the Government commissioned a study of the Deeplish area of Rochdale to investigate whether improvement was physically, socially and financially feasible. The publication of the study led to the implementation of a Pilot Scheme in 1967, which estimated the costs and methods of improving the area. The results showed clearly that improvement was an attractive proposition and the study recommendations formed a basis for the 1969 Housing Act, which introduced the concept of General Improvement Areas. The four streets included in the scheme contained 110 terrace houses in good physical condition but with a monotonous appearance and with attendent problems of on-street parking and through traffic. The scheme reduced traffic intrusion and introduced semimature trees and flower boxes.

Pomona Street, Deeplish, Rochdale – illustrating the traffic management and environmental improvement carried out in the pilot scheme. *P. Anstess.*

Wythenshawe   NW 4/6
OS Sheet 109   GR SJ 8188 (Wythenshawe Centre)

Wythenshawe was the first municipal attempt to implement the garden city principles of Ebenezer Howard. It was built between 1927 and 1941 to the plans of Barry Parker and now houses about 100,000 people. The recent completion of the town centre is a belated recognition of the size and importance of this satellite town which, although now part of Manchester, was conceived on garden city lines with an encircling agricultural zone and ample open space between housing groups. Being later than Parker's plans for Letchworth and Hampstead Garden Suburb, the impact of the motor car is more apparent. Wythenshawe is linked to Manchester by Princess Parkway, a tree and shrub lined arterial road more reminiscent of Chicago or New York than Lancashire.

Blackburn   NW 5/1
OS Sheet 103   GR SD 6828

Like many other Lancashire cotton towns, Blackburn suffered economically from the decline of the cotton industry and has sought to re-establish its prosperity and civic pride through the town centre redevelopment. The complex, begun in 1968 on the site of the old market and surrounding shopping area, contains shops, offices and civic uses, including new council offices, and was designed by the Building Design Partnership.

The new council offices and shopping centre at Blackburn, with the town hall of 1855 in the foreground. *Blackburn Director of Environmental Services.*

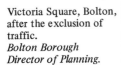

Blackpool Tower.
B.T.A.

Blackpool NW 5/2
OS Sheet 102   GR SD 3036

Although Blackpool had been a small resort since the middle of the eighteenth century, the railway in 1846 really 'created' the town. From then on expansion was rapid as thousands of people from the nearby industrial North West sought to escape from smoke and grime to the bracing climate of this 'fun city by the sea'. The 500 feet tall Tower was built in 1891 as an (inferior) copy of the Eiffel Tower, while the 'Golden Mile' is a seafront shanty town of fortune tellers, food stalls and other entertainments. Blackpool as a 'fun city' provides a welcome fantasy world for its annual millions of visitors.

Bolton NW 5/3
OS Sheet 109   GR SD 7109

A typical Lancashire cotton town, the birthplace of Samuel Crompton, inventor of the 'spinning mule' (a machine which revolutionised the eighteenth century cotton industry), Bolton's nineteenth century prosperity depended on the fact that 'Britain clothed the world'. Later, when other countries learned to clothe themselves, the cotton industry declined and Bolton (like other towns) has had to diversify its economy. The town centre contains some fine examples of Victorian architecture such as the Town Hall which demonstrates the civic pride of the industrial cotton magnates. In recent years it has undergone considerable redevelopment, and Victoria Square and other streets in the centre have been closed to traffic and landscaped.

Victoria Square, Bolton, after the exclusion of traffic.
Bolton Borough Director of Planning.

Preston, Bus Station   NW 5/4
OS Sheet 102   GR SD 5429

Opened in 1969, this is the largest bus station in the country,
built to integrate long distance and local bus services. The complex
is sited between the shopping centre and the inner ring road, and
also contains a multistorey car park. It might almost be called a
'transport interchange', although the railway station is on the
other side of the central area and most interchanging is therefore
from bus or car to foot.

Southport   NW 5/5
OS Sheet 108   GR SD 3317

A nineteenth century seaside resort that developed out of the
desire of industrial workers and their masters to escape from the
smoky city for their leisure. It was fortunate in that its promoters,
the local landowners, laid down rigid rules about the character of
development, for example, every house had to have front and
back gardens. The plan was a flexible grid, based on the spine of
Lord Street — a spacious boulevard running through the heart of
the town. An Act of Parliament in 1825 endorsed this plan and
the control of development needed to carry it out. In character
and origins Southport is the northern equivalent of Bournemouth.

Preston bus station
surmounted by car
parking.
*Building Design
Partnership.*

Lord Street, Southport.
*Sefton District
Planning Officer.*

124

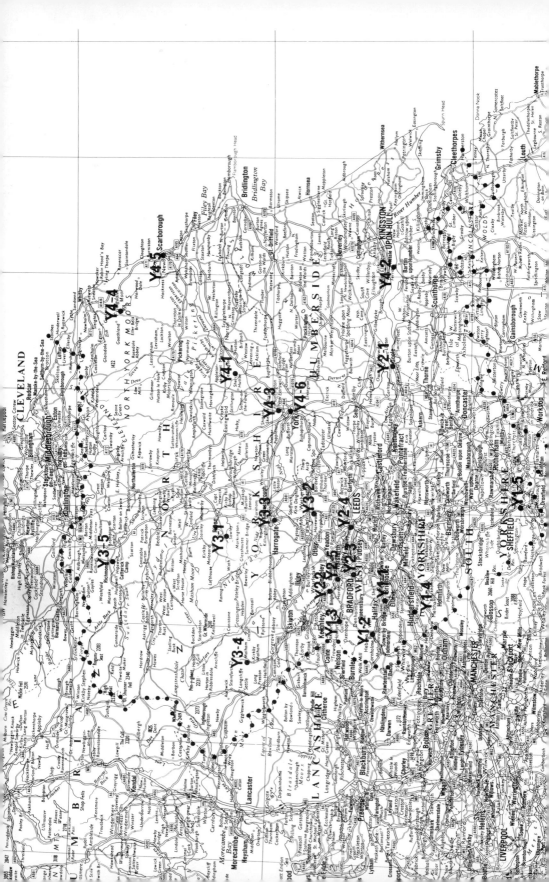

Yorkshire and Humberside

From earliest times, people moved into and about Yorkshire and
Humberside as part of the European migrations, thus developing
the first settlements and lines of communication. The Roman
invasion brought links with other parts of Britain, particularly the
first strategic route up the eastern side of the country.

Waterways too were critical in opening up the region and with
the development of commerce and industry, the rivers,
and later the canals, became the most important routes. The
Humber estuary provided links by the rivers Trent and Ouse to
Nottingham and York. The first canal, in Roman times, linked
the River Trent to the Wash via Lincoln.

The first towns developed at important crossing points of
roads and waterways. York, Doncaster and Leeds have been
important links between water and land since Roman times. The
rivers Aire, Calder and Don were in the forefront of canalised
river transport in the West Riding of Yorkshire, linking the
Humber with Leeds, Wakefield and Doncaster. Eventually, as
trade increased, Bradford, Rotherham, Barnsley and Sheffield
were opened up. The waterways brought in essential fuel needed
to develop industry, and at the same time provided the means to
despatch manufactured goods on their outward journeys.

New roads — the turnpikes — improved communications during
the eighteenth century and, like the motorways of today, cut off
many corners which existed in the historic byways. In the
West Riding these new roads assisted in the development of
Bradford and Wakefield as commercial centres and in other
parts of the region contributed to the development of many
market towns.

In the West Riding, centres such as Halifax and Huddersfield
grew as the wool industry expanded in areas where essential water
was available for power and processing. Until the canals were
built, pack horses and uneconomic road transport were the only
means of transporting the products of the wool textile industry.

Religion also played its part in the development of the region.
Beverley, Ripon, Whitby and Selby flourished round religious
institutions, while the importance of York, Lincoln and Durham
in religious administration provided the impetus for growth and
the need for good communications between them. Some early
religious orders were determined to develop in the seclusion of
the countryside, thus creating Fountains, Reivaulx and other
famous Yorkshire abbeys.

The Industrial Revolution brought a new form of
communications with a major influence on the whole region:
the railway was soon to overtake the canals and roads in its
effect on the development of both towns and villages. York.

was the important railway centre from where George Hudson administered an 'empire' which spread throughout the country. In York, Doncaster and Normanton, whole areas of housing and industry owe their origins to the coming of the railway and many a small village doubled in size when the railway gave easy access to a nearby city. It also started tourism to the east coast towns of Whitby, Scarborough, Filey, Bridlington and Hornsea.

The Yorkshire coalfield has had a special influence on the growth of urban and rural areas in the region. Where a mine was developed, a new village was established, or an existing one was expanded, some of these eventually merging into larger urban areas. Coal was essential to steel and wool textile industries, and its export by way of the Aire and Calder Navigation, was responsible for the growth of the port of Goole.

The local traditions and the hilly terrain strongly influenced the style of the industrial towns. Leeds had its brick 'back-to-back' terraces while, in the Pennines, local stone predominated and the houses of some mill villages, especially Hebden Bridge, were stacked up in hillside terraces with the lower properties 'back-to-earth'.

The industrial prosperity of the nineteenth century and the philanthropy of some industrialists brought about the creation of the 'model village', not only the famous Saltaire at Shipley but others, such as Akroyden and Copley in Halifax. The middle and upper classes of the industrial town were also provided with their garden suburbs such as the 'Avenues' in Kingston-upon-Hull.

The Victorians built splendid civic and commercial centres in nearly all the region's cities and towns and, in spite of the loss of many fine examples such as the Mechanics' Institute and Kirkgate Market in Bradford, the present local authorities have preserved and improved many fine buildings, such as Leeds Town Hall and Bradford Wool Exchange.

Recently, the region's 'Clean-Up Campaign' and 'Operation Eyesore' have provided the incentive to remove the layers of grime from the splendour of many major buildings. Housing Improvement Grants and the designation of General Improvement Areas and Conservation Areas have provided both the finance and a sense of local pride in saving the stock of potentially excellent housing from the compulsory purchase order and demolition contractor.

Changes in rural areas are often overlooked, but the enclosures of open fields and the development of large estates and industrial sites such as quarries, have established the countryside as it is today. In Yorkshire there are many examples of the large estate such as Castle Howard, Harewood House and Sandbeck Park where Capability Brown was responsible for the layout. One of the greatest impacts of this development was the planting of trees and woodland. This has left present day planners with the big task of recording and protecting the tree cover, and planning for its eventual replacement.

Today, the Yorkshire countryside is of special interest to the planner, since pressure from many quarters brings conflict in planning and managing it. On the positive side, the region contains three national parks, parts of the Pennine Way and Cleveland Way and stretches of Heritage Coast.

Before the reorganisation of local government in 1974, the West Riding County Council was responsible for a recreation study of the South Pennines area, lying between the Peak District and Yorkshire Dales National Parks, yet within easy access of industrial Yorkshire and Lancashire. The new local authorities are implementing proposals contained in the Study, and a voluntary coordinating group, The Pennine Park Association, has been formed to promote the development while safeguarding the many local interests.

Apart from Kingston-upon-Hull and Grimsby, no major area needed to be redeveloped because of war damage but, in the postwar period, there has been considerable progress in slum clearance and new council estate development in most cities and towns. Much of this development was of the wrong type and in the wrong place, with resulting social problems. But, in more recent years, more care has been taken in the development of local authority housing, particularly in building to a more human scale and in providing a high standard of landscaping. In this field Sheffield has been a national as well as a regional leader.

Yorkshire and Humberside do not have any new towns, but the local authority planning departments, together with central government and the Regional Economic Planning Council, have been concerned to promote the region on an industrial basis. The South Yorkshire Coalfield and the wool textile towns have declined but new industry has been attracted to take their place. Since 1973, the authorities have combined to form a regional Development Association which will assist in promoting the area at national and international level. To help in attracting industry, the planning departments have improved the environment by clearing derelict land, in many cases the unsightly tips of exhausted coal mines.

The shortage of energy resources has inspired exploration for new coal seams in the Selby area, and the planning authorities are pledged to ensure that their development will not produce the poor environments that resulted from coal mining in the past.

Structure planning is now a responsibility of the new county councils. A start had been made in the Doncaster area by the County Borough and West Riding County Councils, and this is now being expanded by the South Yorkshire County Council, where the planning department is developing many techniques of public consultation. The same county has also pioneered the establishment of a new Environment Department which is responsible for conservation, the countryside, waste disposal and many other essential matters of environmental improvement.

Mark Andrew

OS Sheet 104   GR SE 0925

Halifax made its fortune in the woollen cloth trade, which dates back to the fifteenth century. However, the present town is unmistakably nineteenth century and bears all the hallmarks of a typical northern industrial town. The Piece Hall of 1779 was originally a Cloth Market and consists of 316 separate rooms arranged around a quadrangle. The Town Hall, designed by Sir Charles Barry, dates from 1863. More exotic is Wainhouse Tower, a 253 feet industrial folly, originally a dye works chimney later topped by a Renaissance pinnacle.

The Piece Hall, Halifax, built in 1779 for the sale of woollen cloth. *Calderdale District Planning Officer.*

Heptonstall and Hebden Bridge   Y 1/2

OS Sheet 103   GR SD 9928

Heptonstall is the archetypal Pennine hill village, with buildings clustering around narrow alleys and courts. It developed from the seventeenth century as an early centre for the textile trade, with sheep from the surrounding moors supplying looms in the local farmhouses. The Industrial Revolution led to the eclipse both of the local cottage textile industry, and of the village itself by Hebden Bridge.

Hebden Bridge was originally a packhorse bridge over the River Calder, but the advent of the canal and later the railway allowed the bulk movement of goods and raw materials, and transformed the town into a typical Yorkshire mill town. Use of local materials and vernacular styles has given an overall unity to the town's appearance.

The old pack-horse bridge and mill workers' houses at Hebden Bridge. *Calderdale Borough Planning Officer.*

The main street in
Howarth.
*Bradford District
Planning Officer.*

Haworth, Keighley and Worth Valley Railway   Y 1/3
OS Sheet 104   GR SE 0337

In the mid-nineteenth century Haworth became famous as the
home of the Bronte family, and this literary association has led to
the growth of tourism in the area, which in turn has encouraged
the conservation of the old town. As a result, Haworth is
comparatively free of modern development, but has suffered
greatly from tourist traffic. A bypass is being constructed, after
which the town centre will be closed to through traffic.

   The Keighley and Worth Valley Railway runs at the foot of
the town. The line was closed by British Rail as being
uneconomic, but has been reopened by a private company,
who run steam trains as a tourist attraction. A number of
similar lines have been opened over the last decade,
demonstrating the 'pulling power' of steam engines for the public.

Steam engines on the
Keighley and Worth
Valley Railway.
Keith Smith.

Scammonden Dam and M62 (West of Huddersfield) Y 1/4
OS Sheet 110   GR SE 0516

Scammonden Dam, the highest earth-filled dam in Britain, was
also designed to carry the transPennine motorway (M62) over
the reservoir. The dam was built in the 1960s, and the motorway
opened in 1970. The function of the reservoir is both to supply
water to the conurbations of West Yorkshire , and for recreation
in the form of boating and sailing. This triple function of
motorway, water supply and recreational facility is probably
unique in Britain.

Scammonden Dam
with the M62
Motorway across the
top.
Ronald Taylor.

Sheffield, Hyde Park, Park Hill and Gleadless   Y 1/5
Valley Housing Estate

OS Sheet 111   GR SK 3687   (Hyde Park, Park Hill)
                 SK 3783   (Gleadless)

Three nationally known examples of postwar municipal housing
estates, which demonstrate changing attitudes to density and
design in residential areas. The first two are medium to high
density areas of deck access flat blocks, based on the ideas of
Le Corbusier, and stretching up the hillside above the city centre.
However, over the last decade there has been a reaction against
such housing schemes, because of the social problems they can
create. The emphasis now is on estates such as Gleadless Valley
consisting of more modest low rise developments based on the
time honoured two storey house and garden.

Aire and Calder Navigation   Y 2/1
OS Sheet 105   GR SE 7423 (Goole)

Although competition from rail and road has caused a decline in
the commercial use of narrow canals, ship canals and some
navigable rivers remain competitive. The Aire and Calder
Navigation from Leeds and Wakefield to the 'company port' of
Goole (developed between 1825 and 1830) now carries 540
ton barges. Experiments are currently taking place with the
BACAT system ('barge aboard catamaran') in which canal barges
from Europe are transported across the North Sea for direct
transit to the inland waterways of England. With such systems,
inland waterways can have a commercial future.

Bingley 'Five-Rise' locks   Y 2/2
OS Sheet 104   GR SE 1039

The Leeds and Liverpool Canal was authorised by an Act of
Parliament in 1768, planned by James Brindley and executed by
John Longbottom. When completed in 1816 it provided a
cross-Pennine route linking the ports of Hull and Liverpool.
In order to cross the Pennines — the 'backbone of England' —
extensive flights of locks were necessary and, on the north
western outskirts of Bingley, four locks raise the canal by
120 feet. One of these, the famous Bingley 'Five-Rise', completed
in 1773, has five adjacent lock chambers and is a remarkable
piece of engineering, now preserved as a 'listed building'. The

canal's scenic grandeur and its closeness to large centres of population has given it a new lease of life as a waterway for pleasure boating.

Bradford, Listers Mill Y 2/3
OS Sheet 104   GR SE 1434

A symbol of the prosperity and influence of Victorian Yorkshire, Listers Silk Mill was opened in 1873, replacing an earlier building burnt down in 1870. Built by Andrews and Pepper for Samuel Lister (Lord Masham), the mill is in the Italianate style, with two similar six storey blocks with panelled parapets, a highly ornamented staircase tower and a unique square chimney stack 250 feet high, which has been likened to the Campanile San Marco in Venice. The mill has recently been cleaned and the overall effect is extremely impressive.

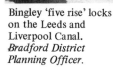

Bingley 'five rise' locks on the Leeds and Liverpool Canal.
Bradford District Planning Officer.

Lister's silk mill, Bradford.
Bradford District Planning Officer.

Leeds Y 2/4
OS Sheet 104   GR SE 3033

Leeds is a natural focus for transport routes and has been famous for centuries for its cloth industry. Its strategic location led to enormous industrial expansion during the nineteenth century. In the middle and late 1960s, Leeds pioneered a new 'Leeds Approach' to transport planning, based on providing a balance between private and public transport, including the introduction of 'park-and-ride' services and the building of an inner ring road. An integral feature of this strategy was the provision of a traffic free shopping area in the city centre, entailing the closure of many streets. The precincted area includes Victorian arcades and the new Merrion Shopping Centre.

Quarry Hill Estate, dating from the 1930s, was one of the earliest large-scale municipal housing estates, based on a series of interlinked blocks of flats. However, the blocks are now considered substandard and structurally deficient and it is planned to demolish the complex after only forty years.

Commercial Street, Leeds, now free of traffic.
Leeds City Planning Officer.

Housing in Sir Titus
Salt's Saltaire.
*Bradford District
Planning Officer.*

Saltaire, Shipley   Y 2/5
OS Sheet 104   GR SE 1438

A pioneering model industrial village built by Sir Titus Salt in
1850 to house the workers at his alpaca woollen mill. Salt
believed that better living conditions and amenities would lead
to happier workers and increased productivity at the mill.
Saltaire was one of the first such schemes and set an example
later followed by Bournville in Birmingham, Port Sunlight near
Liverpool, and others. The street plan is a regular grid iron and
820 houses had been completed by 1872, as well as other social
and cultural amenities. The village, which was originally in
green fields, is now surrounded by later development, but
retains much of its physical and social identity.

Fountains Abbey   Y 3/1
OS Sheet 99   GR SE 2768

Fountains Abbey, dating from 1132, is one of a number of
famous abbeys that were founded in Yorkshire at the beginning
of the Middle Ages. They subsequently became rich and
prosperous through the monks' involvement with the wool trade
of the area, controlling extensive areas of sheepwalks (see also
Malham). Fountains became the richest Cistercian house in
England, and as such was one of the first to be dissolved and
sold by Henry VIII in 1540. The ruins of the Abbey can be
approached through the beautiful grounds of Studley Park.

Fountains Abbey.
B.T.A.

Harewood Village   Y 3/2
OS Sheet 104   GR SE 3245

A planned estate village, built in 1760 to replace the original
settlement which interrupted the view from Harewood House

and was therefore demolished. The village was designed to create
a formal approach to the park gates and its 'urban' feel is a
complete contrast to later 'romantic' estate villages such as
Old Warden (c.f.), or even those of a similar period such as
Milton Abbas (c.f.).

Harrogate   Y 3/3
OS Sheet 104   GR SE 3055

One of the great inland spas which flourished in the eighteenth
and nineteenth centuries. Although Harrogate was the first town
to be designated a 'spa' in the sixteenth century, it was not fully
developed until the Victorian era. Harrogate is, therefore,
essentially Victorian and contains distinguished examples of
urban design and landscape gardening of that period. The town
centre is a patchwork quilt of buildings and public gardens,
including the Stray Lawns. Harrogate still retains its function as
a tourist town, and also specialises in conferences.

Malham and the Dales   Y 3/4
OS Sheet 98   GR SD 9063

Malham is an ancient village set in the Yorkshire Dales amidst
rugged limestone scenery. It is a centre for tourists, and a new
centre provides an information and interpretive service for
visitors. The village dates back to Saxon times and there are
some eighth century 'lynchets' (cultivation terraces). There is
also evidence of Iron and Bronze Age occupation, and
medieval field boundaries can be seen. A number of dwellings
illustrate well the development of local agricultural architecture
in the seventeenth and eighteenth centuries; prevailing weather
conditions and the proximity of construction materials both
influenced design. The wealth created by the wool produced at
villages like Malham was used to build and endow the great
medieval Yorkshire Abbeys such as Bolton and Fountains (c.f.).

Richmond and Catterick Camp   Y 3/5
OS Sheet 92   GR NZ 1701

Richmond is one of Yorkshire's most attractive towns. It owes its

Richmond Castle dominating the town.
B.T.A.

existence primarily to the protection offered by the Castle and to its market and trade in Swaledale lead during the Middle Ages. The town retains much of its historic character and also contains one of England's oldest theatres, built in 1788. In contrast, three miles to the south lies Catterick Army Camp, established in 1915 as a 'temporary' base for 40,000 enlisted soldiers. Today it is one of the largest military concentrations in the country and the basis of the area's economy.

Castle Howard   Y 4/1
OS Sheet 100   GR SE 7170

One of England's grandest country houses, built between 1699 and 1726 by Vanbrugh and Hawksmoor for the Earl of Carlisle. The grounds were laid out at the same time and contain Vanbrugh's Temple of the Four Winds and other monuments. A good example of the early eighteenth century country house and park, before the advent of the picturesque landscape movement.

Castle Howard, designed by Sir John Vanbrugh.
B.T.A.

The Humber Bridge, near Hull   Y 4/2
OS Sheet 107   GR TA 0326

The third of the great trio of modern British estuary road bridges (the other two are the Severn and Forth bridges). Due for completion in the late 1970s, the bridge links Hull to Barton-on-Humber and is twenty miles downstream from the next crossing at Goole. When completed, it is bound to have an enormous impact, both economically and physically, on the now relatively undeveloped area around Barton-on-Humber and is also designed to improve Hull's road links with the south.

135

New Earswick, York

Y 4/3

OS Sheet 105   GR SE 6155

New Earswick is a garden suburb, developed by the Rowntrees in the tradition of Bournville and Port Sunlight. It dates from 1902 and the architect was Sir Raymond Unwin (who was also responsible for Letchworth, the first garden city). New Earswick was, in fact, the first practical expression of Unwin's principles of town planning.

North York Moors National Park

Y 4/4

OS Sheet 94   GR NZ 7619 (Boulby)

Fylingdales early warning radar station in the North York Moors National Park. *B.T.A.*

The North York Moors National Park was one of ten national parks set up under the Act of 1949, whose purpose was to safeguard the most beautiful and unspoilt areas of Britain for public recreation. However, the parks contain a multitude of other uses, principally farming. Beginning in 1920 the Forestry Commission has carried out a programme of afforestation on the moors, in order to reduce dependence on imported timber. Extractive industries are also allowed in national parks — for example, potash mining on the moors at Boulby, near Loftus. Near the coast at Fylingdales is the Early Warning Ballistic Missile Station, a symbol of the 'cold war', but also a striking landmark. A good way to see the moors is to take the restored railway from Grosmont to Pickering.

The surface workings of the Cleveland potash mine at Boulby in the North York Moors National Park. *I.C.I.*

136

South Bay, Scarborough,
from the spa colonnade.
B.T.A.

Scarborough   Y 4/5
OS Sheet 101   GR TA 0488

Scarborough is unusual in that it was first a 'spa' and subsequently
a coastal resort. It has thus been able to prosper from both these
fashions in British tourism over the last 300 years. The springs
were first discovered in 1626 and by the end of the eighteenth
century, the town had all the trappings of a successful spa, plus,
significantly, bathing machines. Scarborough is divided by the
headland on which are the ruins of the twelfth century castle.
South of the headland lies the original fishing port, and to the
north, the later Victorian hotel terraces.

York   Y 4/6
OS Sheet 105   GR SE 6052

York was founded by the Romans as a legionary fortress in
A.D. 71, and later became a colony. It was refounded by the
Normans after a fire in 1069, when the city was replanned and
extended to five times its former size. The medieval walls and
gates are mostly intact and considered, with those of Chester, to
be the best in the country. The Multangular Tower is a Roman
survival from the fourth century. The original street pattern is
also still clearly discernible. The famous Minster dates from
1220 to 1470. There was a good deal of redevelopment during
the Georgian era and again in the nineteenth century so that the
city now contains fine examples of architecture from practically
all periods.

Recently, York has been subjected to all the pressures and problems of modern society, and the need for conservation has become acute. Consequently, York was one of the four historic towns for which detailed studies were carried out in the late 1960s. Many of the recommendations contained in the report are now being implemented.

York Minster and the city walls.
B.T.A.

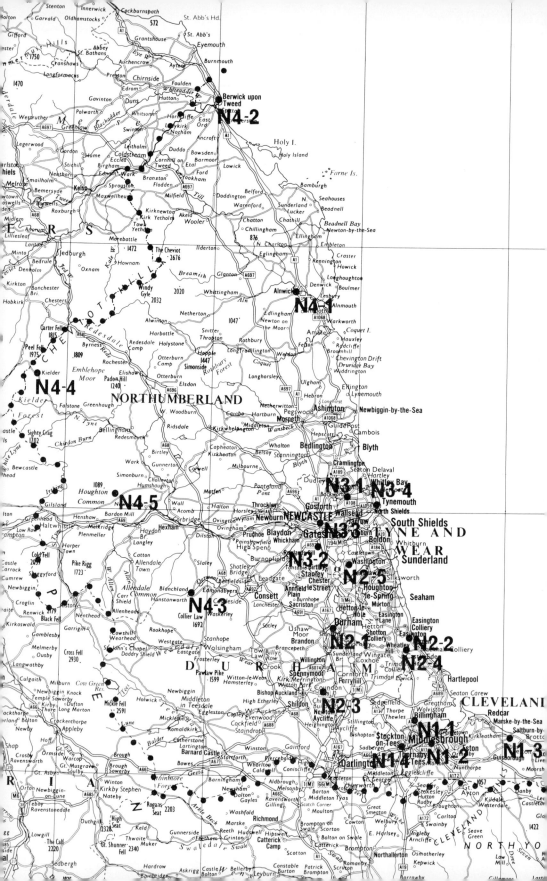

Northumbria

The topography of the North East divides evenly between uplands and sea-bordering lowlands, crossed by three great rivers which, in turn, provide links across the hard back of the Pennines. Early development of the east is associated with colonisation from the mainland of Europe and Scandinavia across the North Sea. The cultural penetration of the country west of the Pennines from the west produced two closely linked northern regions which have in many respects played opposite roles throughout their recent history — a view toward North America and cotton in the west, wool and Europe in the east.

Tangible relics of the early days, both pre-Roman and post-Roman, are widespread, nowhere better represented than by the Stanwick fortification in North Yorkshire, an enormous complex of earthworks with over six miles of banks and ditches. Roman settlements themselves were based either on the fortifications along Hadrians Wall, or are related to the road network which provides access to the Wall from the south.

Anglian settlements marked the last influx of immigration and are related to the area of South Durham and North Yorkshire where the predominant pattern of village development is of large, spacious and often complex 'greens'. West Auckland, in Durham, marks the northern limit of this influence, with other splendid examples at Romaldkirk and Gainford, also in County Durham.

Almost all the villages which exist in the region today, except the later estate and industrial villages, were established by the fourteenth century and occupy the sites of medieval agricultural settlements. In the uplands, they were related to the valley lines sited upon the sand and gravel terraces, or along the base of the escarpments of central Durham and Cleveland. Many were naturally related to major fortifications at strategic points of river crossing or travel network, such as Norham in Northumberland and Barnard Castle in Durham. Others were linear developments allied to a naturally formed enclosure site, such as Yarm in Cleveland or Warkworth in Northumberland. The pattern of street villages and later country towns was clearly and decisively established. Several important monastic sites exist where, after the dissolution of the monasteries, village communities or estate villages developed as at Blanchland in Northumberland.

The towns grew in many cases from the Anglian 'burgh' to medieval towns proper, as at Darlington. Bamburgh, on a headland of the Whin Sill in North Northumberland, was the centre of Anglian organisation, and Corbridge a royal seat. At the Norman Conquest, Newcastle and Durham superseded Bamburgh (now a tiny village) and Carlisle as the real seat of power and control. Newcastle, based on the site of a Roman river crossing, became significant as a fortress in the twelfth century, and quickly developed as a prospering port with a wealthy merchant community.

Markets and towns flourished in the region, related to the village groups or the new patterns of traffic such as Wolsingham and and Morpeth, or were related to the patrimony extended from a fortified town, such as Alnwick or Barnard Castle.

Berwick upon Tweed was the result of continuing interaction and sparring between England and Scotland. It is dramatically sited within the town walls of Edward I and the splendid Elizabethan fortifications begun by Mary Tudor in 1555. The whole situation, by the open sea and flanking an estuary crossed by three bridges, heightens its drama and importance.

The period following the union of the crowns of England and Scotland marked a new era of stability and prosperity based on a steadily developing agriculture and the new coal trade. The market towns grew rapidly during the late seventeenth and eighteenth centuries: the pattern was set for the growth of the county town of Durham with its attempts at provincial fashion and its social hierarchy. Small towns such as Hexham became elegant and civilised architectural entities. The growth of the ports, too, was rapid: Stockton, Sunderland and North Shields all blossomed during the century and promoted a pattern of town development which exists to this day, although in some cases, as in Sunderland, the heart of the town was resited in the nineteenth century, leaving behind decaying eighteenth century structures.

The nineteenth century inspired brave and imaginative schemes in the pursuit of the ideal city: Richard Grainger's and John Dobson's Newcastle, built substantially in the ten years following 1832, was based on speculation allied to high standards of planning and design, and fostered by local initiative and capital. Tynemouth was a new town development based on an older community in which the benefits of fashionable medicine through sea bathing could be enjoyed. Saltburn in Cleveland was a product of railway mania. Devised by Henry Pease, the Quaker ironmaster, it was allied to the arrival of the railway from Middlesbrough in 1860. After a vigorous start, only a small part of the project was completed.

The founding of the new towns in the North East started with Middlesbrough, one of the most striking examples of the phenomenon of industrial growth. The first, modest developments were allied to the extension of the Stockton and Darlington railway in 1831, an enterprise of Joseph Pease of Darlington. New impetus came with the discovery of ironstone in the Cleveland Hills, and what had started as a small, well-ordered community quickly got out of hand: from 1851 to 1871 the population grew from 7,500 to 39,500.

The counties of the North East were, through the centuries, controlled by great landowners who, in turn, took an active part in the creation of new agricultural estate villages, such as Cambo, on the Trevelyan estate at Wallington, and Brancepeth and Hunstanworth in Durham, the latter a curious assembly of High Victorian buildings by S.S. Teulon. The role of promoter of these settlements has, in our own time, been taken over by national agencies such as the Forestry Commission, as at Kielder in Northumberland.

The other agricultural villages were joined by newly developing industrial communities; the thriving towns and villages in the west of the region, based on the lead mining industry, shrank as coal mining drew away their populations to the new or expanding towns and villages of the east. Pit villages were simple and straightforward, often no more than a single row of cottages and an attendant chapel. As a single row amid open countryside they represented a considerable improvement on previous standards of accommodation and sanitation, and the monotony resulting from the interminable repetition of this simple arrangement was not envisaged.

Out of the characterless sprawl of many of the region's Victorian towns and villages grew the realisation that concerted action had to be taken: the Team Valley Trading Estate, a formal but attractive gathering of industrial units, was laid out in 1936, the result of the terrible depression which had laid low so much of the region's industry. It was to become a model for many others.

The new towns which followed in the wake of the establishment of postwar planning start with the designation of Newton Aycliffe in 1946, based on the conversion of a wartime munition works to a peacetime industrial estate. The real virtues of large areas of tree planting are now very evident at Newton Aycliffe. Peterlee, in a bleak windswept position by the coast, was something of an emotive concept from the start: this new city arising from the mining wastes of the coastal belt had as its first aim the provision of an alternative source of employment to the collieries which, even then, were losing importance. The early stages of Peterlee were cheerless, but lessons were soon learned and the mistakes of the first generation of new towns remedied. In the last twenty years it has managed to establish its own identity with some spectacular and original housing. Of the later generations of new townships Killingworth and Billingham have created particular identities — the former through the ingenuity of its housing and the quality of its overall design, and the latter for establishing civilised shopping and leisure facilities as a fundamental part of its community development.

Change, and particularly change through planning, is everywhere evident in Northumbria. The formerly inadequate routes have been replaced by an integrated network of fast roads and motorways. They now provide reliable communications for the many industries now established in the region in accordance with local and national planning policies to replace the declining industries of coalmining and shipbuilding. In the principal urban concentration of Tyneside, a rapid transit system will speed communication using an improved rail loop on north Tyneside, a new railway bridge across the Tyne and an underground section beneath central Newcastle. In the field of urban redevelopment, exciting and original experiments such as the Byker Wall show a real desire by planners to consider the impact of urban motorways on people living nearby. Here a long snaking block of flats with living rooms only on the quiet side screen residents from the motorway to be built alongside. The redevelopment of Newcastle's Eldon Square provides shopping facilities unequalled in the North East, while in Durham City the new precinct by Framwellgate Bridge improves shopping amenities without detracting from the very fine setting of the cathedral and castle.

The decline and indeed extinction of some villages and the disruption caused by the reclamation of derelict land and the rationalisation of the settlement pattern are part of the necessary price to be paid for the rebirth and regeneration of the region.

Neville Whittaker

Billingham Forum.
Cleveland County
Planning Department.

Billingham Town Centre and ICI Works   N 1/1
OS Sheet 93   GR NZ 4622

The development of the large Imperial Chemical Industries works at Billingham, led to the considerable expansion of the town and prompted the local council to promote an ambitious new town centre development. Completed in 1967, the scheme includes a completely pedestrianised shopping centre, large free car park, residential accommodation, civic hall, library, health and sports centres (known as the Forum), pubs, offices and a district heating scheme. The centre operates most successfully and illustrates what can be achieved by an enterprising, but small local council.

Middlesborough Old
Town Hall, built 1846
but redundant by
1883. This view was
taken in the late 1950s.
*Cleveland County
Planning Department.*

Middlesbrough

OS Sheet 93   GR NZ 4920

Originally planned as a coal port for the Stockton and
Darlington Railway, Middlesbrough later became famous (or
notorious) as the first of the 'iron towns', after iron ore had
been rediscovered in the nearby Cleveland Hills in 1850.
Population growth was rapid, rising from 40 in 1821 to 75,000
in 1891, and the quality of the environment was minimal. Forty
iron foundries were opened between 1850 and 1871. The
original concept of Middlesbrough's founders was ordered and
solid, if unexciting: but the town eventually became a symbol
of nineteenth century industrialisation − prosperous but squalid.
This gloomy picture of Victorian exploitation is, however,
enlivened by some impressive civic buildings, such as the
Municipal Buildings of 1883.

Saltburn

OS Sheet 94   GR NZ 6621

As was common near industrial towns of the nineteenth century,
the desire to escape from the smoke and damp of Middlesbrough
led to the founding of Saltburn as a seaside resort in the 1860s
(see also Southport and Blackpool). The railway enabled
Saltburn to be enjoyed, not only by the local ironmasters, but
also by many of their employees. The town was laid out in a
wooded valley and much of the original development is still
visible.

Saltburn-on-Sea.
*Cleveland County
Planning Department.*

The original booking office of the Stockton and Darlington Railway, Stockton. *Cleveland County Planning Department.*

Stockton, Railway Museum

OS Sheet 93   GR NZ 4419

Although an old market town, Stockton is now chiefly remembered for the Stockton and Darlington Railway — the first in the world to carry fare-paying passengers and use steam locomotives. It opened in 1825, and the original booking office is still standing. It is used as a railway museum, and a bronze tablet on one of the gables states 'Here in 1825 the Stockton and Darlington Railway Company booked the first passenger, thus marking an epoch in the history of mankind'.

Durham

OS Sheet 88   GR NZ 2742

Durham was founded in A.D. 995 by Saxon monks as an easily defended shrine for the remains of their patron, St Cuthbert, on a loop of the River Wear. The rocky promontory on which the city stands is an almost perfect natural defensive position. The Normans built the castle in 1072 and the present magnificent cathedral between 1093 and 1133. Because of its good defensive location the city prospered and became a focus for overland routes to Scotland. In medieval times the Bishop of Durham was extremely powerful and the city was the 'capital' of the Northumbrian region. The castle, cathedral and many fine Georgian houses can be seen today. The University was founded in 1832 and now dominates the social and economic life of the the city.

The historic core of Durham in the loop of the River Wear. *Aerofilms.*

Horden

OS Sheet 88   GR NZ 4441

The first coal pits in County Durham were some distance inland,

145

where the coal seams are close to the surface. The seams slope down to the east and, as these first collieries were worked out, other deeper mines were begun towards the coast. Pits still in production, such as Horden, are now on the coastline itself, mining under the sea and coal waste is tipped directly onto the beaches. This gives rise to enormous problems of pollution and environmental damage.

Leasingthorne
OS Sheet 93   GR NZ 2529

A former colliery village, now mostly demolished and laid out as parkland. With the run-down of the inland coal mines in the area after the war, many villages such as Leasingthorne went into decline. The county council decided that new development in these villages would be 'limited to the social and other facilities needed for the life of the existing property' — in other words, the villages would be allowed to 'die'. Leasingthorne is an example of one of these villages.

All that remains of the former village of Leasingthorne. The streets and pavements are now edged with grass and trees. *Ray Taylor.*

Peterlee New Town
OS Sheet 88   GR NZ 4241

An early (1948) new town. In contrast to most recent new towns, whose purpose is to house overspill from nearby conurbations, Peterlee was intended to concentrate the population from the many declining colliery villages of East Durham and to rationalise the previously very dispersed settlement pattern of the area. The large amount of landscaped open space within the town results from the need to avoid areas of mining subsidence. In a unique experiment, the artist Victor Pasmore was called in as a consultant in the initial planning of the town.

Shotton Colliery — one of the villages to be replaced by Peterlee New Town. *Ian Wright.*

Housing in Glebe
village, Washington
New Town.
Photo-Mayo Ltd.

Washington New Town N 2/5
OS Sheet 88   GR NZ 3056

Washington Old Hall was the home of George Washington's
ancestors, but the modern new town dates from only 1964. It
was part of a comprehensive regional plan for the Tyne-Wear
area and was designed for the higher living standards of the
1960s. A grid of urban motorways attempts to allow for the
full use of private cars without traffic congestion, and the town
is divided up into 'villages' of about 4,500 people which are
designed as selfcontained physical and social units. There is
also a less rigid land use zoning than in earlier new towns, with
a closer physical relationship between housing and industry.

Cramlington and Killingworth N 3/1
OS Sheet 88   GR NZ 2676   (Cramlington)
             NZ 2771   (Killingworth)

Two new towns promoted and built since 1960 by Northumberland
County Council to house overspill from the Tyneside conurbation
and act as growth points in the planned economic revitalisation
of the North East. Both towns are still being expanded.
Cramlington was the first new town to be developed by a
partnership of private enterprise and local authority. Killingworth
contains high density deck access housing and some impressive
industrial buildings. The target population of Cramlington is
62,000 and of Killingworth 20,000.

The centre of
Killingworth township.
*Turners Photography
Ltd.*

Team Valley Trading Estate, Gateshead N 3/2

OS Sheet 88   GR NZ 2460

A trading estate built in the 1930s with extensive government aid,
to help solve the unemployment problems of the area during the
Depression and, as such, an early example of government
intervention in industrial location. Its physical layout is a good
example of prewar industrial estate planning. The estate currently
provides 20,000 jobs and a further area has yet to be developed.

The Team Valley
Trading Estate.
*English Industrial
Estates Corporation.*

Newcastle-upon-Tyne N 3/3

OS Sheet 88   GR NZ 2464

Newcastle originally grew up around the 'new castle' of
A.D. 1080, at the lowest bridging point of the River Tyne. The
town walls were built by Edward I to enclose 120 acres, and
for 500 years they were acclaimed as the finest in the country.
Substantial fragments can still be seen today, together with the
remains of the Norman castle. Since the Middle Ages coal has
been shipped from the Tyne, especially to London, and a
flourishing shipbuilding industry grew up along the banks of the
river. During the 1830s and 1840s, a fine new town centre and
commercial area was built in neo-Classical style by Richard
Grainger to the designs of John Dobson. Grey Street is reckoned
to be one of the finest streets in Britain and the whole area is
now extensively conserved.

   During the 1960s Newcastle underwent another period of
extensive rebuilding. A large part of the shopping area has been
rebuilt and a comprehensive pedestrian deck system created at
first floor level. Byker is a substantial redevelopment area, and
includes the famous 'Perimeter Block' of single aspect dwellings
which backs on to a projected urban motorway and is designed
to protect the new housing from traffic noise. Elsewhere, areas
of older housing have been improved, for example Heaton,
which in 1970 was an early GIA under the 1969 Housing Act.

The Byker 'wall',
Newcastle-upon-Tyne.
Newcastle City Engineer.

Grey Street,
Newcastle-upon-Tyne.
*Newcastle City
Engineer.*

Tynemouth

OS Sheet 88   GR NZ 3769

Tynemouth, only five miles from the shipyards of Wallsend and
Jarrow, has the atmosphere of a country village and is regarded
as one of the country's outstanding conservation areas. The
picturesque main street is predominantly Georgian in character
although the village grew up in Norman times round the now
ruined priory and castle. The former, of Saxon origin, was built
on a rocky headland and later enclosed within the Norman
castle. To the north is an interesting area of Victorian and
Edwardian housing laid out to a comprehensive plan by the
Duke of Northumberland. The railway enthusiast and industrial
archaeologist should visit the magnificent Victorian wrought iron
railway station.

*Tynemouth railway
station.*
*South Tyneside District
Planning Officer.*

Alnwick

OS Sheet 81   GR NU 1813

Alnwick developed because of its strategic location as the crossing
place of the River Aln, the first barrier for travellers from
Scotland to England. The castle, originally twelfth century, was
ruined in the border wars and restored in the eighteenth and
nineteenth centuries. In the Middle Ages it guarded the wild no
mans land between Scotland and England, and peace came to the
area only after the two kingdoms were united in 1603. Alnwick
was a market town and the county capital. Very little modern
building has taken place, and the historic character of the town
remains intact.

Berwick-upon-Tweed

OS Sheet 75   GR NT 9953

On the border with Scotland, Berwick, founded in A.D. 870,
changed hands thirteen times before finally becoming English in
1482, although border warfare continued until the unification
of 1603. This turbulent history is graphically illustrated by the
walls of 1565, designed to withstand artillery attack, and still
intact today. Besides being a military town, Berwick was also
a market centre, port and bridging point of the River Tweed.
It is one of the best preserved fortified towns in Europe and its
Elizabethan defences are unique in Britain.

*Berwick-on-Tweed,
defined to the east and
south by its
Elizabethan defences.*
Aerofilms.

Blanchland

OS Sheet 87   GR NY 9650

The Abbey at Blanchland, founded in 1165, was dissolved in 1539 and lay derelict until it came to the Crewe family in 1752. The site was then used for an estate village to house workers at the family's nearby lead mines. The present layout was probably dictated by the plan of the monastic buildings and the church, gatehouse and storehouse (now an inn) enclose a paved square. The unspoilt appearance of the village has made it a showplace and this is maintained by strict control over development and parking restrictions, with the provision of a visitors' car park outside the village.

Blanchland, built in the 18th century on the site of a former monastery.
B.T.A.

Kielder

OS Sheet 80   GR NY 6293

Since the 1920s the Forestry Commission have created Kielder Forest on 145,000 acres of previously barren moorland. In the late 1940s and early 1950s, the Commission built Kielder Village to house the forest workers and their families — it is thus a modern example of the old 'estate village'. The consultant architect planner was Dr Thomas Sharp, an authority on village and rural development, and the general idiom of development is derived from Milton Abbas, Dorset (c.f.).

Kielder forest village.
Forestry Commission.

Hadrian's Wall, between Bowness and Wallsend   N 4/5

OS Sheet 87   GR NY 9865   (Corbridge)
NY 7969   (Housesteads)
NY 7766   (Vindolanda)

The most spectacular Roman relic in Britain, the wall and its accompanying forts were begun by the Emperor Hadrian about A.D. 120 to mark the northern boundary of Roman Britain. There are many interesting sites along the wall, but Corbridge (on the Roman Stonegate, the road which ran parallel to the wall and acted as its communications artery), Housesteads and Chesters have all been extensively excavated. The most interesting current excavation is at Vindolanda (i.e. Chesterholme), where various Roman buildings and works are being reconstructed.

Hadrian's Wall at Cuddy's Crags.
B.T.A.

150

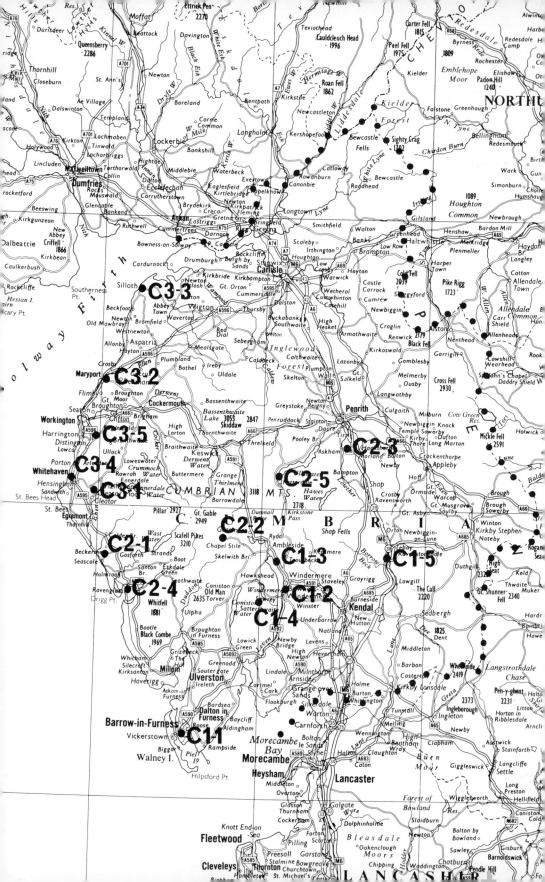

Cumbria

The first conscious planning in Cumbria reflected the military preoccupation of the Romans. The pattern of forts, signal stations and defensive walls, still attracts over 100,000 visitors a year. The best preserved section of Hadrian's Wall, with the fort of Birdoswald, lies between Banks and Gilsland. But the defences extended along the Solway and North Cumbrian coast with a system of forts, milecastles and turrets at strategic sites such as Bowness, Beckfoot, Maryport, Burrow Walls, Moresby and Ravenglass. Inland forts at Hardknott, Ambleside, Brougham, Old Carlisle, Kirkby Thore, Brough and Kendal secured the area. Carlisle itself, on the line of the wall, was the major Roman civil settlement (Luguvalium) north of York but has as yet had no systematic excavation. Evidence of the road system can still be seen in the Maiden Way, High Street, A66, and A595 between Ambleside and Ravenglass, and through the Lune valley between Tebay and Kirkby Lonsdale.

The Anglian and Scandinavian settlers cleared forests and established agriculture, shaping the countryside and founding a pattern of settlements which is still reflected in the old place names of Workington, Brampton, Dalton, Thornthwaite, Esthwaite and Grizedale.

The Norman development of towns at many strategic points — often associated with trade routes — can still be seen at Appleby, Brough, Brougham, Carlisle, Cockermouth, Egremont and Kendal. These towns, with the remains of influential monastic sites of the same period, make particularly fine contributions to the county's history and architecture.

Appleby town centre reflects a very early conscious plan, dating from about 1110, by Ranulph de Meschines, linking church and castle by a wide street. The small market towns of Cumbria present attractive examples of townscape and small-scale urban planning, from the informality of Hawkshead and Brampton to the more formal squares of Broughton-in-Furness and Kirkby Lonsdale. A feature of rural development in the unsettled twelfth and sixteenth centuries was the construction of numerous pele towers, bastle houses, and fortified manors, characteristic of the whole border area. Many of these survive, particularly fine examples being at Dacre (Ullswater), Kirkandrews (Longtown), Yanwath (Penrith) and Dalton-in-Furness.

While the impact of the industrial revolution was not felt until the eighteenth and nineteenth centuries, important evidence of earlier iron smelting remains, now of industrial archaeological interest. Iron smelting can be traced back to the thirteenth century in Furness, and iron furnaces were developed at Duddon Bridge and Backbarrow in the early seventeenth century by Isaac Wilkinson.

In the Pennine foothills on the eastern side of the county, the mining of lead, started by the Romans, produced the mining and farming communities of Alston Moor and the founding by the London Lead Company in 1753 of Nenthead as a mining village 1,400 feet above sea level. The scale of mining in the 18th century here led to the construction in 1776 of a five mile long underground drainage level from Nenthead to Alston which later became a Victorian tourist attraction. The remnants of the former industry in the area contain a wealth of industrial archaeological and social history, since the Company pioneered various welfare schemes at Nenthead.

The most impressive example of urban planning in the county is associated with the early stages of industrial development on the west coast in the seventeenth century. Whitehaven, which Pevsner has called 'the earliest post-medieval planned town in England', presents a striking example of planned development on an ambitious scale. The centre was first developed on a regular grid in the 1660s by Sir John Lowther, and extensively and graciously redeveloped a century later. By the eighteenth century the port of Whitehaven was second in importance only to London. On a smaller scale, Portland Square in Workington, and the grid iron village of Longtown are also interesting examples of conscious formal planning of this period.

In the mid-nineteenth century, stimulated by the development of railways and docks, the manufacture of iron and steel, and shipbuilding, Barrow-in-Furness was developed, again on a grid iron pattern, under the guidance of industrialists such as Ramsden and Schneider. Ramsden's ambitious plan is incomplete, however, and visually disappointing, apart from some imposing individual Victorian buildings and the interesting 'garden city' suburb of Vickerstown. The former mining village of Cleator Moor is an exception to the generally indistinguished small settlements of the industrial era. Its large nineteenth century market square contains a blend of modest old and new public buildings, surrounded by larger scale property and by unselfconscious and colourful terraces overlooking the river Ehen valley and Ennerdale Fells. These epitomise the close compatibility between town and country throughout the county in terms of scale, colour and materials.

The tortuous road and rail links with the west coast have always been an obstacle to the growth of industry in the county. The recent decision to improve the A66 between Penrith and Workington through the National Park is therefore seen as a major solution, and completion of the M6 motorway through the county in 1971 has revolutionised communication with the north and south, with a particularly fine stretch of motorway engineering and landscape where the M6 follows the river Lune valley — a route taken by the Romans and railway navigators. In the process, the bypassing of numerous small villages and the towns of Penrith and Carlisle has greatly eased traffic congestion and its associated environmental problems.

153

Railway development accelerated the exploitation of minerals and associated industrial development, especially along the coast, with viaducts across the estuaries of the Kent, Leven and Solway. The twentieth century has seen a reduction in the railway network but at Carlisle, the Kingmoor marshalling yards, using furnace slag waste from Cleator Moor, form one of the largest complexes of its kind in the country.

Recent planning policies have tried to stimulate new industries to replace the old, declining primary industries. Complementary to the stimulation of economic prosperity has been the implementation of a major land reclamation programme to clear and restore spoil heaps and derelict sites. Previously concentrated in the industrial areas of west and south Cumbria, this is seen as an essential task, not only improving the intrinsic landscape, but in making the areas more attractive to potential industrial development. Treatment of sites has included restoration to agriculture, woodland industry, amenity and recreational use. Major examples are at Maryport (Risehow Colliery spoil heap and Solway Coast slag banks), Lowca, Workington North Shore, Derwent river and Harrington harbour, Whitehaven South Shore, Cleator Moor and Millom. At Millom, the flooded 600 acre Hodbarrow subsidence area caused by extraction of iron ore and contained by the massive outer barrier wall constructed in 1905, could become a major recreation area.

Large-scale urban redevelopment has not been a feature of Cumbrian towns over the last two decades, the emphasis being on slum clearance renewal, conservation and sympathetic new building. Of particular note is the comprehensive conservation scheme for the historic centre of Whitehaven, the first stage of the central shopping precinct at Workington, the Well Lane development overlooking Maryport harbour, and riverside housing at Kendal.

Tourism is by no means a recent phenomenon in the county: the eighteenth century fashion for scenery and the picturesque inspired the first tourist guide to the area in 1778. The age of steam and railways brought an influx of day trippers to the large-scale woodlands and lakes at Derwentwater and Windermere. On the coast, Arnside, Grange-over-Sands, Seascale and Silloth developed rapidly as holiday centres, Silloth, in particular, characterised by fine buildings facing a wide foreshore green. Most of the larger lakes now form part of a comprehensive water supply system serving local domestic and industrial needs, as well as those of Lancashire. Efforts are now being made to develop the recreation and amenity value of man-made reservoirs, but the pressure for recreation and water sports activities is creating problems on Ullswater, Windermere, and Coniston, where policies are now being formulated to protect these attractive areas from overuse.

The late nineteenth century saw the development of the countryside preservation movement and the founding of the National Trust by Octavia Hill and Canon Rawnsley. The National Trust now owns and manages extensive lands, especially

within the Lake District National Park. The Trust also owns
ten important buildings and their grounds, such as Sizergh
Castle and gardens in Kendal, and Wordsworth's house at
Cockermouth, while Fell Foot Park (Newby Bridge) has been
developed as a holiday centre with chalets and recreation
facilities. The acquisition of land for public use, the establishment
of nature trails, warden services, recreational facilities,
information centres and, in particular, the first National Park
Centre at Brockhole, near Windermere in 1966, indicate a positive
approach by the planning authorities, the National Trust, the
Forestry Commission, the Nature Conservancy Council and
private landowners to the problems of improving recreation
opportunities while conserving landscape quality.

The increasing pressure on the central Lake District area has
meant that more emphasis is now being given to the study of
areas outside the National Park to establish their potential for
recreation and tourist development. This change of emphasis
could be as significant for the economy and prosperity of
peripheral areas as eighteenth and nineteenth century tourism
was for the central parts.

Gordon Fanstone

Barrow-in-Furness   C 1/1
OS Sheet 96   GR SD 2069

Barrow grew from a village of 300 people in 1841 to a thriving
town of 7,000 in 1881 and 74,000 in 1921. Its growth was based
on the coming of the railway in 1846, the discovery of a very
rich deposit of iron ore in 1850 and the dynamism of James
(later Sir James) Ramsden. In 1856 he prepared plans for a new
town with spacious avenues and squares and this was enlarged
after 1865. The wide tree lined streets convey to this day 'a sense
of space and ease which even the casual visitor is likely to comment
on' (Pevsner). Although founded by the Furness Railway Company
(the first railway cottages of 1847 can still be seen in Salthouse
Street) it was the establishment of iron ship building after 1869
that brought the greatest growth.

The relative isolation of Barrow and its original dependence
on ship building — which has since declined — have created
difficulties in attracting new industry and maintaining full
employment. But Barrow still remains one of the few examples
in England of a nineteenth century town planned on a grandiose
scale which is more common in Europe.

Ramsden Square,
Barrow — with a
statue of Sir James
Ramsden — terminating
the main axis of the
formal street plan.
*Cumbria County
Planning Officer.*

Bowness and Windermere   C 1/2
OS Sheet 97   GR SD 4097

Bowness and Windermere developed as a response to the increase
in visitors at the start of the nineteenth century when the writings
of poets such as Thomas Gray, Wordsworth, Southey and Coleridge
helped to popularise the Lake District. In the 1830s the romantic
scenery similar to, yet more accessible than Switzerland and
the Italian lakes, provided a picturesque setting for 'Italianate'
villas for the well-to-do, particularly on the slopes above Lake
Windermere.

In 1844, the railways, although opposed by Wordsworth,
opened up the Lake District to a wider and more distant range of
visitors and Bowness, on the lake shore, and Windermere, at the
terminus of the railway, began to acquire the range of
accommodation and services which have made them the principal
tourist resorts of the Lake District today.

Villas on the hillside
above Lake Windermere
at Bowness.
Aerofilms.

Brockhole, National Park Visitor Centre   C 1/3
OS Sheet 90   GR NY 3901

Brockhole National Park Visitor Centre was opened in 1969 by
the Lake District Special Planning Board to encourage visitors to
develop an understanding and appreciation of the Lake District.
Housed in a country house between Windermere and Ambleside,
the Centre is surrounded by thirty-two acres of grounds including
six acres of woodland and a stretch of Windermere lake shore.
It has an information centre, bookshop and lecture facilities and
houses an imaginative exhibition on the geology, natural history,
local history and recreation of the Lake District. The grounds
contain picnic sites, nature trials and refreshment points.

Such centres were recommended by the Hobhouse Committee
on National Parks in 1947. Brockhole is the first centre to be
opened but increased public awareness of countryside affairs and
the strengthened management of National Parks under the
1972 Local Government Act should ensure the opening of
comparable centres.

Grizedale Forest   C 1/4
OS Sheet 96 or 97   GR SD 3394

Acquired by the Forestry Commission since 1937, Grizedale
Forest now comprises 7,590 acres of land, including 5,766 acres
of coniferous plantations and 718 acres of broadleaved
woodlands. Its scale and variety, and its situation in the heart
of the Lake District, have provided many opportunities for the
recreation and education of visitors. The site of the former
Grizedale Hall is being used as a camping and picnic site and
outbuildings house a wildlife centre and forest centre, open to
all visitors. One building has become 'The Theatre in the Forest'

An open air lecture theatre on the terrace of the former Grizedale Hall within Grizedale Forest. *Cumbria County Planning Officer.*

presenting plays and concerts in an unusual setting. Nature and geology trails have been laid out throughout the forest and fishing and controlled deer stalking are permitted.

Grizedale Forest shows as clearly as any Forestry Commission property how timber production, ecology, education and recreation can be undertaken with mutual advantage.

Lune Valley, M6 Motorway C 1/5

OS Sheet 91 and 97   GR NY 6102 (Lune's Bridge)

South of Tebay, the M6 motorway, which is part of the principal road link between Scotland and England, passes through the spectacular scenery of the Lune Valley. To lessen the impact of the road works on the landscape and to reduce the otherwise steep gradient, the carriageways have been separated in places and the earthworks moulded into the natural contours. The result is so attractive that car parks have been created along the A685 road between Kendal and Tebay to provide viewing points where the road, motorway and railway run a parallel course through the valley.

Calder Hall Nuclear Power Station. *U.K.A.E.A.*

Calder Hall and Windscale C 2/1

OS Sheet 89   GR NY 0304

Opened by the Queen in October 1956, Calder Hall became the first commercial nuclear power station in the world. It is operated by the UKAEA in conjunction with the adjoining Windscale works where research and nuclear fuel processing are undertaken. Like the Dounreay establishment in Caithness (see S 4/3), Calder Hall and Windscale provide welcome employment in an area with few alternative job opportunities.

Langdale Fells and Valley C 2/2

OS Sheet 90   GR NY 2806 (Head of Great Langdale)

Increasing threats to the character and appearance of the

countryside led to the founding of the National Trust in 1895. Many of its early acquisitions were in the Lake District and today the Trust owns about 80,000 acres of land in Cumbria. Among its estates, it owns or leases virtually the whole of Great and Little Langdale Valleys and the surrounding fells, including the Langdale Pikes. It is thus able to control development through its powers of ownership and the right of inalienability, granted by the National Trust Act, 1907. Unlike most other landowners, the Trust's primary task is to preserve the scenic beauty of its property and it has, therefore, relocated or extinguished unsightly camping and caravan sites and provided discreet car parks in Great Langdale.

Lowther   C 2/3
OS Sheet 90   GR NY 5323

With his wealth from the West Cumberland coalfield, (see Whitehaven C 3/4) Sir John Lowther bought the Lowther Estate in 1682 and built the houses known as Lowther New Town to replace the previous village which had spoiled the view from his house. A descendent, James Lowther, Earl of Lonsdale, needing further estate houses, commissioned Lowther village, built between 1765 and 1773. Although uncompleted, the small-scale but formal closed terraces of one and two storey houses and the unfinished 'circus' at the eastern end provide a most attractive example of eighteenth century estate housing. Lowther Castle, set amid extensive parkland, was designed by Sir Robert Smirke in 1806 but has now been abandoned to the elements as too large and unmanageable for modern needs. Pevsner has pleaded for the shell to be safeguarded since he feels that the county can ill afford to lose so spectacular a ruin.

Lowther Village laid out in 1765 for Lord Lonsdale. *Cumbria County Planning Officer.*

The view from
Hardknott Roman Fort
dominating the
strategic route down
Eskdale to Ravenglass.
*Cumbria County
Planning Officer.*

Ravenglass and Hard Knott   C 2/4

OS Sheet 96 (Ravenglass) and 89 (Hard Knott)
GR SD 0896 (Ravenglass)   NY 2101 (Hard Knott)

The Roman defensive system of Hadrian's Wall had its western
termination at Bowness on Solway. Beyond this, the frontier was
defended by a chain of forts, fortlets and watchtowers along the
coast towards St Bees Head. Further south, defence was
fragmentary and mainly associated with the Roman road network.
At Ravenglass, the well-preserved remains of a fort and bathhouse
can be seen in association with a civilian settlement. The Roman
road linking Ravenglass with Ambleside traverses the Hard Knott
and Wrynose Passes. At Hard Knott is one of the most impressive
Roman sites in Britain — a spectacularly sited three acre fort
which had a tower at each corner and an entrance in each side.
Outside the fort was a bath house and parade ground. It is now
an Ancient Monument in the care of the DoE.

Ullswater, which despite
its use as a reservoir,
has retained much of
its natural beauty.
B.T.A.

Thirlmere and Ullswater   C 2/5

OS Sheet 90   GR NY 3213   (Head of Thirlmere)
               NY 4624   (Polley Bridge, Ullswater)

Water was first transported from Thirlmere to Manchester by
aquaduct in 1894. The need to ensure purity of water and
to maintain flow throughout the year resulted in restriction of
public access to the lake with extensive conifer plantation of
the catchment area and an unsightly tide mark caused by seasonal
drawdown. Thirlmere has, therefore, become one of the less
attractive lakes in the Lake District. By contrast, public opposition
to the use of water from Ullswater led to a solution whereby
water is only extracted at time of excess flow while subsequent
purification ensures that public access to the lake is not impeded.

Cleator Moor   C 3/1

OS Sheet 89   GR NY 0215

Cleator Moor represents an attempt to establish an urban
community based on iron mining, following the enclosure of
common moorland in 1825. By contrast, most mining
settlements in west Cumberland were either straggling hamlets

or extensions to existing towns. The establishment of ironworks at Cleator Moor in 1842 and the coming of the railways in the 1860s produced a rapid growth accompanied by strong civic pride and community spirit. Schools, an Institute and an infirmary were built and, in 1882, the Market Place was laid out, later enclosed with civic buildings and a surprisingly impressive Cooperative Society shop with a fine iron verandah. The civic buildings now house a government sponsored community development project which is attempting to restore the civic dignity and attitudes of self help which were destroyed with the decline of iron mining in the area.

Maryport   C 3/2
OS Sheet 89   GR NY 0336

Maryport was founded in 1749 by Humphrey Senhouse to accompany his development of Ellenfoot Harbour for the export of coal. The earliest housing was at the foot of the cliffs but, by 1850, a larger town had been laid out on the cliff top with a rectangular street plan culminating in Fleming Square on the higher ground to the north. The street plan and much of the original housing remain, but the docks and the railways built to serve them lie unused. Following the loss of the Irish coal trade after 1918 the railway works, blast furnaces and iron works all closed and, by the 1930s, unemployment was as high as 80 per cent. With Government aid and local initiative, industry has now diversified and much dereliction has been removed. Maryport, therefore, represents in one small town the rise, fall and subsequent rebirth of an industrial economy.

19th century housing in the local style fronting onto the cobbled Fleming Square, Maryport. *Cumbria County Planning Officer.*

160

Criffel Street, Silloth, still retaining its granite setts, overlooking the greens and seafront. *Cumbria County Planning Officer.*

Silloth
C 3/3

OS Sheet 85   GR NY 1153

The progressive silting up of the Solway estuary led to the abandonment of Carlisle and the later Port Carlisle as ports. Silloth Docks were established in 1857 and linked to Carlisle by railway but the town never grew as its promotors had hoped. But Silloth was developed concurrently as a holiday resort with a wide grassy 'flat' facing the sea and backed by terraces of houses and hotels.

Because of its isolated location and the small population of its hinterland the resort, like the port, has not expanded very much beyond its original extent. It therefore gives a good impression, not often achieved elsewhere, of a mid-Victorian seaside resort in its prime.

Whitehaven
C 3/4

OS Sheet 89   GR NX 9718

The rectangular street pattern and harbour at Whitehaven. *Aerofilms.*

Important coal exports from west Cumberland in the eighteenth century made Whitehaven the second port in Britain (after London). Founded in the 1660s by Sir John Lowther (see

Lowther C 2/3) it is the earliest post-medieval planned town in England. Like simple planned towns of most periods its plan was a rectangular grid, squeezed into the narrow valley behind the coastal indentation that was developed as a harbour. The commercial success of Whitehaven has ensured its intensive redevelopment, but the grid plan remains intact today with the church occupying one block and many interesting nineteenth century houses, shops and warehouses close to the harbour.

Workington, Lillyhall Strategic Industrial Estate   C 3/5
OS Sheet 89   GR NY 0225

To replace jobs lost with the decline of the coal and iron industries in West Cumbria, the Government has made the area a 'Special Development Area'. It provides grants for new factories, for industrial training and for improved infrastructure, especially new roads and environmental improvements (such as derelict land clearance). Local authorities are providing sites for new factories such as the Lillyhall Estate on the A595 road near Workington. This estate, opened in 1969, contains a wide range of industries including the Leyland National bus factory which makes a high proportion of the country's buses. Such new industries depend on good road links with the rest of the country, a fact which, in the case of West Cumbria, can conflict with the desire to preserve the scenic beauty of the nearby Lake District.

The Leyland/National bus factory on the Lillyhall industrial estate near Workington. *Cumbria County Planning Officer.*

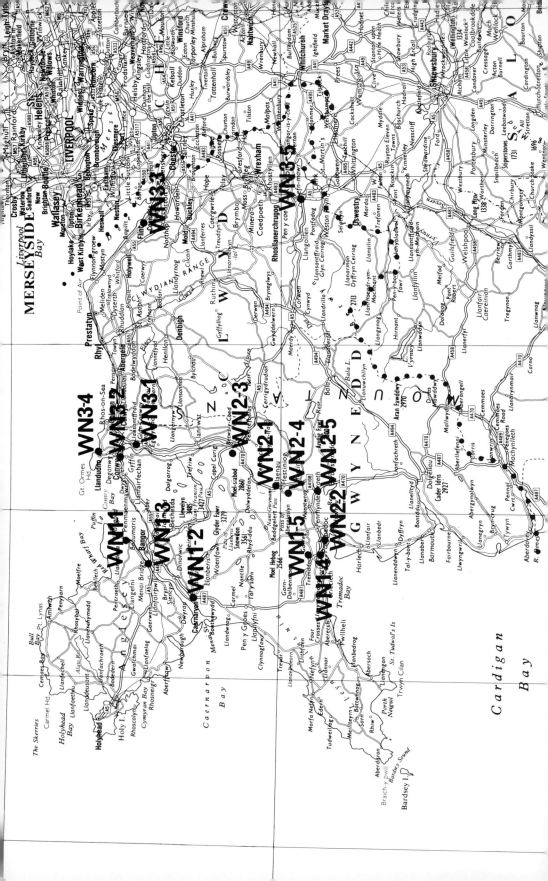

North Wales

North Wales's economic and social history could never have
encouraged town building and planning. There is, quite simply,
no such thing as a true 'Welsh town' in a physical or historical
sense as opposed to a community sense; there are only the
plantations of military and commercial venture — knots
tying Wales more tightly to England. None of the *maerdrefi* of the
chieftains ruling between the departure of the Imperial Eagle and
Anglo-Norman conquest form the germ of any present day town.
The ports and the resorts were planted, the junctions and
markets, even the industrial towns, built to oil the wheels of the
Industrial Revolution and encourage miners from Redruth and
Derby to Merthyr and Swansea. Probably, the only true Welsh
'town' is the smallholding, subsistence-based settlement, such as
Llanddona on Anglesey: a type more common in Ireland and
patently unplanned.

The first Neolithic or New Stone Age farmers were great
innovators in building, and it was their demand for word for
construction which led to the development of the so called
'axe-factories' of Graig-lwyd above Penmachmawr and
Myhyad Lhin on the top of the Lleyn Peninsula. The scatter
of axe-head finds suggests a highly organised trade with
the Severn Valley forming an important commercial route
to Southern Britain.

The most familiar pre-Roman feature, the hill fort, belongs to
Bronze and Iron Age times. Some like Tre'r Ceiri on the Rivals
and Pen-y-gaer above Manbedr-y-ennin, are obviously planned
military installations with ditch and rampart defences. Others,
like the chain along the Clwydian Hills, may have played
some role in a cattle-herding economy.

During the Roman occupation, planned development was
predominantly inspired by military aims — Din Lligwy on
Anglesey is one of the few examples of an estate settlement
of the Pax Romana, so common in the south. There, is however,
only one really interesting Roman remain for our purposes — the
auxiliary fort Tomen y Mur just north of Trawsfynydd. An oval
amphitheatre and a huge, unfinished parade ground lie a few
hundred yards north east of the walls.

Another conqueror, coming nearly nine centuries after the
departure of the legions, was responsible for what is still the
pre-eminent feature of planning in North Wales — the *villes
neuves* (commonly called 'bastides'). Edward I's solution for the
pacification and settlement of North Wales was to establish a
string of castles and castle towns — Flint, Rhuddlan, Conway,
Caernarvon, Beaumaris, Criccieth, Harlech and the private
lordships of Denbigh and Ruthin in the north, closely modelled

164

on the new towns he and his immediate predecessors had built in their French territories of Gascony and Aquitaine. They formed loyal enclaves in subversive territory; the ground inside the walls of the new boroughs was split into burgages on equal plots — the basis of the 'grid iron' street pattern — and offered with commercial concessions to English settlers. Each of the castles is worth visiting, each is outstanding in architectural and military terms and unique in some way, but the best example of the *ville neuve* with its close relationship of town and castle is, without doubt, Caernarvon. In both Caernarvon and Conway, the grid iron skeleton of street remains, more obvious in the overall shape of the walled borough of Caernarvon, distinguishing it sharply from the unplanned Victorian town outside the walls. By any criterion the building of the *villes neuves* and castles is impressive. Most of them were completed by the mid-1290s. Work on six of them was going on simultaneously, and Caernarvon, Conway and Harlech were started within weeks of one another in 1283. In sheer physical terms, they are still the most imaginative development programme carried out in the area. In relative cost terms, they exceeded even the nineteenth century schemes described below, virtually bankrupting the throne.

Militarily, too, they were extremely efficient, but they were not planted for exclusively military reasons. During Edward's reign there were nearly forty new foundations in England and Wales and over fifty in the French territories — the encouragement of commerce and the resulting increase in revenue were a vital part of the policy, and towns such as Newborough, Caerwys and Bala were to follow.

It was, again, economic motives which fired the next great era of planned development in North Wales during the nineteenth century. Raw materials — ores, coal, slate — put North Wales at the forefront of the Industrial Revolution, attracting such men as the ironmaster Hazeldene — who ran Kynaston and Upton Magna foundries and made the iron channel for the Pont-Cysyllte Aqueduct and the chains for the Menai Suspension Bridge — and Wilkinson. Economic penetration by the English took on all the aspects of an invasion — less violent than Edward's but no less far-reaching in its consequences. Lord Penrhyn — like the Nantlle slate quarry owners and the Assheton-Smiths who owned Dinorwic — planned and built a horse tramway, later replaced by a railway, and port facilities to handle the industry's growth. Port Penrhyn, just east of Bangor, lies on the northern edge of the family estate and has a very attractive late Georgian harbour office designed by Benjamin Wyatt. Penrhyn Castle, the family seat, is now a National Trust property.

While shipping from Caernarvon, Portdinorwic and Port Penrhyn choked the Menai Straits, William Madocks was developing Portmadoc in the south of the county as part of his grand scheme to secure the Irish packet connection for Porthdinllaen on the Lleyn Peninsula. Last staging post on his route from London was to be his new town of Tremadoc, built on the reclaimed lands behind his massive civil engineering work — the Portmadoc Embankment. Although extremely successful visually, with a formal layout and elegant but restrained use of local materials, Tremadoc never developed as its founder hoped.

The solution, and settlement of what competition there was, was Telford's Holyhead Road, very largely the basis of the present A5 — particularly the Anglesey stretch which rules a straight line across the island from his Menai Suspension Bridge to his Stanley Embankment, a causeway connecting Holy Island. The road has been referred to as Britain's first 'route nationale', funded by Government and overriding the host of inefficient turnpike trusts, it brought a status to road building unknown since Roman times; however, it was not to be a precedent. Although open all the way by 1830 and halving the journey time, the railway came hot on its heels: by 1850 it was possible to travel twice as quickly by train as by coach to Holyhead.

The commercial failure of the schemes Telford was involved in does not detract from his greatness. When we look at the Holyhead Road and the Ellesmere Canal, despite their long periods of disuse, what we see is not discontented bands of ratepayers and creditors but Telford's genius as engineer, surveyor and designer. His Chirk Aqueduct, the even more impressive Pont-Cysyllte Aqueduct, the Menai Suspension Bridge and the Conway Bridge, are all imaginative engineering feats, using materials in new ways, and beautiful pieces of architecture, as are the superb tollhouses and tollgates of the Holyhead Road in Anglesey and at the mainland end of the Suspension Bridge.

A mile west of Telford's Menai Bridge is what remains of Robert Stephenson's physical more impressive Tubular Bridge. In 1970 the tube was destroyed by fire and has been replaced by a steel arch, making Stephenson's massive Egypto-Victorian stone piers look hopelessly out of scale. As an engineering achievement the Tubular surpassed the Suspension Bridge: both faced very strict Admiralty conditions relating to obstruction to shipping and in the Antelope Inn, on the Bangor side of Telford's, there are some good lithographs showing the raising of the tube sections at slack water on enormous hydraulic lifts.

Like the road bridge, the rail link to Anglesey is only the highlight in a grander scheme, in this case the Chester to Holyhead railway along the rugged coastline. It improved the link to Ireland, but was far more important for spawning a string of sprawling seaside resorts beside its tracks — Prestatyn, Rhyl, Colwyn Bay, Llanfairfechan and Llandudno, laid out on the Gloddaeth estate.

Llandudno is, in fact, an ideal in resort planning — a balance between the urban jostle of Brighton and Arcadian Bournemouth. Lord Mostyn planned the town on a grid with stringent regulations about road and pavement widths and building plot sizes which still give the streets and sweeping promenade an airy boulevard feeling on traffic-choked summer days. It makes a nice comparison with two holiday developments of this century. Clough Williams-Ellis's Italianesque village, Portmeirion, sited on a wooded peninsula overlooking the Glaslyn estuary was set down with the highly individual touch of the owner, a selfconfessed romantic architect. Most of the buildings serve as annexes to a quayside hotel. Nearby, on the former slate quay of Portmadoc harbour, holiday homes with a nautical air successfully reflect the local idiom of colour washed stonework and a pleasing arrangement of slate roofs.

The demand for this holiday accommodation, predominantly from English people is yet one more example of the relationship between Welsh development and English influence so evident throughout history. Edward I and English and Welsh industrialists exploited the land and people of Wales; the natural and scenic resources of North Wales have recently been developed to satisfy demand from the east. Nuclear and hydroelectric power stations feed power to the national grid. Reservoirs in upland Wales supply water to Liverpool and Birmingham. The whole of North Wales now forms a playground for those from England and further afield. Planning policies must therefore take account of these outside pressures while ensuring that local residents receive the benefits that our comprehensive planning system can confer.

Colin Jacobs with N. Thomson, F. Lynch,
F.A. Usher, M. Hughes.

Beaumaris

OS Sheet 115   GR SH 6076

WN 1/1

Beaumaris was the last of eight castles built by Edward I for the permanent administration of North Wales. It was positioned to guard the northern entry to the Menai Strait as Caernarvon guarded the southern. With no site restrictions the castle, built between 1295 and about 1330, shows the ultimate development

Beaumaris, showing the castle and grid iron street plan. *Aerofilms.*

of concentric defences. The contiguous town, however, while still displaying the characteristic grid plan, was never fortified in the manner of Caernarvon or Conway.

Caernarvon WN 1/2
OS Sheet 115   GR SH 4863

Undoubtedly influenced by similar developments in Gascony, Edward I sought to subdue North Wales by creating a ring of castles and fortified towns. Caernarvon, Conway and Harlech were started within weeks of each other in 1283. At Caernarvon the castle and town walls were built concurrently and the town laid out on a grid plan within. The size, splendour and historical connections with the Prince of Wales have ensured the fame of the castle, and today it survives as one of the top tourist attractions in Wales. This inevitably creates problems of congestion which must be solved within the constraints of its historical importance.

Caernarvon Castle. The walled town is beyond the castle.
Crown Copyright. Reproduced with the permission of the Controller of Her Majesty's Stationery Office.

Menai Bridges and Waterloo Bridge, near Bettws y Coed WN 1/3
OS Sheet 115   GR SH 5571

The confirmation of Holyhead at the start of the nineteenth century as the principal embarkation port for Ireland necessitated the improvement in land transport to the port. First Telford rebuilt the London-Holyhead road (now the A5, much of it on the line of the Roman Watling Street) incorporating such bridges as the Waterloo Bridge near Bettws y Coed (1815) and his masterpiece, the suspension bridge across the Menai Strait. The later railway line by Stephenson was obliged to follow the coast of North Wales, but his technical ingenuity was tested in the use of tubular bridges across the River Conway and the Menai Strait (now rebuilt after a recent fire).

Telford's Menai Suspension Bridge on the London to Holyhead Road.
B.T.A.

Holiday homes on the former slate quay, Portmadoc. William Maddock's embankment is in the background.
Gwynedd County Planning Officer.

Portmadoc

WN 1/4

OS Sheet 124   GR SH 5838

Portmadoc was developed by William Maddocks in about 1810 as the harbour for exporting slate from Blaenau Ffestiniog. This necessitated a tramway on an embankment, 'the Cob', and entailed the reclaiming of 7,000 acres of land. In a total change of fortune Portmadoc is now a thriving holiday centre; the slate railway has become the Festiniog Railway — one of the 'Great Little Trains of Wales' — and the slate quay has been developed very successfully with holiday homes. To safeguard the fine view of Snowdonia from the Cob, a major electricity transmission line has been buried under the estuary at an additional cost of £2 million.

The former town hall dominating the square at Tremadoc.
Gwynedd County Planning Officer.

Tremadoc

WN 1/5

OS Sheet 124   GR SH 5640

Tremadoc was established in 1798 by William Maddocks as a market centre at the junction of two roads from England to the Irish Sea coast. Left isolated by the failure of Port Dinlleyn to capture the Irish trade and by the later development of Portmadoc, Tremadoc remains fossilised at its initial extent. Today, the formal market square with its stone built town hall, hotel, inns and cottages show the impressive but unfulfilled ambitions of Maddocks.

Blaenau Ffestiniog

WN 2/1

OS Sheet 115   GR SH 7047

The town building which followed the Industrial Revolution required large quantities of building materials, not least roofing slates. In North Wales, the extensive slate deposits were quarried and mined and their products carried initially by tramways and later by railways to coastal ports. Blaenau Ffestiniog, now surrounded by waste slate tips, was dependent

A trainload of visitors in the Llechwedd slate caverns, Blaenau Ffestiniog.
Bruno de Hamel.

169

totally on slate production and the collapse of the industry led to the town's decline. However, its situation in an important holiday area has provided the opportunity to reopen the Lechwedd Slate Mine as a fascinating tourist attraction.

Portmeirion   WN 2/2
OS Sheet 124   GR SH 5937

Portmeirion.
B.T.A.

Determined to prove that development of a coastal site need not entail depoliation. Clough Williams-Ellis set out in 1926 to create an Italianate village run as an hotel. Situated on a dramatic hillside site with steps up from the quayside, it has become a 'home for attractive but unwanted buildings' transported from elsewhere and re-erected with other buildings designed by the owner. The number of visitors is controlled by a fluctuating admission charge, a technique which has possibilities for use elsewhere.

Snowdonia Forest Park   WN 2/3
OS Sheet 115   GR SH 7956 (Bettws y Coed)

As the largest landowner in Britain the Forestry Commission believes that its land, primarily acquired for commercial planting, should be open for public enjoyment. To this end it has designated seven Forest Parks, the first, in Argyll, opened in 1935 and predating National Parks by sixteen years. The Snowdonia Forest Park, covering 23,400 acres around the village of Bettws y Coed, provides facilities for walking, climbing, fishing and sailing, as well as tent and caravan sites. Within Forest Parks great effort is taken to ensure the integration of new woodlands into the landscape which is often in contrast to early Forestry Commission planting elsewhere. This is very evident between Bettws y Coed and Blaenau Ffestiniog.

Tan-y-Grisiau   WN 2/4
OS Sheet 124   GR SH 6945

Ffestiniog Power Station above Tan-y-Grisiau Reservoir with the Stwlan Dam one thousand feet above.
C.E.G.B.

Nuclear power stations are most economic when run continously. However, demand shows marked daily peaks. Surplus power from Trawsfynddd is therefore used during offpeak times to pump water from Tan-y-Grisiau reservoir up to Llyn Stwlan 1000 feet above. During peak times the flow is reversed and the same turbines generate 360 megawatts of power for transmission through the national grid. Such a pumped storage project makes technical sense. The principal objections are environmental — for example, the visual impact of the Stwlan dam and the daily changes of level of 73 feet in the upper lake and 18 feet in the lower.

To reduce visual intrustion, the water is carried in tunnels and buried pipes and the power station is partially buried.

Trawsfynydd   WN 2/5
OS Sheet 124   GR SH 6938

The principal siting requirements of nuclear power stations are large quantities of water for cooling, sufficient land area with adequate bed rock for foundation, suitable linkages to existing or proposed transmission lines and Government imposed safety requirements. So all nuclear power stations are built near large water masses, mostly on the coast and often in areas of attractive landscape. Trawsfynydd, completed in 1969, is actually within the Snowdonia National Park and its proposal aroused much hostility. However, the resultant development is clad in concrete made from local stone and incidental structures such as switchgear are on lower ground surrounded by three thick belts of trees. The CEGB acknowledges the recreational importance of the area and welcome visitors to the station (by appointment) and provides for fishing on the lake.

Trawsfynydd Nuclear Power Station.
C.E.G.B.

Bodnant Gardens   WN 3/1
OS Sheets 115 and 116   GR SH 8072

Of Bodnant Gardens Edward Hyams claims: 'if a visitor, anxious to know what the "English Garden" has become at last, had time for but a single garden, this is the one . . . I would send him to'. In view of the importance of gardens in the British landscape, Bodnant justifies mention. Laid out between 1875 and 1914 the gardens have now reached maturity and show both formal terraces and informal 'wild gardens' sloping down to a tributary of the

River Conway and giving extensive views to the mountains of
Snowdonia. Its sheltered position enables an extensive range of
plants to be grown, and it contains one of the most famous
rhododendron gardens in Britain.

Conway   WN 3/2
OS Sheet 115   GR SH 7877

The selection by Edward I of the site for Conway Castle and town
was based on defence needs. Since the thirteenth century its
natural advantages have become the headaches of succeeding
generations. Telford built a suspension bridge in castellated gothic
style, to carry the coast road over the Conway below the castle
and Stephenson was later obliged to tunnel under the walled
town for his Holyhead railway. The recent road bridge, using the
same promontories of land to ensure a narrow span, dominates
the famous view across the river and forces all coastal traffic
through the walled town. The appearance and character of such
towns as Conway can only be maintained at enormous cost.

The strategic site of
Conway, chosen by
King Edward I and
confirmed by Telford,
Stephenson and
modern road builders.
Aerofilms.

Flint Castle
overlooking the
Dee Marshes.
*Clwyd County
Planning Officer.*

Flint   WN 3/3

OS Sheet 117   GR SJ 2473

Flint, overlooking the Dee estuary, was one of the earliest of
Edward I's ring of *villes neuves* surrounding North Wales.
It was started in 1277 in almost perfect rectangular form but with
only an earth bank and wooden defences. It has suffered many
changes due to industrial growth and the bisection of the town
by the railway. However, the castle ruins and much of the street
plan remain as evidence of Edward's intentions, which were not
influenced by physical site restrictions as at Caernarvon or
Conway.

The sea-front at
Llandudno from the
Great Orme.
*Aberconwy District
Council.*

Llandudno   WN 3/4

OS Sheet 115   GR SH 7882

A private Act of Parliament in 1854 by the landowner E.M.L.
Mostyn initiated the resort development of Llandudno to a plan
which can still be clearly discerned. Behind the spacious
promenade lay the shopping district and residential areas of

progressively lower densities. Size and disposition of streets were strictly controlled and high standards of housing (for the period) were maintained. It remains an attractive seaside town which, because of the provisions of its original plan, maintains both 'urban' and 'rural' characteristics.

Pontcysyllte Aqueduct WN 3/5

OS Sheet 117   GR SJ 2742

The Pontcysyllte Aqueduct, isolated on a branch canal which was never a commercial success, is still one of the most dramatic monuments to the canal age. Started in 1795, it took ten years to build, and carried the Ellesmere Canal on nineteen arches 121 feet above the River Dee. The graceful lightweight structure was made possible by using cast iron water channels in place of the traditional puddled clay, a technique pioneered by Thomas Telford. The aqueduct is an impressive sight, arching over the wooded valley of the Dee and carrying a canal which, today, is well used by pleasure craft.

Pont-Cysyllte aquaduct carrying the Shropshire Union Canal over the River Dee.
Clwyd County Planning Officer.

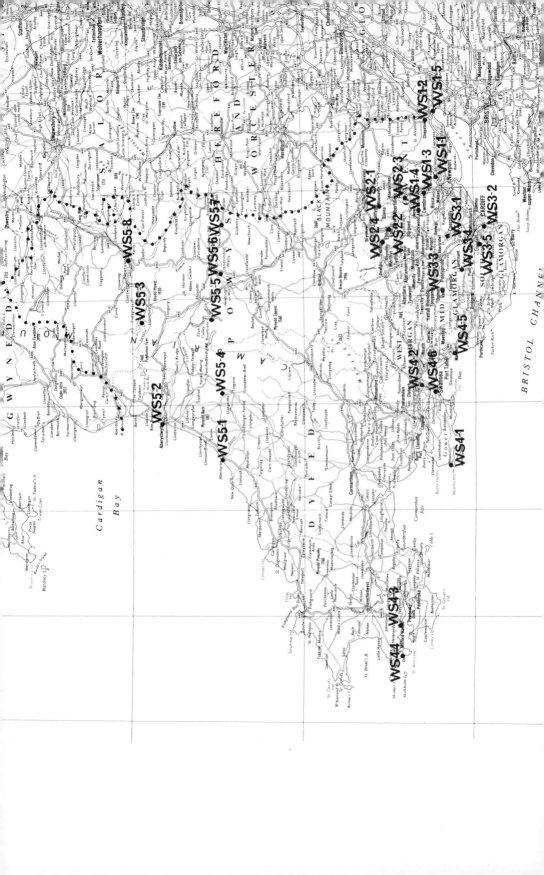

South Wales

Geographically and economically, South Wales comprises two areas of striking contrast. Industrial South Wales — East Dyfed, the three Glamorgan counties and Gwent — contains three fifths of the population and is highly urbanised. West South Wales and mid-Wales are rural, sparsely populated, hilly areas, delimited to the north by the boundaries of the former counties of Cardigan and Montgomeryshire.

The urban south shows little evidence of pre-nineteenth century planning. In both areas, the Roman occupation was essentially military, the only true town being Caerwent, between Chepstow and Newport, Elsewhere, at Brecon, Caersws and Carmarthen, for example, only isolated forts were established.

The invading Normans came via the Glamorgan coastal belt, the Talgarth Gap and the Severn Valley, and established castles at strategic points, such as Brecon, Cardiff and Pembroke. Later settlement resulted in town plantation with development based on preconceived plans. Aberystwyth, Rhayader, Lampeter and New Radnor came into being in this way. But what is now popularly regarded as South Wales came into existence in the nineteenth century, when a number of industrial settlements grew rapidly. The population of Merthyr, the first industrial town, grew from 7,700 in 1801 to 49,794 in 1861, but the market towns of mid-Wales did not expand in this way. Welshpool, Llandovery, Newtown, for instance, grew relatively slowly, serving agricultural hinterlands of scattered population.

From the very beginning of the Industrial Revolution there were examples of planned urban development. One of the earliest was Morriston, dating from 1811. Now part of the City of Swansea, it provided accommodation for employees in the local collieries and copper works. In mid-Wales, Aberaeron was a unique attempt at development in the grand manner with formal terraces and a square.

Apart from this isolated venture into the Renaissance, however, planned development in the nineteenth century tended to take the form of model villages of terraced houses built by the coal and iron masters in the valleys of the south, as at Butetown in the Ryhmni Valley and at Pentre-bach near Merthyr. Later attempts to improve the living conditions of industrial workers inspired a number of small garden suburbs. One of the biggest of the garden villages is at Rhiwbina in Cardiff, where nearly 200 houses were built between 1912 and 1923.

These low density estates were, as in England, a reaction to the congested and inferior conditions which were typical of so much of the industrial housing of the nineteenth century. As the industries which gave rise to the low standard housing declined, an appreciation of the need for a more comprehensive planning approach developed. Since the 1920s, because of the continued decline of its basic industries, South Wales has been the subject of several regional plans and studies. Various strategic plans have been prepared and individual local authorities have attempted to improve commercial and employment opportunities independently.

Rural mid-Wales, too, has had its share of problems, in particular, depopulation. Planning authorities are trying to attract new industry to the country towns and larger villages, to stimulate small-scale urban growth in selected centres, to develop recreation and tourism, and to improve communications. With the encouragement and support of central government, over 100 factories are being built between 1957 and 1977, providing about 3,500 jobs. The public image is of an underdeveloped agricultural area: in fact, three people now work in manufacturing industry for every one in agriculture.

To rationalise the settlement pattern, a mid-Wales Development Corporation was established in 1966 to expand the population of Newtown to 11,000 by 1980, thus doubling its size. Industry has been attracted there, and a recent study has shown a healthy pattern of immigration with a satisfactory social balance. Smaller scale expansion is taking place at Aberystwyth, Rhayader, Llandrindod Wells, Brecon, Bala and Welshpool.

Tourism and recreation play a vital role in the Welsh economy but there is a basic need to preserve and enhance the natural resources upon which the industry is based. In many instances, these resources have not yet been effectively developed. They include the Cambrian mountains, the uplands of Radnorshire, the reservoirs of the Elan and Claerwen valleys, together with large afforested areas. Unfortunately, tourist development is frequently a source of conflict and a recent proposal to designate 500 square miles of the Cambrian mountains as a national park was not proceeded with because of the strong objections from the farming community and other vested interests.

On the other hand, the Forestry Commission has made a positive contribution in the area by creating picnic sites, caravan parks, nature reserves and making accessible several hundred miles of forest roads. The water and planning authorities are considering the potential of the Elan and Claerwen valleys for recreational development.

The obvious advantage of national park designation is that scarce resources can be properly managed. In established national parks — the Brecon Beacons and the Pembrokeshire Coast — provision is made for the holidaymaker by creating caravan and camping sites, picnic sites and nature trails. In the Brecon Beacons, a mountain centre has been built which caters for educational and leisure activities, and along the Pembrokeshire coast one of the few long distance footpaths in Britain has been created.

One of the difficulties still facing both mid-Wales and South

Wales is the paucity of modern communications. An improved
road network is being built that includes wider carriageways
and by-passes. This will facilitate cross-country journeys,
particularly in mid-Wales, and will help to revitalise the area.
Wales, as a whole, is still only just penetrated by national
strategic routes. The M50 and an improved A449 connect
the Valleys, Cardiff, and Newport with the West Midlands, but
the M4 still does not extend beyond Cardiff. A route to Swansea
is now agreed but until it is constructed Wales's second city will
remain relatively isolated. With the possibility of exploitation of
oil in the Celtic Sea, and the continued expansion and potential
of Milford Haven, it is imperative that there should be an
improvement of the road system into West South Wales.

The commercial centres of Cardiff, Newport and Swansea, are
all the subjects of large-scale redevelopment schemes. Swansea,
with forty-three acres of its centre, was devastated in 1941
and redeveloped in the early 1950s. This reconstruction did not
separate pedestrians from traffic, but recent plans to extend the
shopping centre into the Quadrant make full provision for the
pedestrian. The central area plan for Newport provides for a
system of interconnected pedestrian ways and provides for the
complete exclusion of vehicles from pedestrian precincts, with
a primary distributor road surrounding 7,000 car parking spaces,
new shops and entertainment facilities. Cardiff's central area
proposals have now been approved and provide for an increase in
shopping floor space by 1981, with new car parks, offices and
public buildings.

Throughout South Wales, General Improvement Areas are being
designated so that large numbers of nineteenth century houses in
declining areas will have another thirty years or so of active life.
A successful example is the pilot scheme implemented by the
Welsh Office at Francis Street in Caerphilly. Local authorities
continue to provide new housing, but there has been a reaction
against the high rise blocks of flats of a few years ago. One of the
more interesting developments is the new neighbourhood unit
at Llanedeyrn on the outskirts of Cardiff. Some three and a half
thousand dwellings are being built by private and public
enterprise according to an overall plan prepared by the City
Planning Department.

The search for an overall solution to urban growth still
continues and Cwmbran remains the only new town in South
Wales. The proposal to locate the University of Wales Institute
of Science and Technology there will inevitably add to its growth
potential. Situated only five miles from the centre of Newport
and built to help to revitalise the mining industry and rationalise
employment in the area, Cwmbran has developed a dormitory
function with considerable journey-to-work commuter problems.

Wales has been described 'as a country where failure
constitutes an art form'. Certainly, to its continuing economic
problems, can be added the failure to gain acceptance of a
number of recent planning proposals. Paradoxically, perhaps,
these failures represent the success of a new ingredient in the

planning process. Community involvement has undoubtedly had a significant part to play in these decisions. However, despite such setbacks, the increasing effectiveness of planning action reinforced by various forms of government assistance has resulted in greater confidence and certainly in South Wales.

Tom Hughes and Richard Mordey

The Roman amphitheatre at Caerleon.
B.T.A.

Caerleon Roman Fort and Caerwent WS 1/1
OS Sheet 171   GR ST 3490 (Caerleon)
                   ST 4790 (Caerwent)

Caerleon was the military headquarters of the Roman Second Augustan Legion from A.D. 80, and Caerwent, nine miles east, was the accompanying civilian city. The legionary fortress covered fifty acres and included an amphitheatre, now fully excavated. Remains of other buildings can also be seen. Caerwent, the only Roman walled civilian town in Wales, has also been substantially explored and the walls and gates can be seen. First the fort and then the town were built to subdue and civilise the Silures, the local tribe, and Caerwent replaced their earlier hill fort capital. Both sites were abandoned in the fifth century.

Chepstow WS 1/2
OS Sheet 162   GR ST 5393

Chepstow originated in the Middle Ages as a fortress border town guarding the old Roman road leading to South Wales. England and Wales were separate countries until after 1300, and the border, like that with Scotland, was subject to raids and minor warfare. The castle was built in 1067, and the town walls date from the thirteenth century, with the impressive gate house dating from 1524. The walls and castle are now in a ruined condition, but the gatehouse is maintained as a museum.

Sunken water gardens in the shopping centre of Cwmbran New Town.
Cwmbran Development Corporation.

Cwmbran WS 1/3
OS Sheet 171   GR ST 2995

An early (1949) new town, located to act as a growth point in an area of high unemployment and physical obsolescence. The site enclosed a number of small industrial villages. The town centre is traffic free, with associated car parking; there are some well designed housing developments and the town is well landscaped in a fine setting beneath the surrounding hills. Additional growth will undoubtedly be encouraged by the decision to establish there the University of Wales Institute of Science and Technology.

Cwmcarn Scenic Forest Drive, NW of Newport   WS 1/4
OS Sheet 171   GR ST 2293

The original site of a colliery and working forest roads, Cwmcarn
Scenic Drive illustrates current imaginative use of such redundant
areas for recreation, and the widening interests of the Forestry
Commission who own and manage the area. The Drive enables
car borne visitors to enjoy magnificent forest scenery, and the
area contains viewpoints, picnic areas, play areas and way
marked walks.

Severn Bridge   WS 1/5
OS Sheet 172   GR ST 5590

One of the great trio of modern British road bridges (see Forth
and Humber Bridges), the Severn Bridge was opened in 1966 and
designed to improve road communications between South Wales
and England. A journey of fifty-five miles or a ferry crossing was
saved. The impact on the economy of south east Wales has been
considerable and the bridge has helped to bring new life to this
previously depressed area. The subsequent opening of the M4
has completed the modern road link between London, Bristol
and South Wales.

Blaenavon Ironworks, Pontypool   WS 2/1
OS Sheet 161   GR SO 2409

The iron smelting industry of the South Wales valleys based on
locally mined ore dates from the beginnings of the Industrial
Revolution. A good example of one of the early ironworks (1789)
and associated workers' housing, can be seen at Blaenavon, north
of Pontypool. The ruined works, which are being restored as an
industrial museum, consist of furnaces, cast house, balance pit
and houses (Stock Square).

Ebbw Vale.
Aerofilms.

Ebbw Vale Steelworks WS 2/2
OS Sheet 161   GR SO 1708

Ebbw Vale has been a main coal mining and iron/steel producing
area since the nineteenth century. During the 1930s
unemployment was extremely high and in 1938 the steelworks
were built to help provide jobs and stimulate new investment.
It was the first hot strip mill in Europe and, in 1947, the first
electrolytic tinning line outside the USA was established there.
The works are two and a half miles long and constitute one of the
most spectacular industrial sights in Britain.

ICI Chemical Works, Pontypool WS 2/3
OS Sheet 171   GR SO 3002

An early postwar (1948) development designed to bring
employment to a previously depressed area, the Imperial
Chemical Industries' plant was the first in Britain to produce
nylon yarn commercially. The design and layout of the works
is good and the industrial buildings are set in twenty acres of
landscaped gardens which are open to the public one Sunday in
July every year.

I.C.I.'s nylon works at
Pontypool.
I.C.I. Fibres.

Tredegar, Mining Town WS 2/4
OS Sheet 161   GR SO 1409 (Tredegar)
              SO 1403 (New Tredegar)

The South Wales coal mining industry produced its planned
new towns, as well as its organic ribbon development, along the
valleys. Tredegar was built in the mid-nineteenth century to
serve the local iron and coal interests. It is laid out on a grid iron
pattern with a central 'circus' complete with town clock. During
the last quarter of the nineteenth century an area of new colliery
housing was built at New Tredegar. The whole area is now subject
to housing improvement and land reclamation.

Caerphilly WS 3/1
OS Sheet 171   GR ST 1587

Caerphilly grew up round its castle, founded in 1271 and with a
very advanced design. The castle, which has the largest outer

bailey in Europe as well as many other interesting features, has been partly restored. Caerphilly has recently become famous for its new shopping hypermarket, with a floor space of 110,000 square feet and 980 car parking spaces. This is interesting as one of the main new shopping trends is towards car based, out-of-town centres such as Caerphilly, although generally such centres have been resisted by local authorities seeking to protect existing shopping areas from competition, and to protect the countryside from such radical intrusions.

Caerphilly Castle.
*Mid Glamorgan
County Planning
Officer.*

Cardiff   WS 3/2
OS Sheet 171   GR ST 1877

Although Roman in origin, Cardiff dates primarily from the building of the Castle in 1081-93. The town was laid out on a grid plan which can still be traced, and the castle and part of the walls survive. Modern Cardiff dates from the opening of Bute West Dock in 1839, after which the city expanded rapidly. In 1875 a new commercial centre was established at Butetown, one and a half miles south of the historic centre, to capitalise on the boom in coal exports. Much of the original development survives, for example, Mount Stuart Square, although showing signs of decay. As in other cities, parks were established to act as 'lungs', for example, Reath Park, presented to the city in 1887 by the Marquess of Bute. The city's prosperity at this time is illustrated by the imposing houses of Cathedral Road. Later, the commercial centre returned to its present position, beginning with the building of the Civic Centre complex from 1900 onwards. In 1922 the attractive old village of Llandaff, with its Norman cathedral, became part of Cardiff. More recent modern redevelopments include the BBC Centre (Llantrisant Road), opened in 1966, and the National Sports Centre (Sophia Gardens) opened in 1972, which is a modern multipurpose sports and recreation centre.

The Civic Centre of Cardiff, seen from the Castle keep.
B.T.A.

Tip heaps and land dereliction as a result of coal mining at Gilfach Goch.
Mid Glamorgan County Planning Officer.

Gilfach Goch   WS 3/3
OS Sheet 170   GR SS 9889

This part of South Wales was until recently a major coal mining area and was ruthlessly exploited, resulting in much derelict land and slum housing. The area is now being improved — housing is being rehabilitated, and derelict land reclaimed, partly as a country park (the scheme won the Prince of Wales Award for Reclamation in 1973). Up to 1973 reclamation has cost £253,000, covers 86 acres and has included the planting of 26,000 trees. Gilfach Goch was the setting for Llewellyn's documentary novel *How Green was my Valley* which exposed the physical and social effects of coal exploitation.

Gilfach Goch after the regrading of tip heaps and extensive tree planting.
Mid Glamorgan County Planning Officer.

Llantrisant   WS 3/4
OS Sheet 170   GR ST 0483

Llantrisant marks the norther limit of the vale of Glamorgan and developed from about 1250 as a typical Welsh hill town and castle. Recently it has become famous as the site of the new Royal Mint, moved from the City of London in the mid-1960s as part of the Government's decentralisation of offices policy. The present works at Llantrisant provides badly needed employment in a relatively depressed area.

Welsh National Folk Museum, St Fagans   WS 3/5
OS Sheet 171   GR ST 1277

The original buildings at St Fagans date from 1730, although a thirteenth century castle was previously on the site. The Museum contains examples of Welsh building, such as a sixteenth century barn and an eighteenth century woollen mill, which have been brought from other areas of the country and re-erected. It also

183

contains costumes, cultural exhibits and other items reflecting the history of the Welsh people.

The Gower Peninsula WS 4/1
OS Sheet 159   GR SS 5894

Perhaps the most unspoilt and attractive part of South Wales, close to the industrial area of Swansea and mid-Glamorgan, and just across the bay from the steel works at Port Talbot. The Gower Peninsula is used primarily for agriculture, but has a very important function as a holiday and recreation area. A balance has to be found between those two competing uses. Gower is especially important as it was the first Area of Outstanding Natural Beauty to be designated under the 1949 National Parks Act.

Three Cliffs Bay and Pennards Pill, on the Gower Peninsula. *South Glamorgan County Planning Officer.*

Lower Swansea Valley Reclamation Scheme WS 4/2
OS Sheet 159   GR SS 6796

The Lower Swansea Valley was an important copper smelting and later, steel making, centre from 1717 to the 1950s which resulted in 60 per cent of the valley becoming derelict by 1961. It was then probably the United Kingdom's largest contiguous area of industrial dereliction. Initiated in 1967, reclamation schemes have attempted to restore this land to useful life: afforestation and flood prevention measures have been carried out and the environment of the area is gradually being improved. Most of the work has been undertaken by Swansea Council who, in 1973, owned 995 acres and had spent £679,000 on seven reclamation projects, including the former White Rock copper works which is now mainly amenity open space.

Milford Haven Oil Port WS 4/3
OS Sheet 157   GR SM 9305 (Waterston)

Until recent years, Milford Haven was a small port and fishing village. Because of its magnificent deep water harbour, it was chosen to be a major oil terminal and a great deal of development has taken place over the last decade. The modern harbour takes tankers of up to 250,000 tons and Milford Haven is now one of the most important oil ports in Britain. But this expansion has had a significant cost in environmental terms — oil refineries, small villages and scenic coastlines make uneasy neighbours.

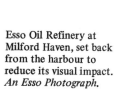

Esso Oil Refinery at Milford Haven, set back from the harbour to reduce its visual impact. *An Esso Photograph.*

184

Pembrokeshire Coast National Park WS 4/4
OS Sheet 157   GR SM 8612 (Broadhaven)

The Pembrokeshire Coast National Park is the smallest of the ten
national parks in England and Wales, covering 225 square miles.
Its coastal scenery is as beautiful and impressive as any in Europe.
To encourage visitors to appreciate it, the Pembrokeshire
Countryside Unit provides guided walks through the park and
study information facilities at Broadhaven. A fare paying bus
service which links car parks along the coastal footpath is being
provided on an experimental basis until 1975. The aim is to
encourage greater use of the path by walkers, to distribute use
along a greater length of the path and to ease congestion from car
parking in narrow roads. The deep sheltered water of Milford
Haven is now dominated by oil terminals and refineries but the
national park committee have restricted development to the
central portion and persuaded the oil companies to take great
pains with landscaping.

Margam Steelworks on
the coast at Port Talbot.
*West Glamorgan
County Planning
Officer.*

Margam Steelworks, Port Talbot WS 4/5
OS Sheet 170   GR SS 7887

Britain's biggest steelworks and an impressive industrial complex,
the Margam and Abbey works contain three and a half miles of
blast furnaces and rolling mills. A large tidal harbour has recently
been built for ships carrying ore to the works. The steelworks are
owned by the British Steel Corporation, which organises guided
tours round the complex.

Swansea City Centre Redevelopment WS 4/6
OS Sheet 159   GR SS 6593

Swansea, like many British industrial cities, suffered heavy bomb
damage during the Second World War and was faced with a large
rebuilding programme. Some cities like Coventry were rebuilt to
imaginative and progressive plans which separated traffic and

pedestrians, whereas most perpetuated the old pattern of shopping streets that were also main traffic routes. Swansea was one of the latter group, and its central area redevelopment (1949-56) is characterised by wide streets and a regular layout. Now, twenty years later, as in many other cities, the council is adopting a 'Coventry' solution and has closed some of the main shopping streets to traffic.

Oxford Street, Swansea, 21st February 1941. *Swansea City Planning Officer.*

Aberaeron WS 5/1
OS Sheet 146   GR SN 4663

A new town – or more exactly 'new port' – planned and developed from 1807 by the Reverend Alban Thomas Jones Gwynne, who recognised the potential of the site for commerce. The town became the exporting port and shipbuilding centre for the area around Cardigan Bay, but the improved land communications which followed the development of the railways prevented its further expansion. The town today still reflects the original design concept and survives as a pleasant resort and small fishing port.

Oxford Street, Swansea, after reconstruction. *Swansea City Planning Officer.*

Aberaeron Harbour. *Ron and Phil Davies.*

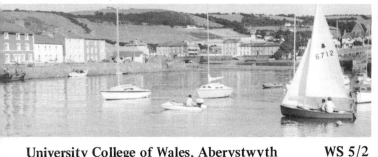

University College of Wales, Aberystwyth WS 5/2
OS Sheet 135   GR SN 5881

The University College of Wales was established in the 1860s by public subscriptions collected throughout Wales. It was a symbol of the growing national pride of the Welsh after centuries of neglect. The first college building was originally designed as a hotel, but was converted and opened in 1872 as a 'College by the Sea'. It dominates the seafront at Aberystwyth and has a coloured mosaic on its south western wall. The University buildings are now spread throughout the town and tours can be arranged.

Llyn Clywedog WS 5/3
OS Sheet 136   GR SN 9088

In contrast to the reservoirs of the Elan Valley, Llyn Clywedog, completed in 1967, does not provide direct supply of water but regulates the flow in the River Severn. Discharge in dry weather

186

Clywedog reservoir and
dam controlling the
flow of the River
Severn.
*Clywedog Reservoir
Joint Authority.*

Cors Tregaron National
Nature Reserve.
Ron and Phil Davies.

Craig Goch reservoir
and dam. Part of the
Elan Valley scheme
to supply Birmingham
with water.
B.T.A.

ensures water supply for downstream abstraction (e.g. for
Birmingham) while storage in wet weather prevents downstream
flooding. Reduced need for purity at the reservoir permits
extensive agricultural and recreational use of the water and
catchment area. Fifteen miles of new and improved roads, picnic
sites, car parks, footpaths and a viewing area.

Cors Tregaron WS 5/4
OS Sheet 146   GR SN 6761

To the north of Tregaron lie the 1,842 acres of Cors Tregaron,
one of the best actively growing raised peat bogs in England and
Wales. As at Wicken Fen (q.v.) the natural features and the plant
and animal life they support can only be preserved through
intensive management practice. The Nature Conservancy Council
controls access to this national nature reserve by issuing permits.
Drainage, clearance and cultivation are prevented by agreement
with the land owners.

Elan Valley, near Rhayader WS 5/5
OS Sheet 147   GR SN 9164 (Garreg Ddu bridge)

The Elan Valley has been transformed since 1892 from an area of
bare sheep walks into a series of reservoirs and impounding dams
to provide water for Birmingham. Unlike the water from the
Clywedog reservoir, the Elan Valley water is supplied direct by a
73½ mile pipeline and therefore retains its purity. The wooded
valley sides, planted as part of the overall scheme, the 1,491 acres
of reservoirs and the dams themselves attract numbers of tourists,
bringing life and financial benefits to the nearby town of Rhayader.

Llandrindod Wells WS 5/6
OS Sheet 147   GR SO 0661

The fashion for spas was common to both Wales and England, and
Llandrindod Wells is the largest of the Welsh Spas. The town
reached the height of its popularity in the late nineteenth century,
later than most spas, and contains many late Victorian buildings
and parks. It is now an administrative centre, but is still popular
with tourists and for conferences.

New Radnor WS 5/7
OS Sheet 148   GR SO 2160

The 'new town' of Old Radnor was established in about 1100,
but never grew beyond village size. New Radnor was established
around 1250, approximately two and a half miles west of the

Llandrindod Wells.
*Building Design
Partnership.*

old town, which then decayed. The town did not prosper either, and by the seventeenth century there were many empty plots within the walls. The remains of the town wall can still be seen in the fields to the south and west of the village, and the castle mound is visible. New Radnor demonstrates that not all medieval new town plantations were successful.

Newtown   WS 5/8
OS Sheet 136   GR SO 1191

The size of Newtown and its scale of expansion makes it unique amongst the new towns of Britain. From an initial population of 5,500 in 1968 it is expected to double by the 1980s. The Government saw this expansion as the answer to depopulation in mid-Wales by concentrating growth into fewer and larger settlements so that more varied employment and social opportunities can be provided. Certainly the wide range of industries and housing to be found in Newtown is untypical of comparable Welsh towns and would not have occurred without such extensive government aid.

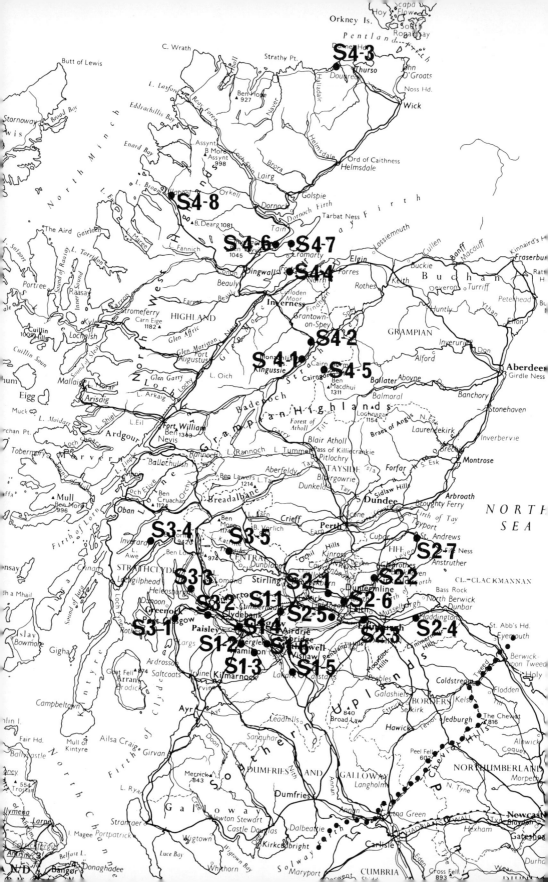

Scotland

The landmarks of Scottish planning are legacies and reflections of the highland topography of the country and the strains and surges in Scotland's social and economic history: the settlement of the Highlands in the eighteenth century; the first 'overspill' from the late medieval towns incorporated in eighteenth century Edinburgh and nineteenth century Glasgow; the twentieth century overspill from the congested tenements of the Industrial Revolution, and the current initiatives to counter the economic difficulties of the underdeveloped areas of West Central Scotland and the Highlands.

Before the year 1000, Scotland was occupied by five separate peoples, descendants of the Picts, Angles, Scots, Britons and Norwegians who had invaded in previous centuries, some three thousand years after the settlement of Skara Brae in Orkney. In the five hundred years from the mid-eleventh to the mid-sixteenth century, the separate peoples were merged into a recognisable nation by four forces: Malcolm Canmore's assumption of the monarchy of Scotland, his federalisation of the old Kingdom of Strathclyde, the Episcopalian colonisation of Scotland under the shadow of the great cathedral at St Andrews and the foundations of burghs, or towns, on the English model in the twelfth and thirteenth centuries.

The burghs developed in a landscape which lacked villages, except in the south east of the country. Many burghs grew in the primarily rural economy of the sixteenth and seventeenth centuries, but there were few sizeable towns. The small burghs associated with farming or in the pocket of a noble landowner — as Inveraray was in the keeping of the Duke of Argyll — were characteristic of Scotland until industrial communities, based upon the fuel sources of the Industrial Revolution, emerged in the coal and salt towns of the Forth valley. Culross, for example, sprang from the mining of coal, but its now pleasant environment is in direct contrast with the nineteenth century pit villages and towns on the coalfield of central Fife.

In 1786, the British Fisheries Society moved to set up three fishing stations at Ullapool, Tobermory and Lochbay in Skye, but the piers and storehouses did not attract sufficient settlers to occupy all the plots. By this time the Industrial Revolution had already taken root in the Lowlands and, with the rise of the cotton industry after the American War of Independence, blossomed fully and shifted the emphasis of trade from the Forth to the Clyde and Glasgow.

The first distinguished landmark of the parallel Urban Revolution came with the founding of the New Town in Edinburgh in 1767. The New Town was at first regarded as being too English but, as the old town became too overcrowded and socially embarrassing for the times, the well-to-do spilled beyond its tenement cliffs, which had reached fourteen storeys in height in places, into the dignified squares and terraces which were laid out north of the old town. The Urban Revolution reversed the reputations of Edinburgh and Glasgow. Glasgow had previously been one of the most stately and handsome cities of Britain, whose elegance contrasted with the overcrowded insanitariness of Edinburgh. Glasgow built its own new towns at Blythswood in the 1820s and at Park Circus in the 1850s, but the colonisation of the south side of the city was prevented by the overwhelming spread of the Gorbals slums which were already obvious in the early nineteenth century.

The prosperity of the Industrial Revolution was based on the cotton industry and David Dale founded the first great cotton mills in Scotland at New Lanark in 1786. Helensburgh had been founded to attract stocking, linen and wool weavers but, with the advent of cotton, the plan for the town was adapted to attract a more affluent population. Eaglesham kept its artisan character until the twentieth century, when it filled a new role as a commuter village which New Lanark has not emulated.

The twentieth century has seen the most powerful drive to make new communities in Scotland. East Kilbride was the first new town — one of four in an orbit round Glasgow proposed in the Clyde Valley Plan of 1946 as a means of relieving the congestion of the unfit, overcrowded Victorian sandstone tenements of Glasgow and North Lanarkshire. It was established against Glasgow's objections and, not until several years after the Corporation had come to accept the impracticability of their City Engineer's extraordinary plan to retain the city's population within its boundaries, was a second new town for Glasgow established at Cumbernauld in 1956. By this time, architectural taste had moved from garden cities to fortified urbanism. Although Glasgow's population reached a peak of 1,100,000 in 1947, evacuation of the most crowded central parts of the city was already under way in the 1930s. In seventeen of the central wards of the city, a population of 580,000 in 1931 had fallen to 223,000 in 1971. Although scarcely half as many families as expected moved from Glasgow to the new towns and other sponsored overspill schemes in the 1960s, three times as many families moved away from the city of their own accord. By 1973, the city's total population had fallen to 850,000, and although an end to overspill might be reached by 1981, it could leave Glasgow with fewer than 700,000 people.

Whether the city and the Government could meet the cost and provide the effort to create a fit environment for even this much reduced population was a question which was becoming more urgent in the early 1970s. The Corporation's 1973 estimate of the cost of improving the residential environment of 'Areas in Need' in the city was £94 million. The cost of £1/3 million for improving 400 yards of riverside at Custom House Quay was a measure both of the potential and problem of the banks of the

Upper Clyde, abandoned now by both shipbuilders and steamer services as shipyards and port facilities have moved downriver in search of deeper water.

By the late 1960s, the Scottish Office was finding its policy of fostering 'growth areas' was not sufficiently developed to offset worsening economic conditions. The slow growth of population in West Central Scotland which had reached a peak in 1966 turned into a decline and, by the early 1970s, confirmation of a sustained decline in the birth rate brought even the Registrar General to accept the possibility that the region's population was unlikely to be restored to the level of the mid-1960s for twenty years, if ever. This prospect radically altered the assumptions of sustained growth of population upon which the new towns of Livingston and Irvine had been established, subsequently to be joined by the New Community of Erskine, sponsored by Renfrew County Council. The prospects of completing the comprehensive motorway network for the Greater Glasgow area — of which the main artery across the conurbation will be completed by the mid-1970s — were also being reduced by the decline of population.

An essential issue to be proved in the next ten years is whether the new towns can create economic growth which would not have arisen in Scotland in their absence, or whether they simply serve to spread growth more thinly than is economically or socially justifiable in changed circumstances. This was a question raised by the West Central Scotland Plan in 1974, which made the first comprehensive review of regional strategy since the Clyde Valley Plan over twenty-five years before.

Also in the 1960s, the Government revived its attempts of two centuries before to colonise or, at least, to resettle the Highlands. Tourism and winter sports were expanding but more significant even than the conference, tourist and winter sports centre at Aviemore was the setting up of the Highlands and Islands Development Board in 1965. The Board's most obvious mark has been on the shore of the Cromarty Firth, where the establishment of an aluminium smelter had, within a few years, been overshadowed by the important discoveries of oil in the North Sea, and by their implications for rig and platform building, for refineries and servicing bases.

In the West of Scotland, where the great programme of rehousing and overspill of Glasgow's people anticipated by the Clyde Valley Plan is now two thirds completed, only a beginning has been made to what was intended to be a parallel attack on the depressed environment in and surrounding Glasgow and the towns of North Lanarkshire. In Glasgow, particularly, the attack is being mounted on the residential environment, both of areas of solid tenements and of some of the great peripheral housing estates built around the city since the Clyde Valley Plan was published. The Strathclyde Park in the valley of the Clyde between Hamilton and Motherwell had been held back for twenty-five years until started in 1973, delayed by the overwhelming emphasis on rehousing which has brought the proportion of publicly rented housing in the West of Scotland up to 60 per cent of all housing, some twice the British average and a marked influence on the Scottish urban landscape.

Urlan Wannop

Cumbernauld town centre crowning the hill-top above terraced housing in the Carbrain area. *Cumbernauld Development Corporation.*

Cumbernauld   S 1/1
OS Sheet 64   GR NS 7674

Unlike the earlier new towns Cumbernauld, which was commenced in 1955, was designed on the principle of maximum private car ownership and easy access for all inhabitants to the town centre. The town is, therefore, built to a higher density with very extensive footpath systems. The town centre straddles the main dual carriageway road with servicing, car and bus parking at ground level and shops, offices and flats above. The inflexibility of the original plan and its dominant hill top location make it unique as a 'second generation' new town, while its interesting architectural features have won it numerous awards. The Seafar housing area, for example, incorporates a very high standard of landscaping and the houses are very 'human' in scale and design. Many of the churches in the town reflect the architectural ingenuity which made Cumbernauld an international showplace.

Eaglesham   S 1/2
OS Sheet 64   GR NS 5752

Scotland lacks the village tradition so evident in England. Most Scottish villages were consciously developed in response to a particular need. Eaglesham was developed between 1769 and 1797 for the spinning and weaving of cotton. Thread was produced in the mill for hand loom weaving and therefore represents a transition between cottage and factory production. The village has now lost its industrial function but many original

Weavers cottages facing
across the common at
Eaglesham.
*Renfrewshire County
Planning Officer.*

buildings and the plan form — two diverging roads with buildings
facing across the triangular Common — remain. The survival of
Eaglesham's attractive environment has been assured by its
colonisation as a commuter village.

East Kilbride   S 1/3
OS Sheet 64   GR NS 6354

Like Stevenage, East Kilbride, Scotland's first new town, is now
nearing maturity. Originally proposed as one of four new towns
to absorb the population and industry which would inevitably be
displaced by redevelopment in Glasgow, its growth since 1948 has
made it a regional growth point in its own right. Changing ideas
on shopping centres in the 1960s resulted in the conversion of
a dual carriageway road into the pedestrian precinct of today.

Princes Street, East
Kilbride. Part of the
town centre of
Scotland's first new
town.
B.T.A.

Glasgow   S 1/4
OS Sheet 64   GR NS 5964

Founded in A.D. 543, Glasgow remained a relatively small
university and cathedral town until the seventeenth century,
when it developed as a port. Great expansion occurred in the
nineteenth century, and it is now essentially a Victorian city.
The Victorian development contained some very distinguished
examples of urban design such as Park Circus (*c* 1850),
designated in 1971 as the city's first Conservation Area. But it

194

The redeveloped
Hutcheson Gorbals,
Glasgow.
*Director of Planning,
Glasgow Corporation.*

also contained some of the worst slums in Britain, for example,
the infamous Gorbals, a tenement area close to the city centre.
Most of the tenements have now been redeveloped, the first such
area south of the city centre having recently been completed
to designs by leading architects Sir Robert Matthew and Sir
Basil Spence. Glasgow is also constructing one of the most
comprehensive urban motorway networks in Britain made possible
by the comprehensive redevelopment of the large slum areas of
the inner city. The eight lane Kingston Bridge over the River
Clyde was opened in 1970. The obsolete sheds and warehouses
of Custom House Quay in the old port of Glasgow have been
replaced by a new complex of public parks and promenades.
Glasgow is a city with a great architectural heritage — perhaps
the best Victorian city in Britain — but is also trying to establish
a dynamic modern image through office, residential and
motorway redevelopment.

New Lanark. Robert
Owen's school of 1817
(left), 'The New
Institution for the
Formation of Character'
(1816) and housing
built in 1792 and 1798.
*Lanarkshire County
Planning Officer.*

New Lanark   S 1/5
OS Sheet 72   GR NS 8843

The most famous of industrial model communities, and the
inspiration of all such later developments, New Lanark was
founded by David Dale in 1784. He built both cotton mills and

village and, to attract workers, he offered low rents and other amenities. In 1799 he was joined by his son in law, Robert Owen, who ran the mills for twenty-five years. Owen proved that efficiency in business and concern for employees were not incompatible, for he not only built a school, bakery, cooperative store, workers' institute and houses of a high standard for the time, but also increased the firm's profits considerably. In later years, the village declined, the mills closed in 1967 and the buildings decayed. Current proposals are for a scheme of improvement and conservation to be carried out so that this unique monument can be given a new and useful lease of life.

Strathclyde Regional Park S 1/6

OS Sheet 64   GR NS 7357

The mining dereliction between Hamilton and Motherwell inspired ambitious postwar proposals for land reclamation for recreational use. With Government help, the 1,600 acre Strathclyde Regional Park, comprising a sport and country park, is now under construction. The River Clyde has been diverted, and low lying land is being excavated to form a loch of Olympic rowing proportions (see Holme Pierrepont). The Park will eventually include recreation and leisure facilities and a 335 acre bird sanctuary. It will also offer a much more pleasant entry to industrial Lanarkshire for travellers on the M74 motorway.

Diverting the River Clyde during the construction of the Strathclyde Regional Park.
Lanarkshire County Planning Officer.

Culross S 2/1

OS Sheet 65   GR NS 8598

Although Roman in origin, Culross was primarily developed in the early seventeenth century to serve Sir George Bruce's industrial enterprises of salt panning, coal mining, fishing and weaving. His 'palace' forms one of the two foci of the town, the other being the thirteenth century abbey. Culross is therefore a very early example of a 'company town' of a kind later to become common in the eighteenth and nineteenth centuries. Many original houses survive and some have been recently restored.

Culross on the northern shore of the Firth of Forth.
B.T.A.

Restored cottages and
alley way (Hie Gait)
at Dysart.
*National Trust for
Scotland.*

Dysart

S 2/2

OS Sheet 59   GR NT 3093

The south coast of Fife contains a number of small fishing ports
whose character has remained intact despite the changing
fortunes of the fishing industry. To preserve this character the
National Trust for Scotland has encouraged the rehabilitation of
housing by creating a revolving fund which enables houses to
be bought, rehabilitated and sold; the profit being reinvested
in other properties. In 1967, a scheme was initiated at Dysart by
the Crown Estate Commissioners and Kirkcaldy Council.
A picturesque group of old fishermen's cottages and other historic
buildings have been improved and a new terrace of houses built
on a site which had stood derelict for some years.

Edinburgh

S 2/3

OS Sheet 66   GR MT 2673   (Old Town)
                      MT 2574   (New Town)

Edinburgh, the ancient capital of Scotland, was granted its charter
in the twelfth century. The first castle was built in the seventh
century but the existing buildings date from the thirteenth to
fifteenth centuries. The other focus of the old town was the
Abbey of Holyrood and the town grew up as a linear formation
between the two. Much of this development, based on a series
of courts and closes with a wide variety of building types, can
still be seen, and some of it has recently been restored. The threat
of invasion by the English prevented Edinburgh developing beyond
its walls until the eighteenth century, when the Nor' Loch was
drained and the New Town laid out. Founded in 1766, this was
one of the largest and most complete areas of Georgian planning
in Europe. James Craig devised the plan of squares and broad
thoroughfares, to a basic grid pattern. He also created the Princes
Street Gardens. Work in the New Town continued throughout the
nineteenth century, although some of the later work is less
distinguished than Craig would have wished. Of interest are the
Outlook Tower and Ramsay Gardens, the work of Sir Patrick
Geddes, one of the founders of modern British town planning.

Squares, crescents and
circuses of the 18th
century New Town,
Edinburgh.
Aerofilms.

Haddington town centre, showing the continuous Georgian facade of the High Street fronting onto the triangular market place, now much encroached by buildings. *Aerofilms.*

Haddington   S 2/4
OS Sheet 66   GR MT 5173

Haddington was originally developed as a market centre in the twelfth century to a long narrow triangular plan, which can still be seen in the lines of High St, Market St and Hardgate. There was much further development, especially in the eighteenth century, so that the town now possesses one of the finest Georgian small town centres in Scotland. It is a good example of growth and conservation going hand in hand. The population increased from 4,518 in 1951, to 7,787 in 1971, largely as a result of an overspill agreement with Glasgow. This growth has enabled some sixty of the town's 129 historic buildings to be restored and now the future of only ten is in doubt.

Livingston New Town   S 2/5
OS Sheet 65   GR NT 0668

Informal housing groups at Craigshill, Livingston New Town. *Livingston Development Corporation.*

The fourth new town in Scotland (designated 1962), designed to relieve congestion in overcrowded Glasgow and create a new industrial focus in central Scotland, Livingston has a target population of 100,000. The town is developed on a linear strip basis along the axis of the town centre. The road network allows for 100 per cent car ownership, with the maximum amount of pedestrian segregation. The design of housing areas attempts to offset some of the less attractive results of a high level of car usage.

Forth Bridges   S 2/6
OS Sheet 65   GR MT 1278 (South Queensferry)

For centuries, the Firth of Forth constituted a formidable barrier to travel between Edinburgh and Fife. Ferries were established early (at Queensferry) but, in 1851, a 'floating railway' enabled trains to be loaded on to large flat steamers for the crossing. This

198

was followed by the present cantilever railway bridge, opened
in 1890, which was a gigantic engineering achievement for the
time. But road traffic continued to use the ferry until the present
road bridge was opened in 1964. This, too, is a masterpiece of
engineering — at one and a half miles in length it is the longest
suspension bridge in Britain (the Humber Bridge will be longer)
and took six years to complete. The two bridges together make an
impressive contribution to the landscape.

St Andrews S 2/7

OS Sheet 59   GR NO 5116

King David I (1124-53) initiated a national plan for the creation
of burghs and churches throughout Scotland. He established the
archbishopric at St Andrews and commissioned his 'town planner',
Mainard, to lay out the town. The result was Mainard's greatest
achievement. He set the huge cathedral on the height above the
harbour at the focus of the three gently radiating main streets.
The central street was widened in the middle to form the market
place. This unique eleventh century street plan is intact today.
Later St Andrews became the site of Scotland's first university
(1410) and the oldest known golf course (*c* fifteenth century).

Clyde-Muirsheil Regional Park   S 3/1
OS Sheet 63   GR NS 3660 (Castle Semple)

The Clyde-Muirshiel Regional Park, covering a total of
30,000 acres, is designed to provide for countryside recreation
in the Glasgow region. The park consists of several distinct
recreation areas, connected by footpaths and roads. The first
area, Muirshiel Country Park, was opened in 1970 and has been
followed by the Castle Semple Water Park and Cornalees Bridge.
Other recreation areas are planned for the future. The landscape
of the park is very varied, and includes high moorland with
magnificent views over the Clyde estuary, steep wooded gorges
and large inland lochs and reservoirs.

Shielhill Glen and the
Firth of Clyde from
above Inverkip in the
Clyde-Murshiel
Regional Park.
*Renfrewshire County
Planning Officer.*

Erskine   S 3/2
OS Sheet 64   GR NS 4771

On the south bank of the Clyde eight miles west of Glasgow,
Erskine, a 'new community', is being developed to receive
overspill population from Glasgow and provide for local
expansion and growth. The construction of the most graceful
high level Erskine Bridge across the Clyde has now put this
formerly isolated corner of Renfrewshire into a strategic position
between the Glasgow conurbation and the west of Scotland.

The Erskine Bridge
across the River Clyde.
*Renfrewshire County
Planning Officer.*

Helensburgh   S 3/3
OS Sheet 56   GR NS 3083

A Georgian new town begun in 1776, to a conventional grid iron
plan. The purpose of the town was to share in the trade of the
River Clyde, but it seems that it flourished more as a resort than
a port, although early steamship trials were made here in 1812.
The town's proximity to Glasgow meant that after the introduction
of the railway it developed as an early commuter settlement for
affluent Glasgow merchants and industrialists. Hill House, in
Upper Colquhorn St, was designed by the late nineteenth century
'arts and crafts' architect, C.R. Mackintosh, and is open to
the public.

Helensburgh has hardly
grown beyond the area
of the original town,
laid out as a regular
grid in 1776.
Aerofilms.

Inveraray, built on a
new site between 1750
and 1790 by the
Dukes of Argyll.
Aerofilms.

Inveraray   S 3/4

OS Sheet 56   GR NN 0908

The first 'new town' in Scotland, built between 1750 and 1790
by the Dukes of Argyll. The Third Duke decided in 1747 to
rebuild the existing village, which he considered to be too close
to his castle. He also wished to create a new administrative centre
for the county and a flourishing fishing port. The concept was
essentially artificial in that economic or locational considerations
were not important, the town being based on the whims and
omnipotence of its creator. The plan is cruciform, with a church
at the focus. Inveraray was extensively restored between
1958 and 1973.

The Trossachs   S 3/5

OS Sheet 57   GR NN 4907 (Loch Katrine Pier)

Romanticised by Sir Walter Scott and made accessible by the
coming of the railways to Aberfoyle and Callender, the
Trossachs became the first area of the Highlands to receive large
numbers of tourists. Improved mobility caused further
incursions into the Highlands and the present frontier of
intensive tourist development lies at Aviemore, ninety miles to
the north. However, with sensitively planted forest areas within
the Queen Elizabeth Forest Park and the development of
Lock Katrine to supply Glasgow's water, the landscape has lost
some of its rugged grandeur. But it still remains a pre-eminent
attraction for day visitors from the cities of central Scotland.

Mixed woodlands
adding variety to the
scenery in the Queen
Elizabeth Forest Park.
B.T.A.

Aviemore

OS Sheet 36   GR NH 8912

A modern holiday development (1960s) stimulated by the
Highlands and Islands Development Board in order to open up
the Cairngorms as a holiday area, the Aviemore Centre is now
complete and contains facilities for all kinds of recreation, such
as skiing, walking and pony trekking. The complex was developed
to a comprehensive plan, with hotels, theatres, ice rinks, bars and
shops set round a pedestrian plaza. The architecture is boldly
modern, based on local granite and wood materials.

The Aviemore Centre.
B.T.A.

Carrbridge, Landmark Visitor Centre   S 4/2

OS Sheet 36   GR NH 9022

The Landmark Visitor Centre at Carrbridge alongside the A9 road
between Aviemore and Inverness was the first visitor centre
established in Britain on the lines of the US National Park visitor
centres. The Landmark Centre, opened in 1970 at a cost exceeding
£150,000, provides a vivid exhibition of man's impact on the
Highlands and a complementary tape/slide show. In the
thirty-five acres surrounding the centre nature trails have been
laid out and a book stall and craft shop encourage visitors to take
away reminders of their visits.

Landmark visitor
centre, Carrbridge.
B.T.A.

Dounreay   S 4/3

OS Sheet 11   GR NC 9967

The Dounreay Experimental Reactor Establishment is situated
ten miles west of Thurso where the strict siting requirements of a
low coastal site with ample supplies of fresh water in an area of
low population density are amply met. Work began in 1955, and
two reactors are now in operational use, producing electric power
and experimenting with fast breeder reactors which produce
nuclear fuel. The 2,000 employees have brought a new community
and prosperity to Caithness, and the results of the Dounreay
experiment are proving of interest and value to social as well as
nuclear scientists.

The experimental fast
reactor at Dounreay.
U.K.A.E.A.

The star-shaped defences of Fort George, built in 1748.
Aerofilms.

Fort George   S 4/4
OS Sheet 27   GR NH 7656

Following the Jacobite rebellion of 1745 Fort George was built in 1748 to protect the narrow entry to the Moray Firth. It remains as one of the finest late artillery fortifications in Europe, built on a star pattern with water on three sides. It still houses army units but is also open for public inspection as an Ancient Monument.

Cairngorms and Glenmore   S 4/5
OS Sheet 36   GR NH 9709

The Cairngorm Mountains, south of Aviemore, have been declared one of the largest nature reserves in Europe but, with the tourist development at Aviemore, suffer great pressures from summer visitors and winter sportsmen. On the northern slopes of the Cairngorms the Forestry Commission have created the Glenmore Forest Park, with 3,300 acres of pine and spruce woods and 9,200 acres of mountainside. Camping sites and hostels, together with an outdoor training centre, have been established around the attractive Loch Marlich.

A caravan and camping site established by the Forestry Commission within Glenmore Forest Park.
J.A. McCook.

Invergordon   S 4/6
OS Sheet 21   GR NH 7270

The Aluminium Smelter at Invergordon lies not far from the oil platform yards of Nigg Bay. Aluminium smelting is not new in the Highlands, but the plant at Invergordon is particularly extensive. The factory, opened in 1971, is situated in the midst of farmland

and has been landscaped to lessen its impact on the surrounding area. A covered conveyor brings the ore from the pierhead on the Cromarty Firth. Recent industrial developments, in particular those associated with North Sea oil, have had a considerable effect on the Easter Ross area of north east Scotland.

Nigg Bay Oil Platform Fabrication Yard S 4/7
OS Sheet 21   GR NH 8072

The discovery in the 1960s of natural gas, and later oil, in the North Sea, has led to something approaching a 'gold rush' by oil companies. Since many of the oil fields are off the Scottish Coast and because the specialised topographical conditions needed are found there, much of the on-shore development is taking place in northern Scotland. One of the first yards to be opened was at Nigg Bay (1972). The 130 acre site contains the largest graving dock in Europe, with an area of 600,000 square yards, a depth of 50 feet and dock gates 400 feet wide, together with workshops and a steel rolling mill. Such large industrial developments are not universally popular as their impact on the environment of the Scottish Highlands is considerable.

The North Sea oil production platform 'Highland One' nearing completion at Nigg Bay, Spring 1974.
Ross and Cromarty County Planning Officer.

Ullapool S 4/8
OS Sheet 19   GR NH 1394

Following the abortive Highland rebellion of 1745-6, measures were taken by the government to repress and subdue the clans, with the result that the economy of the Highlands, based on small farms (crofts) declined. Efforts were made to create alternative employment, for example by the British Fisheries Society, which founded Ullapool and Tobermory in 1788 to encourage the displaced clansmen to take up fishing as a livelihood. Ullapool was comprehensively planned to a grid layout, with wide streets. The venture was successful and the town became a major herring port. Today it is also a tourist centre.

Ullapool.
Ross and Cromarty County Planning Officer.

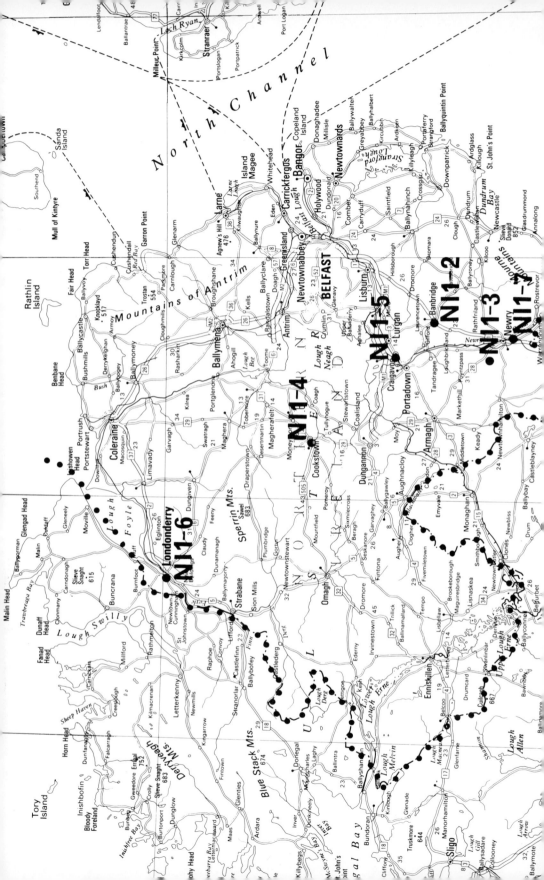

Northern Ireland

In the early seventeenth century, the Government in London promoted a scheme, known as 'The Plantation of Ulster', for the creation of twenty-three new towns in Northern Ireland and settled them with inhabitants from England and Scotland. Several of these towns continue to prosper while others have remained villages.

Londonderry, established in 1609, was the most important urban centre in the Plantation Scheme. The site for this 'new town' was chosen because of its strategic location, its practical advantages as a defensive site, and its situation on a navigable river. A planned grid of streets converging on a central square was laid out behind a defensive wall. The historical significance of Londonderry is two-fold: it was one of the last urban centres in the British Isles to be provided with a defensive wall, and it may truly be regarded as London's first 'new town'.

In the eighteenth century a number of impressive town squares and many attractive villages such as Cookstown and Banbridge were built by large landowners. During this period, the construction of the Newry Canal — one of the first designed canals in the British Isles — connected Lough Neagh with the Irish Sea. It is sad to relate that, in common with much of the canal system in the United Kingdom, the Newry Canal is now derelict.

In Victorian times, the first model industrial villages were built at Bessbrook, in County Armagh. Then came the rapid change of the industrial revolution and the development of Northern Ireland as a major centre of manufacturing industry. The recent decline in the basic industries of linen and shipbuilding has stimulated a planning policy of diversifying the industrial structure. Many new industries have come to Northern Ireland and, during the last few years, there has been considerable emphasis on the synthetic fibre industry.

The first planning legislation came with the Planning and Housing Act (Northern Ireland), 1931, which was similar to the 1932 Act in England. Permissive in nature, the Act enabled local authorities to draw up planning schemes for their areas, but it made little impact. It was not until 1944 that the development of land in Northern Ireland was brought fully under planning control. The 1944 Act was limited in scope and aimed solely at controlling development, the powers of control being vested in local planning authorities — the county councils, the two county boroughs, the boroughs and the urban district councils. But it proved impossible to prepare the statutory schemes with the staff available at that time so in the late 1940s outline advisory plans were prepared as an interim measure to guide planning authorities and prospective developers.

Air raid damage, and a general desire to see better living conditions in the postwar era, had led the Northern Ireland Government to set up two groups to advise on planning and reconstruction. Officials to the Planning Commission and local authority representatives and people from various organisations on the Planning Advisory Board studied and reported on water supply, sewerage facilities, housing, industrial location, tourism, recreational facilities and the countryside.

From the end of the war until 1960 planning did not make much headway in Northern Ireland other than in the day-to-day business of development control. But the growing congestion and sprawl of the Belfast area in the 1950s was making it increasingly obvious that the benefits of a positive planning approach could no longer be ignored.

So, in 1960, Professor Sir Robert Matthew was commissioned to prepare a Survey and Plan for the Belfast region. The publication of his report in 1962 proved to be the impetus which in a relatively short period of years put Northern Ireland firmly on the planning map. The Matthew Plan was accepted by the Government and formed the basis of a new regional policy based on the concept of concentrating growth at specific locations. New legislation was passed to provide for the preservation of the countryside, to allow for the creation of new towns, and to deal with the vexed question of planning compensation for land development. Work began on the preparation of plans for large parts of Northern Ireland, and this upsurge of interest in planning work in the 1960s was accompanied by a significant increase in the number of professional planners working for Northern Ireland planning authorities.

In 1963, work began on the preparation of the master plan for Craigavon, Northern Ireland's first new town, in County Armagh, twenty-five miles south west of Belfast. The brief was to develop a town capable of accommodating 120,000 people by 1981, with growth potential of around 180,000 by the year 2000, with the objectives of relieving congestion in Belfast, providing a new base for attracting industry, and forming a service centre contributing to the regeneration of the south and west of the region. The first ten years of the Craigavon scheme have seen an intense period of activity with substantial progress being made in housing, industry and recreation. Work has now commenced on the construction of the town centre which will include Northern Ireland's first environmentally controlled office block which will convert heat from fluorescent light fittings. At the edge of Craigavon, an artificial lake has just been completed which will provide boating, aqua sports and restaurant facilities for many of the new residents.

In the early part of this activity Northern Ireland still lacked a basic planning code similar to the 1947 Act. It was not until the whole of local government administration was put under review in 1969, in the shape of the Macrory Review Body, that the final impetus was given to the writing of comprehensive planning law. The Government of Northern Ireland accepted that all planning powers should be vested in the Ministry of Development (now the Department of Housing, Local Government and Planning) in place of some thirty-seven local planning authorities. The change in administration took place in 1973, so bringing Northern Ireland planning law broadly into line with that operating in Great Britain.

It has taken many years for planning in Northern Ireland to gain the general acceptance which is evident elsewhere in Great Britain, but it is fair to say that the Province is now well equipped in terms of organisation and law to plan for the future.

Geoffrey Booth

The Ulster Plantation (1608-10)   NI 1/1

One of the earliest 'regional planning' schemes in Europe was the seventeenth century settlement of Northern Ireland (Ulster) where six hitherto sparsely populated counties were divided up into agricultural holdings and given to English and Scottish settlers. The purpose was primarily political and the plantation's influence on the history of Ireland is still only too apparent.

On a technical level the plan was remarkably successful. Twenty three new towns were begun, each to a prepared plan, and with a stated target population. Provision was made for such amenities as churches, schools, markets and water supply. Many Ulster towns still retain the original street pattern. The size of the new farms was carefully calculated to be economically viable, but not sufficiently large to support absentee landlords. The settlement was partially financed by the wealthy London Guilds, and many settlers came from overcrowded London (an early example of planned overspill). Although interrupted by periodic civil wars between 1641 and 1690, the plantation was substantially completed and the results are visible to the present day.

Banbridge   NI 1/2

A 1767 new town and an early example of a traffic 'flyover'. The 1767 plan sited the main cross roads on the crest of the steep hill overlooking the River Bann. In 1832, as the wide main street permitted it, the centre of the street was lowered to pass the north-south main road under the minor east-west road, leaving slip roads on either side. This lessened the main road's slope for coach traffic and provided grade separation. The present town retains the original layout and many fine Georgian buildings. Banbridge was the subject of a very successful Civic Trust scheme in 1962.

The main street of Banbridge with one of the first traffic underpasses, built in 1832.
Aerofilms.

208

John Richardson's model industrial village of Bessbrook, founded in 1846.
Aerofilms.

Bessbrook   NI 1/3

An early industrial model village begun in 1846 by Quaker linen manufacturer John Richardson. The standard of housing and amenity was high; houses were lit by gas and the village contained a community centre, shops, school, churches and doctor's dispensary, but no pub, pawnshop or police station. The layout consists of two open greens, connected by a main street, and was originally of 'Radburn' design, with green and footpaths in front and service road behind, although this has now been altered. The village preceded Saltaire by four years, and was used as a model for Bournville in Birmingham (c.f.).

Cookstown, the unsuccessful rival to Dublin.
Aerofilms.

Cookstown   NI 1/4

Cookstown was begun in 1750 by William Stewart to rival Dublin as a commercial centre. The original plan was grandiose in design, consisting of a main street, one and a quarter miles long and 130 feet wide, with many lesser cross streets. However, the town did not fulfill its promoter's hopes and never grew beyond a market town of 6,000 people. The 'fossilised' eighteenth century street plan is retained, with its long main street, but many of the cross streets have become country lanes, resulting in the creation of a 'linear' form of development.

Craigavon

Craigavon is Northern Ireland's first modern new town, situated thirty miles south west of Belfast on the southern shores of Lough Neagh. It was designated to create a new settlement capable of alleviating pressures on the Belfast area and forming a new service centre which could contribute to the regeneration of the south and west of the Province. The initial population of 40,000, living in the thriving towns of Lurgan and Portadown which would be incorporated into the new town structure, will be increased to 100,000 by 1981. The first new township, Brownlow, was commenced in 1965 and will house about 20,000 people. It will be provided with its own schools, shops and community facilities and, like all the new townships, will have easy access to the recreational facilities between the new town and Lough Neagh.

Housing and schools in the Brownlow township of Craigavon New Town. *Northern Ireland Department of Housing, Local Government and Planning.*

Londonderry

The original name of this old town was Derry, but following the Ulster Plantation it was adopted for development by the Guilds of London, who altered the name. It became the chief town and port of the plantation and the immigrant population came chiefly from London. The new city was laid out to a specific plan and enclosed by a defensive wall. The original street layout, the walls and the cathedral of 1628 (in a style called Planters Gothic) can still be seen. Londonderry is a uniquely preserved example of seventeenth century planning, and part of the city is subject to a model conservation scheme for EAHY 1975.

Newry Canal

Built in 1741, the Newry canal runs twenty-one miles from Newry to Portadown, connecting Lough Neagh with the Irish Sea. Its purpose was to 'open up' the centre of Ulster by facilitating the movement of goods, especially coal. The canal is significant because it was built twenty years before the generally acknowledged start of the 'canal age' in England. It contains ten locks and was designed for barges rather than narrow boats. Although now derelict, it constitutes a unique piece of industrial archeology, and may eventually be restored for recreational use.

The clearly defined walled town of Londonderry. *Aerofilms.*

210

SITE INDEX

Civic, Royal and Religious Sites

Conservation in Towns

Conservation of the Countryside

C	1/3	Brockhole Visitor Centre
S	4/5	Cairngorms Nature Reserve
WM	3/2	Cannock Chase AONB
S	4/2	Carrbridge, Landmark Centre
SE	2/3	Chichester Harbour AONB
SW	2/2	Countisbury Hill and Foreland Point
TC	3/2	Cublington, abortive airport site
SW	2/3	Dartmoor National Park
EA	4/2	Dedham Vale AONB
EM	1/2	Gibraltar Point Nature Reserve
WS	4/1	Gower AONB
NW	3/3	Goyt Valley
C	2/2	Langdale Valleys
EM	4/3	Laxton
NW	3/4	North Lees Hall Estate
Y	4/4	North York Moors National Park
WS	4/4	Pembrokeshire Coast National Park
SE	2/6	Seven Sisters Country Park
WM	5/6	Slimbridge, Wildfowl Trust
EA	2/6	Wicken Fen Nature Reserve

Country Estates

SE	1/1	Beaulieu
TC	2/5	Blenheim Palace
WN	3/1	Bodnant Gardens
Y	4/1	Castle Howard
EM	4/1	Clumber Park
EM	3/3	Elvaston Castle
Y	4/1	Harewood House
SE	1/3	Hursley (IBM)
C	2/3	Lowther
EM	3/4	Newstead Abbey
TC	2/2	Rousham House
SW	4/4	Stourhead
TC	2/3	Stowe
TC	3/5	Woburn Abbey
TC	1/5	Windsor

Defence Sites

N	4/1	Alnwick
WN	1/1	Beaumaris
N	4/2	Berwick-upon-Tweed
WN	1/2	Caernarvon
EA	5/3	Castle Rising Castle
Y	3/5	Catterick Camp
WN	3/2	Conway
SW	2/3	Dartmoor, military training
SE	4/2	Dover

N	2/1	Durham
WN	3/3	Flint
S	4/4	Fort George
Y	4/4	Fylingdales
NI	1/6	Londonderry
WM	4/3	Ludlow
SW	2/6	Plymouth, Devonport Dockyard
SW	2/5	Portsmouth, Dockyard and defences
TC	1/5	Windsor Castle

Housing Developments

L	2/2	Barnsbury
L	1/1	Becontree Estate
L	4/2	Bedford Park
L	3/1	Belgravia
EM	3/1	Belper, mill housing
WM	1/1	Birmingham, redevelopment areas
L	1/2	Blackheath, Span housing
L	2/3	Bloomsbury
WM	1/3	Bournville
L	3/2	Churchill Gardens
WM	5/4	Cirencester
S	1/4	Glasgow, The Gorbals redevelopment
NW	4/2	Glossop, Howard Town
L	3/3	Hampstead Garden Suburb
L	1/5	Harold Hill Estate
L	1/7	Lansbury Estate
L	3/2	Lillington Gardens
Y	2/4	Leeds, Quarry Hill flats
EM	4/4	Lincoln, Swanpool garden suburb
NW	4/4	Manchester, Hulme
L	4/6	'Metroland'
N	3/3	Newcastle, Byker Flats and Heaton GIA
SE	3/3	New Ash Green
Y	4/3	New Earswick
EA	5/5	Norwich, Friars Quay
SE	2/4	Peacehaven
NW	1/4	Port Sunlight
NW	4/5	Rochdale, Deeplish
L	4/1	Roehampton, Alton Estate
Y	2/5	Saltaire
Y	1/5	Sheffield, Gleadless Valley and Park Hill
WM	1/1	Solihull, Chelmsley Wood
L	1/8	Thamesmead
NW	4/6	Wythenshawe

Industry and Power and Industrial Towns

SW	2/1	Appledore, shipyards
EA	5/1	Bacton, natural gas terminal
C	1/1	Barrow
EM	3/1	Belper
NI	1/3	Bessbrook
N	1/1	Billingham, ICI
WM	1/3	Birmingham, Bournville
WM	1/2	Black Country
WS	2/1	Blaenavon
WN	2/1	Blaenau Ffestiniog, slate mines
Y	4/4	Boulby, potash mine
Y	2/3	Bradford, Listers Mill
C	2/1	Calder Hall
C	3/1	Cleator Moor
EM	1/1	Corby, ironstone working
EM	3/2	Cromford
L	1/3	Dagenham, Ford's
S	4/3	Dounreay UKAEA
SE	4/3	Dungeness
S	1/2	Eaglesham
WS	2/2	Ebbw Vale
SE	1/2	Fawley, oil refinery and power station
N	3/2	Gateshead, Team Valley Trading Estate
WS	3/3	Gilfach Goch
NW	4/2	Glossop
Y	1/1	Halifax
Y	1/2	Hebden Bridge and Heptonstall
N	2/2	Horden colliery
Y	1/3	Howarth
S	4/6	Invergordon, aluminium smelter
WM	3/3	Ironbridge/Coalbrookdale
WS	3/4	Llantrisant, Royal Mint
WS	4/2	Lower Swansea Valley
C	3/2	Maryport
N	1/2	Middlesbrough
WS	4/3	Milford Haven
S	1/5	New Lanark
WS	2/4	New Tredegar
EM	3/4	Newstead Colliery
S	4/6	Nigg Bay, oil platform fabrication yard
EA	1/3	Old Fletton
L	4/7	Park Royal
WS	2/3	Pontypool, ICI
NW	1/4	Port Sunlight
WS	4/5	Port Talbot, Margam Steelworks
SW	1/2	Redruth, East Pool Mine
Y	2/5	Saltaire
TC	1/3	Slough Trading Estate
EA	4/6	Snape Maltings
TC	4/5	Stewartbẏ, brickworks

NW	2/6	Styal
WN	2/4	Tan-y-Grisiau, HEP Scheme
WN	2/5	Trawsfynydd, nuclear power station
WS	2/4	Tredegar
EM	4/5	West Burton, power station
C	3/4	Whitehaven
C	3/5	Workington, Leyland/National bus factory

Land Reclamation

EM	1/1	Corby, restoration of ironstone workings
WM	5/5	Cotswold Water Park
EA	2/2	Fens, Bedford Rivers
EM	2/1	Holme Pierrepont
L	1/6	Lea Valley Regional Park
WS	4/2	Lower Swansea Valley
EA	1/3	Old Fletton
WN	1/4	Portmadoc embankment
SE	2/5	Portsmouth, North Harbour reclamation
EM	3/5	South Wingfield, colliery reclamation
WM	3/4	Stoke-on-Trent, Westport Lake and Hanley Forest Park
S	1/6	Strathclyde Regional Park
L	1/8	Thamesmead
EM	1/4	Wash, coastal marsh reclamation

Medieval Towns

N	4/1	Alnwick
SW	4/1	Bath
WN	1/1	Beaumaris
EA	4/1	Bury St Edmunds
WN	1/2	Caernarvon
WS	3/1	Caerphilly Castle
SE	4/1	Canterbury
WS	1/2	Chepstow
NW	2/1	Chester
SE	2/2	Chichester
WM	5/4	Cirencester
EA	3/3	Colchester
WN	3/2	Conway
S	2/1	Culross
N	2/1	Durham
S	2/3	Edinburgh
EA	2/4	Ely
SW	2/4	Exeter
WN	3/3	Flint
S	2/4	Haddington
SE	4/4	Hastings
EA	5/4	Kings Lynn
EA	4/3	Lavenham
EM	4/4	Lincoln

EA	4/3	Long Melford
WM	4/3	Ludlow
N	3/3	Newcastle-upon-Tyne
WS	5/7	New Radnor
EA	5/5	Norwich
TC	2/1	Oxford
EA	1/4	Peterborough
SW	2/6	Plymouth
SW	3/5	Poole
Y	3/5	Richmond
SW	5/2	Salisbury
SE	4/5	Sandwich
SE	1/5	Southampton
EM	1/3	Stamford
S	2/7	St Andrews
WM	2/4	Stratford-upon-Avon
N	3/4	Tynemouth
TC	2/4	Wallingford
SE	4/6	Winchelsea
SE	1/6	Winchester
TC	1/5	Windsor and Eton
Y	4/6	York

Garden Cities

Modern New Towns and Town Expansion Schemes

EA	3/1	Basildon, NT
SE	3/1	Basingstoke, TE
N	1/1	Billingham, LANT
EA	4/1	Bury St Edmunds, TE
WM	1/1	Chelmsley Wood, LANT
NI	1/5	Craigavon, NT
N	3/1	Cramlington, LANT
SE	3/2	Crawley, NT
S	1/1	Cumbernauld, NT
WS	1/3	Cwmbran, NT
WM	4/1	Droitwich, TE
S	1/3	East Kilbride, NT
S	3/2	Erskine, LANT
S	2/4	Haddington, TE
EA	3/5	Harlow, NT
N	3/1	Killingworth, LANT
EA	5/4	Kings Lynn, TE
TC	4/1	Letchworth, GC
S	2/5	Livingston, NT
TC	3/3	Milton Keynes, NT
WS	5/8	Newtown, NT
EA	1/4	Peterborough, NT
N	2/4	Peterlee, NT
NW	2/5	Runcorn, NT

TC	4/4	Stevenage, NT
SW	5/4	Swindon, TE
WM	3/5	Telford, NT
N	2/5	Washington, NT
TC	4/6	Welwyn, GC and NT
NW	4/6	Wythenshawe, LAGC

Footnote:

GC	=	Garden City
NT	=	New Town
TE	=	Town Expansion scheme
LANT	=	Local Authority New Township
LAGC	=	Local Authority Garden City

Modern Town Centre Redevelopment

TC	3/1	Aylesbury, Friars Square
WM	1/1	Birmingham, redevelopment areas, Bull Ring etc.
NW	5/1	Blackburn
WM	2/1	Coventry
L	4/3	Croydon, Whitgift Centre
S	1/4	Glasgow, housing redevelopment, Custom House Quay
TC	1/1	High Wycombe, The Octagon
NW	1/3	Liverpool, City Centre
L	2/1	London, Barbican and Paternoster
NW	4/4	Manchester, King Street
N	3/3	Newcastle, pedestrian deck system
SW	2/6	Plymouth
SE	2/5	Portsmouth, Guildhall Square
SE	1/5	Southampton
WS	4/6	Swansea City Centre

Prehistoric Sites

SW	5/1	Avebury
SW	1/1	Chysauster
EM	4/2	Cresswell Crags
EA	2/5	Grimes Graves
SW	3/3	Maiden Castle
SW	5/3	Stonehenge

Recreation Sites

S	4/1	Aviemore
SE	1/1	Beaulieu
N	1/1	Billingham Forum
SE	2/1	Brighton Marina
C	1/3	Brockhole Visitor Centre
WM	3/2	Cannock Chase
WS	3/2	Cardiff National Sports Centre
S	4/2	Carrbridge Landmark Centre
EM	4/1	Clumber Park

S	3/1	Clyde & Murshiel RP
NW	4/1	Compstall CP
WM	5/5	Cotswold Water Park
WS	1/4	Cwmcarn Forest Drive
SW	2/3	Dartmoor NP
NW	3/2	Edale, Fieldhead Information Centre
EM	3/3	Elvaston Castle CP
EA	3/4	Epping Forest
S	4/5	Glenmore and Cairngorms
NW	3/3	Goyt Valley
C	1/4	Grizedale Forest
Y	1/3	Haworth, literary associations and Keighley and Worth Valley Railway
EM	2/1	Holme Pierrepont, National Water Sports Centre
WM	3/3	Ironbridge Gorge Museum
C	2/2	Langdale Valleys
L	1/6	London, Lea Valley RP
L	3/6	London, Regent's Canal
L	2/7	London, South Bank complex
SW	2/5	Minehead, Butlins Holiday Camp
SE	1/4	New Forest
EM	3/4	Newstead Abbey
NW	3/4	North Lees Hall Estate
Y	4/4	North York Moors NP
NW	3/2	Pennine Way
WS	4/4	Pembrokeshire Coast NP
WN	1/4	Portmadoc, Festiniog Railway
SE	2/6	Seven Sisters CP
EA	4/6	Snape Maltings
SW	1/5	St Agnes, Little Orchard Village
WS	3/5	St Fagans, National Folk Museum of Wales
WM	3/4	Stoke-on-Trent, Gladstone Pottery Museum
WM	2/4	Stratford-upon-Avon
S	1/6	Strathclyde RP
NW	3/5	Tissington Trail
S	3/5	Trossachs, Loch Katrine, Queen Elizabeth Forest Park and Aberfoyle and Callender
WM	2/4	Upper Avon Navigation and Stratford Canal
TC	3/4	Whipsnade Zoo
NW	1/6	Wirral Way CP
TC	3/5	Woburn Abbey

Footnote:

NP	=	National Park
CP	=	Country Park
RP	=	Regional Park

Renaissance, Georgian and Regency Sites

WS	5/1	Aberaeron
NI	1/2	Banbridge
SW	4/1	Bath
L	3/1	Belgravia
TC	2/5	Blenheim Palace
L	2/3	Bloomsbury
SE	2/1	Brighton and Hove (Brunswick Town)
SW	4/3	Bristol, Clifton
SE	1/1	Bucklers Hard
Y	4/1	Castle Howard
WM	5/2	Cheltenham
SE	2/2	Chichester
L	2/8	City of London, St Paul's and Wren churches
NI	1/4	Cookstown
L	2/4	Covent Garden
S	2/3	Edinburgh, New Town
S	1/4	Glasgow, Park Circus
L	1/4	Greenwich, Royal Naval Hospital
S	2/4	Haddington
SE	4/4	Hastings, St Leonards
S	3/3	Helensburgh
S	3/4	Inveraray
EA	5/4	Kings Lynn
EM	2/2	Leicester, New Walk
NI	1/6	Londonderry
N	3/3	Newcastle, Grainger and Dobson's Grey St.
L	3/7	Regent St and Regent's Park
TC	2/2	Rousham
WM	4/5	Stourport
TC	2/3	Stowe
WN	1/5	Tremadoc
SE	3/6	Tunbridge Wells
N	3/4	Tynemouth
SW	3/7	Weymouth
C	3/4	Whitehaven
TC	3/5	Woburn Abbey

Resort Developments

S	3/5	Aberfoyle and Callender
S	4/1	Aviemore
SW	4/1	Bath
SW	3/2	Bournemouth
NW	5/2	Blackpool
C	1/2	Bowness
SE	2/1	Brighton
NW	3/1	Buxton
WM	5/2	Cheltenham
WM	4/1	Droitwich
Y	3/3	Harrogate

SE	4/4	Hastings, St Leonards
WM	2/3	Leamington
WS	5/6	Llandrindod Wells
SW	2/5	Minehead, Butlins Holiday Camp
WM	1/4	Portmadoc
WN	2/2	Portmeirion
SW	1/5	St Agnes, Little Orchard Village
Y	4/5	Scarborough
C	3/3	Silloth
NW	5/5	Southport
SE	3/6	Tunbridge Wells
SW	3/7	Weymouth
C	1/2	Windermere

Roman Sites

SW	4/1	Bath
WS	1/1	Caerleon and Caerwent
EA	1/1	Car Dyke
WM	5/1	Chedworth
NW	2/1	Chester
SE	2/2	Chichester
WM	5/4	Cirencester
EA	3/3	Colchester
WM	4/1	Droitwich
SW	2/4	Exeter
N	4/5	Hadrians Wall, Housesteads, Vindolanda and Corbridge
C	2/4	Hard Knott
EM	4/4	Lincoln
C	2/4	Ravenglass
SE	3/4	Silchester
WM	3/6	Wroxeter

Rural Land Use

EA	5/1	Bacton gas terminal
SE	1/1	Beaulieu
WN	2/1	Blaenau Ffestiniog, slate mines and tips
WN	3/1	Bodnant Gardens
WM	3/2	Cannock Chase
EM	4/1	Clumber Park and Sherwood Forest
WS	5/3	Clywedog Reservoir
WS	5/4	Cors Tregaron Nature Reserve
WS	1/4	Cwmcarn, forest drive
SW	2/3	Dartmoor
SE	4/3	Dungeness
WS	5/5	Elan Valley reservoirs
EA	3/4	Epping Forest
EA	2/2	Fens, Bedford Rivers
Y	3/1	Fountains Abbey
S	4/5	Glenmore Forest Park
EA	1/2	Grafham Water

C	1/4	Grizedale Forest
N	4/4	Kielder Forest
EM	4/3	Laxton
SE	3/5	London Green Belt
WS	4/3	Milford Haven
SE	1/4	New Forest
Y	4/4	North York Moors
EA	1/3	Old Fletton
SE	3/5	'Ribbon development'
WM	5/6	Slimbridge Wildfowl Trust
WN	2/3	Snowdonia Forest Park
WM	1/5	Solihull, National Exhibition Centre
SW	1/6	St Austell, china clay pits
WN	2/4	Tan-y-Grisiau, HEP scheme
C	2/5	Thirlmere and Ullswater reservoirs
S	3/5	Trossachs, Loch Katrine and Queen Elizabeth Forest Park
EM	1/4	Wash, coastal marsh reclamation
TC	3/4	Whipsnade Zoo
EA	2/6	Wicken Fen Nature Reserve

Shopping and Commercial Developments

TC	3/1	Aylesbury, Friars Square
WM	1/1	Birmingham, Bull Ring and City Centre
NW	5/1	Blackburn
NW	5/3	Bolton
SW	3/2	Bournemouth, Hampshire Centre
SE	2/1	Brighton, The Square
WS	3/2	Cardiff, Bute Town
WS	3/1	Caerphilly, hypermarket
NW	2/1	Chester, Rows, Arcade, Grosvenor Centre
WM	2/1	Coventry, Precinct
SW	2/4	Exeter, Princesshay
TC	1/1	High Wycombe, The Octagon
EA	5/4	Kings Lynn, Town Centre
Y	2/4	Leeds, City Centre
EA	5/5	Norwich, London Street and Magdalen Street
EM	2/3	Nottingham, Victoria Centre
SW	3/5	Poole, Arndale Centre
SW	5/2	Salisbury, Old George Mall
SE	1/5	Southampton, City Centre
WM	3/5	Telford, hypermarket
EM	2/4	West Bridgford, Asda Shopping Centre

Traffic Management Schemes

SW	3/2	Bournemouth, sea front, pier approach and town centre bypass bridges
WM	2/1	Coventry, inner ring road and precincts
WS	1/4	Cwmcarn, forest drive
NW	3/3	Goyt Valley

Y	2/4	Leeds, city centre
EA	5/5	Norwich, London Street
EM	2/3	Nottingham, city centre
TC	1/2	Reading, town centre

Transport and Communication Sites

Y	2/1	Aire and Calder Navigation
C	1/1	Barrow, shipyards
Y	2/2	Bingley, 'Five-Rise' locks
WM	1/4	Birmingham, 'Spaghetti Junction', Midland Links Motorway and inner ring road
WM	1/2	Black Country canals etc.
SE	1/1	Bucklers Hard, shipyard
TC	4/3	Cardington, airship hangars
EA	1/1	Car dyke
NW	2/2	Crewe
TC	3/2	Cublington, abortive airport site
SE	4/2	Dover
SW	2/4	Exeter, canal
WM	2/2	Fosse Way, Roman road
SE	3/2	Gatwick Airport
S	1/4	Glasgow, urban motorways
SW	1/3	Goonhilly, satellite station
Y	1/3	Haworth, Keighley and Worth Valley Railway
Y	4/2	Humber Bridge
NW	2/3	Jodrell Bank
EA	5/4	Kings Lynn
NW	1/3	Liverpool, Albert Dock
L	4/5	London, Heathrow Airport
L	4/6	London, 'Metroland'
L	3/5	London, Post Office Tower
L	3/6	London, Regent's Canal
L	2/5	London, St Katherine's Dock
L	2/6	London, St Pancras and Euston Stations
C	1/5	Lune Valley, M6 Motorway
NW	2/4	Manchester Ship Canal
NW	4/3	Manchester, Castlefields Canal Basin and Liverpool Road Railway Station
WN	1/3	Menai Bridges
NI	1/7	Newry Canal
NW	3/2	Pennine Way
EA	1/4	Peterborough, railway village
WN	3/5	Pontcysyllte Aquaduct
WN	1/4	Portmadoc, Festiniog Railway
NW	5/4	Preston, Bus Station
S	2/6	Queensferry, Forth road and rail bridges
Y	1/4	Scammonden, M62 Motorway
NW	1/5	Seaforth Docks
WS	1/5	Severn Bridge
SE	1/3	Southampton, Docks
N	1/4	Stockton, Stockton and Darlington Railway

WM	4/5	Stourport, canal town
SW	5/4	Swindon, railway village
NW	3/4	Tissington Trail
WM	2/4	Upper Avon Navigation and Stratford Canal

Urban Parks

NW	1/2	Birkenhead Park
L	2/3	Bloomsbury, squares
WS	3/2	Cardiff, Bute Park
WM	5/2	Cheltenham
L	1/4	Greenwich Park
L	4/4	Kew Gardens
L	1/6	Lea Valley Regional Park
NW	1/3	Liverpool, Sefton Park
L	3/7	Regent's Park
L	3/8	Royal Parks
WM	3/4	Stoke-on-Trent, Hanley Forest Park and Westport Lake

Villages

EA	2/1	Bar Hill
NI	1/3	Bessbrook
N	4/3	Blanchland
EA	5/2	Castle Acre
EA	5/3	Castle Rising
EA	3/2	Cavendish
NW	4/1	Compstall
NI	1/4	Cookstown
EM	3/2	Cromford
S	1/2	Eaglesham
SW	1/4	Halsetown
Y	3/2	Harewood
N	4/4	Kielder
N	2/3	Leasingthorne
EA	4/4	Little Wenham
C	2/3	Lowther
SW	3/4	Milton Abbas
SE	3/3	New Ash Green
S	1/5	New Lanark
EM	3/4	Newstead Colliery Village
TC	4/2	Old Warden
WN	2/2	Portmeirion
EA	4/5	Rushbrooke
TC	4/3	Shortstown
SW	1/5	St Agnes, Little Orchard Village
TC	4/5	Stewartby
NW	2/6	Styal
SW	3/6	Talbot Village
TC	1/4	West Wycombe
TC	3/5	Woburn
WM	2/5	Wormleighton

GLOSSARY OF ABBREVIATIONS AND PLANNING TERMS

Ancient Monument A building or structure specified under the Ancient Monuments Consolidation and Amendment Act 1913, or other Acts of 1931, 1937, 1943 and 1953. Ancient monuments include such structures as prehistoric barrows and tumuli, henges such as Stonehenge and Avebury, and later buildings, e.g. medieval castles, They are invariably either uninhabited, or inhabited by a custodian only. Ancient Monuments were the first man-made structures to be protected from alteration or demolition, under the Ancient Monuments Protection Act, 1882. The list of Ancient Monuments is kept by the Department of the Environment and the appropriate local authorities.

AONB Area of Outstanding Natural Beauty. The National Parks and Access to the Countryside Act, 1949, set up the National Parks Commission (now the Countryside Commission) among other things to advise on and designate such areas, outside National Parks. Within AONBs, local authorities endeavour to protect the landscape by exercising high standards of development control, and by positive measures such as the removal of eyesores, tree planting, etc. The ownership of the land, however, remains in private hands.

Backland Land at the rear of development which fronts onto a road. Parcels of 'backland' may well have very poor access onto the road, and in some cases no access at all. They are consequently very often difficult, if not impossible, to develop.

CDA Comprehensive Development Area. An area defined by a local planning authority, under the Town and Country Planning Act 1947, as being in need of development (or redevelopment) as a comprehensive unit. CDAs were defined in the development plans drawn up by planning authorities, and were then subject to compulsory acquisition. CDA plans have now been replaced by Action Area plans under the 1971 Town and Country Planning Act.

CEGB Central Electricity Generating Board. The national authority responsible for the generation and bulk distribution of electricity.

Civic Amenities Act 1967 A Private Members Act, promoted by the President of the Civic Trust, Duncan Sandys. Planning authorities were obliged to designate Conservation Areas (q.v.) and to prepare policies to 'preserve and enhance' their environment. The Act also gave added powers to planning authorities to stimulate tree planting and protect existing trees. The Act was incorporated into the 1971 Town and Country Planning Act.

Civic Trust A society founded in 1957 by Duncan Sandys to promote better standards of planning and architecture, and the conservation of buildings and areas of architectural and historic importance. The Trust works at the national level, but subsidiary Trusts have been established in the North West, North East, Scotland and Wales. In addition, the Trust keeps a register of local amenity societies (of which there are now well over 1,000).

Conservation Area Introduced in the Civic Amenities Act 1967. Under the Act, planning authorities were required to determine 'which parts of their area are areas of special architectural or historic interest, the character or appearance of which it is desirable to preserve or enhance'. These areas were designated as Conservation Areas, and policies were to be drawn up to 'preserve and enhance' their character and appearance. The powers contained in the Act have been incorporated in the 1971 Town and Country Planning Act, and have been further strengthened in the Town and Country Planning (Amendment) Act 1972, and the Town and Country Planning Amenities Act 1974. The number of Conservation Areas now exceeds 3,000.

Countryside Act 1968 This Act supplemented the 1949 National Parks and Access to the Countryside Act (q.v.), extending its provisions to the countryside as a whole. The National Parks Commission was also replaced by the Countryside Commission. Planning authorities were also encouraged to provide country parks (q.v.) for the outdoor recreational needs of urban populations within easy reach of their homes, thus complementing the 'long distance' facilities provided by the National Parks.

Country Park The 1968 Countryside Act enabled local authorities and others to acquire stretches of open countryside and make them accessible to the public for informal recreational use. Such areas were to be designated as Country Parks. The Parks so far established differ widely in character, from the Wirral Way in Cheshire (q.v.), formed from a disused railway line, to Elvaston Castle (q.v.), a country house and parkland.

Countryside Commission The Commission was set up under the 1968 Countryside Act (q.v.) to take over the functions of the National Parks Commission with regard to National Parks and AONBs (q.v.). In addition, the Commission have the duty to 'review, encourage, assist, concert or promote the provision and improvement of facilities for the enjoyment of the countryside generally, and to conserve and enhance the natural beauty and amenity of the countryside and to secure public access for the purpose of open air recreation'. The Commission receives its funds from central government.

DoE Department of the Environment. The central government department which deals with all 'planning' matters. It was set up in 1970 with the amalgamation of the Ministry of Housing and Local Government, the Ministry of Transport and the Ministry of Public Building and Works.

Enclosure of Land The system whereby the old 'open fields' of the Middle Ages, which were communally owned, were 'enclosed' by local landowners with hedges and fences to form the well known regular field pattern of today. The process began about the fourteenth century, and was completed by the General Enclosure Act of 1845.

EAHY 1975 European Architectural Heritage Year 1975. The Council of Europe have designated 1975 as European Architectural Heritage Year in an attempt 'to halt the steady loss of irreplaceable monuments and the erosion of character in historic European towns'. In Britain, the campaign is being coordinated by the UK Council for EAHY, with the Civic Trust playing a leading role. Many projects are being undertaken by central and local government and by local amenity societies to protect and improve the environment of historic areas.

Four Towns Studies In 1966, the Minister of Housing and Local Government commissioned consultants to carry out studies of four historic towns (York, Chester, Bath and Chichester) to identify the problems of historic buildings and areas caused by modern development and traffic pressures and to suggest how these might be overcome.

226

General Improvement Area (GIA) Areas of poorer housing and lower environmental standard, but which are not so bad as to require redevelopment, can be designated as General Improvement Areas under the 1969 Housing Act. Local authorities encourage house improvements by giving grants and loans, and carry out environmental improvements (such as street closures, planting trees etc.) with the aid of central government grants.

Green Belt The increase in urban sprawl during the interwar period led to the setting up of Green Belts around major cities during the 1940s and 1950s. Within the Green Belts development is strictly controlled or often not allowed at all. In this way urban sprawl can be prevented.

High, Medium and Low Rise Refers to the height of buildings. In general, low rise is up to three storeys, medium rise is four to six storeys and high rise is seven storeys and over.

Housing Act 1969 A link in a long chain of legislation aiming to increase and improve the country's housing stock. It enabled local authorities to give grants for house improvements and to carry out environmental improvements, thus giving a new complexion to the rehabilitation of older housing areas, and shifting the emphasis from redevelopment. The Act introduced General Improvement Areas (q.v.).

Hypermarket A large shop, selling both food and non-food goods, and having a minimum floor area of 50,000 square feet, and free parking for several hundred cars. They are often sited on the edge of, or outside, urban areas rather than in town centres.

Linear Development Development of a limited width, stretching along a central transport 'spine', such as a road or railway. The resulting urban area is long and narrow in plan.

LCC London County Council. Until 1965 the old County of London was under the control of the London County Council. In 1965, the LCC area was extended and is now administered by the Greater London Council.

Listed Building Any building on a List of Buildings of Architectural or Historic Interest, drawn up by the DoE (q.v.). Listed Buildings, which were introduced in the 1947 Planning Act (q.v.), may not be demolished or altered without permission from the relevant local planning authority. The List is divided into three grades, I, II*, and II in descending order of merit. In addition, there is a list of buildings of local interest, which is not given any statutory protection.

MHLG Ministry of Housing and Local Government. Planning affairs (except transport) were dealt with by this ministry until 1970, when it was absorbed into the DoE (q.v.).

MoT Ministry of Transport. Set up in 1919, the Ministry of Transport was responsible for road planning (among many other things) until 1970, when it was absorbed into the DoE (q.v.).

National Parks and Access to the Countryside Act 1949 In 1945, John Dower submitted a private memorandum to the Minister of Town and Country Planning proposing the setting up of National Parks. After a long and sometimes bitter battle, the National Parks Act was passed in 1949, and established the National Parks Commission whose task it was to set up and oversee the proposed National Parks. The Act, as its name implies, also dealt with wider aspects of access to the countryside.

National Trust Founded in 1895 and incorporated by act of parliament in 1907, its full title is the National Trust for Places of Historic Interest or Natural Beauty. The Trust, which is financed by private subscriptions, buys buildings or land to be held in trust 'inalienably' for the enjoyment of the public, including members of the Trust.

Neighbourhood A relatively selfcontained area within a town. The term originated in America and usually applies to residential districts with their own shopping, recreational and other facilities, schools etc. The idea of creating neighbourhoods was very popular in the 1940s and 1950s, and most early new towns were planned on this basis.

New Town Any town which is consciously founded and built to a specific plan. The modern new towns movement grew out of Sir Ebenezer Howard's concept of garden cities embodied in the planning and building of Letchworth (1903) and Welwyn (1920) (q.v.). The New Towns Act (q.v.) provided the powers and finance to establish new towns and by 1950 fourteen had been designated in England, Wales and Scotland, mainly to accommodate population and industry displaced from congested conurbations. Since then a further nineteen new towns have been designated, varying in size from Newtown in mid-Wales (planned population 11,000) to the Central Lancashire New Town, incorporating Preston, Leyland and Chorley, with a planned population of 430,000.

New Towns Act 1946 The original act (since amended) setting up the legislative and administrative machinery for the designation of land for new towns and their construction and management. The act authorised the creation of an independent development corporation, financed directly by Central Government, to develop each town, after which its assets would be handed over to the central Commission for New Towns.

Nonconforming Use A land use which does not conform to the general land use zoning of an area, and which is invariably an intrusion into the area — e.g. a factory in a housing area. There is machinery in the various planning acts for mitigating the undesirable effects of nonconforming uses.

Overspill The 'planned' movement of population from an overcrowded urban area to a less highly developed area under the control of another local authority, often as a result of a joint agreement between the two authorities. The most obvious example is movement from conurbations to new towns (q.v.).

Park and Ride A system of travelling to town centres (often for work, but also for shopping etc.) whereby the traveller drives his car to a transport 'interchange', parks it there and completes his journey by public transport, thus decreasing traffic congestion close to the central area.

Pedestrianisation The exclusion or restriction of vehicles from a street. Often refers to shopping streets, but may also be used in housing areas. The street is then safer and more pleasant for pedestrians.

Planning Blight Uncertainty over the future of an area, or the existence of redevelopment proposals which may not be carried out for some years, depresses the value of property in the area. The result is that such areas become run-down and unsightly, and property in them sometimes becomes unsaleable. This is one of the less pleasant effects of our modern planning system.

Plantation Has two meanings — it can either be a group of trees consciously planted for the production of timber to improve the landscape; or it refers to the founding or 'planting' of a new town, or group of towns. Its most specific reference is the Plantation of Ulster (q.v.) — meaning the carrying out of a regional plan which required the 'planting' of a whole series of new towns, together with new farms, and a new population as well.

Pocket Borough A Parliamentary Constituency which was under the patronage or control of the local landowner — i.e. it was in his pocket. Pocket Boroughs were supposedly abolished in 1832, but some lingered on until the secret ballot was established in 1872.

Radburn Layout A form of residential development in which vehicles and pedestrians are kept separate, usually by confining vehicles to the rear of houses, and pedestrians to the front. It was named after a satellite town of New York, where the idea was first given practical expression.

Revolving Fund A system used for financing the improvement of historic buildings. Given a starting sum, a run-down building is purchased, renovated and sold (usually for a higher price). The money from the sale is then used to buy and renovate another building, which is then sold etc.

Sports Council Set up by the government in 1965 to advise on matters relating to the development of sports and physical recreation facilities, and to foster cooperation between the statutory authorities and voluntary organisations concerned. Regional and local councils have subsequently been established to supplement the national council.

Town and Country Planning Act 1947 Probably the most far reaching measure in the history of town planning, this act established most of our present system of planning. A new administrative system was set up making county and county borough councils the local planning authorities for their area. The two main measures in the act were the requirement for councils to draw up and submit Development Plans for their area within three years, and the introduction of the present system of control of development over all land. A number of the more radical proposals in the act were subsequently removed by later governments.

Town and Country Planning Act 1968 This act set up the present system of structure and local plans, in place of the old development plan system introduced in the 1947 Act (q.v.). The new structure plans were to be primarily statements of policy, rather than land use plans as the development plans has tended to become. The 1968 Act has since been incorporated into the 1971 Planning Act.

Town Development Act 1952 Provided powers to enable two (or more) local authorities to carry out town expansion schemes designed to relieve the overcrowding in older conurbations and urban areas. A pioneering agreement between Salford — the exporting authority — and Lancashire — the receiving authority — initially led to the passing of the act, since when many further agreements and expansion schemes have been carried out (see also Overspill).

Town Expansion Scheme An expansion scheme usually carried out under the Town Development Act 1952 (q.v.).

UKAEA United Kingdom Atomic Energy Authority. The national body responsible for the development and production of atomic energy.

White Land Land where the existing uses will for the most part remain undisturbed. So called because on the old development plans, such areas were uncoloured — i.e. they were white.

BIBLIOGRAPHY

Armytage W.H.G. (1961). *Heavens Below: Utopian Experiments in England (1560-1950)*, Routledge and Kegan Paul.
Ashworth G. (1973). *Encyclopaedia of Planning*, Barrie and Jenkins.
Ashworth W. (1968). *The Genesis of Modern British Town Planning*, Routledge and Kegan Paul.
Bell Colin and Rose (1972). *City Fathers*, Penguin.
Benevolo L. (1967). *The Origins of Modern Town Planning*, Routledge and Kegan Paul.
Beresford M. (1967). *New Towns of the Middle Ages*, Lutterworth Press.
Beresford M. and St. Joseph J.K.S. (1958). *Medieval England: An Aerial Survey*, CUP.
Bor W. (1972). *The Making of Cities*, Leonard Hill.
Briggs A. (1963). *Victorian Cities*, Penguin.
Buchanan C. (1963). *Traffic in Towns*, HMSO and Penguin.
Buchanan C. (1968). *Bath: A Study in Conservation*, HMSO.
Buchanan C. (1972). *The State of Britain*, Faber.
Burke G. (1971). *Towns in the Making*, Arnold.
Burrows G.S. (1969). *Chichester: A Study in Conservation*, HMSO.
Chadwick G.F. (1966). *The Park and the Town*, Architectural Press.
Cherry Gordon (1972). *Urban Change and Planning*, Foulis.
Cherry G.E. (1974). *The Evolution of British Town Planning*, Leonard Hill.
Cresse W.L. (1966). *The Search for Environment*, Yale University Press.
Cullingworth J.B. (1972). *Town and Country Planning in Britain*, George Allen and Unwin.
Davis T. (1960). *The Architecture of John Nash*, Studio Books.
Dyos H.J. (1968). *The Study of Urban History*, Arnold.
Esher Viscount. (1969). *York: A Study in Conservation*, HMSO.
Everitt A. (1973). *Perspectives in English Urban History*, Macmillan.
Fairbrother N. (1970). *New Lives, New Landscapes*, Architectural Press.
Geddes P. (1949). *Cities in Evolution*, Williams and Norgate.
Gregg P. (1971). *A Social and Economic History of Britain*, Harrap.
Gresswell P. (1971). *Environment: an Alphabetical Handbook*, John Murray.
Hatfield C. (1950). *British Canals*, Phoenix House.
Holliday J. (ed.) (1974). *City Centre, Redevelopment: a Study of British City Centre Planning and Case Studies of Five English City Centres*, Charles Knight.
Hoskins W.G. (1970). *The Making of the English Landscape*, Penguin.
Howard E. (1965). *Garden Cities of Tomorrow*, Faber.
Insall D. (1969). *Chester: A Study in Conservation*, HMSO.
Lindsay I.G. (1948). *Georgian Edinburgh*, Oliver and Boyd.
McLaughlin J.B. (1969). *Urban and Regional Planning: a Systems Approach*, Faber.
Martin G. (1961). *The Town*, Vista Books.
Morris A.E.J. (1972). *History of Urban Form*, George Godwin.
Mumford L. (1966). *The City in History*, Penguin.
Rasmussen, S.E. (1948). *London: The Unique City*, Jonathan Cape.
Rivet A.L.F. (1958). *Town and Country in Roman Britain*, Hutchinson.
Shaffer F. (1970). *The New Towns Story*, MacGibbon and Kee.
Sharp T. (1946). *Anatomy of the Village*, Penguin.
Stewart C. (1968). *A Prospect of Cities*, Longmans.
Summerson J. (1948). *Georgian London*, Penguin.
Thomas R. (1969). *Aycliffe to Cumbernauld: a study of Seven New Towns in their Regions*, P.E.P.
Trevelyan G.M. (1966). *Illustrated English Social History*, Penguin.